11/25
STRAND PRICE
$5.00

Comparative Feminist Studies

Series Editor
Chandra Talpade Mohanty
Syracuse University
Syracuse
New York
USA

COMPARATIVE FEMINIST STUDIES foregrounds writing, organizing, and reflection on feminist trajectories across the historical and cultural borders of nation-states. It takes up fundamental analytic and political issues involved in the cross-cultural production of knowledge about women and feminism, examining in depth the politics of scholarship and knowledge in relation to feminist organizing and social movements. This series draws on feminist thinking in a number of fields, targeting innovative, comparative feminist scholarship; pedagogical and curricular strategies; community organizing, and political education. Volumes in this series will provide systematic and challenging interventions into the (still) largely Euro-Western feminist studies knowledge base, while simultaneously highlighting the work that can and needs to be done to envision and enact cross-cultural, multiracial feminist solidarity. CHANDRA TALPADE MOHANTY is Professor of Women's Studies and Dean's Professor of the Humanities at Syracuse University. Her work focuses on transnational feminist theory, cultural studies, and anti-racist education. She is the author of Feminism Without Borders: Decolonizing Theory, Practicing Solidarity and co-editor of Third World Women and the Politics of Feminism, and Feminist Genealogies, Colonial Legacies, Democratic Futures. Mohanty has worked with three grassroots community organizations, Grassroots Leadership of North Carolina, Center for Immigrant Families in New York City, and Awareness, Orissa, India, and has been a consultant/evaluator for AAC & U and the Ford Foundation.

More information about this series at
http://www.springer.com/series/14906

Chielozona Eze

Ethics and Human Rights in Anglophone African Women's Literature

Feminist Empathy

Chielozona Eze
Northeastern Illinois University
Chicago, USA

Comparative Feminist Studies
ISBN 978-3-319-40921-4   ISBN 978-3-319-40922-1 (eBook)
DOI 10.1007/978-3-319-40922-1

Library of Congress Control Number: 2016951317

© The Editor(s) (if applicable) and The Author(s) 2016
This book was advertised with a copyright holder in the name of the publisher in error, whereas the author holds the copyright.
This work is subject to copyright. All rights are solely and exclusively licensed by the Publisher, whether the whole or part of the material is concerned, specifically the rights of translation, reprinting, reuse of illustrations, recitation, broadcasting, reproduction on microfilms or in any other physical way, and transmission or information storage and retrieval, electronic adaptation, computer software, or by similar or dissimilar methodology now known or hereafter developed.
The use of general descriptive names, registered names, trademarks, service marks, etc. in this publication does not imply, even in the absence of a specific statement, that such names are exempt from the relevant protective laws and regulations and therefore free for general use.
The publisher, the authors and the editors are safe to assume that the advice and information in this book are believed to be true and accurate at the date of publication. Neither the publisher nor the authors or the editors give a warranty, express or implied, with respect to the material contained herein or for any errors or omissions that may have been made.

Cover illustration: © Francisco Rivotti / Alamy Stock Photo

Printed on acid-free paper

This Palgrave Macmillan imprint is published by Springer Nature
The registered company is Springer International Publishing AG
The registered company address is: Gewerbestrasse 11, 6330 Cham, Switzerland

Preface

This is a book about African women and human rights. It examines women's rights as a synecdoche for universal human rights. Chimamanda Ngozi Adichie, a prominent name among third-generation African women writers, has been credited with reviving some interest in feminism not only in Africa but also in other parts of the world. Her TEDx talk, "We Should All Be Feminists," has become a popular teaching resource for undergraduates in African literature in the USA. Adichie states that all fair-minded people should be feminists. I believe that her call represents the concerns of the African women writers and activists of her generation who identify as feminists, and who interpret their feminism in terms of human rights.

African literature has always addressed human rights. Increasingly, scholars have begun to pay attention to that. Works that come easily to mind include Joseph R. Slaughter's *Human Rights, Inc: The World Novel, Narrative Form, and International Law* (2007); Elizabeth S. Anker's *Fictions of Dignity: Embodying Human Rights in World Literature* (2012), Zoe Norridge's *Perceiving Pain in African Literature* (2012), Odile Cazenave and Patricia Célérier's *Contemporary Francophone African Writers and the Burden of Commitment* (2011), and Rosemary Joll's *Cultured Violence: Narrative, Social Suffering, and Engendering Human Rights in Contemporary South Africa* (2010). None of these works, however, focuses on feminism as a rich source of understanding of human rights. My book seeks to fill this gap.

This book is based on the assumption that third-generation African women writers believe that gender equality in most African societies has not yet been realized. Indeed, in most African cultures women are still viewed largely through the lenses of culture and tradition rather than as individuals with distinct wishes, rights, and dignities. Focusing on selected fiction and poetry of Anglophone women writers in the new millennium, it examines how African patriarchal societies have disabled women's bodies by subjecting them to needless pain and privation.

My book celebrates the humanist ideals captured by the African concept of *ubuntu* and those expressed in the Universal Declaration of Human Rights (UDHR); it argues that literature can help us interpret those ideals. What I seek to articulate, therefore, are the stirrings of complex interrogations of societies whose ideas of resistance to oppression are beginning to move beyond the resistance to the West. Africa increasingly turns attention to self without the gaze of the West, and one of the areas it does so is in gender politics and women's rights. Whereas it is expedient to address queerness as a human rights issue, I focus chiefly on male–female relations to the degree that they prevent women from thriving and living morally fulfilling lives. Where African politics normalizes polygamy as in Kenya, female genital mutilation as in Sierra Leone, girl-children forced into marriage as in Nigeria, or women's subservient positions in families, African women writers express the impact of such aspects of African cultures in women's lives. There is nothing typical about African gender relations. They are guided by patriarchal norms, and, as in other patriarchal and sexist cultures, women are disadvantaged. When African women writers expose gender inequality and outright sexism in their cultures, they do so, not because they believe these to be specific to Africa, but because they want to expose those behaviors in order to enhance human flourishing.

My choice of these writers was guided primarily by the degree to which their works best exemplify the new turn toward ethics and women's rights in African literature in the new millennium. In works of this nature, there are obviously important literary works to be left out. Their absence is not a statement on their value; it is rather that it would be impossible to include all important works.

The chapters are arranged in a rhetorical sequence that highlights various ways the writers confront the systems that disable African women's bodies. After establishing my theoretical parameters in the introduction, I move from micro (Chapters 2–5) to macro (Chapters 6–8) instances of pain and the abuse of human rights, from the disabling of women by their culture and tradition to the disabling of society by military regimes and civil wars.[1] In the introduction "The Ethical Turn in African Literature," I situate my uses of the concepts: feminism, ethics, empathy, human rights. How are these terms related? The architecture of the argument is simple:

Feminism is the belief in the moral equality of men and women. Ethics recognizes the other and the quality of relation between humans as ends in themselves, rather than as means to other humans' ends. In narrating stories of women incapacitated by the ideologies of tradition and patriarchy, the writers demand that the women be recognized for who they are. In their feminism, these writers propose fairness as a starting principle in the relationship between men and women. One of the ways to conceive of that fairness is through empathy; that is, switching perspectives with women who have been disadvantaged by their gender. Empathy is not a mere intellectual exercise. Nor does it seek to patronize the other. Its goal, in this context, is to identify and address the pain of the other. Feminist empathy is the ability to feel oneself into the experience of a woman in unwarranted suffering, that is, suffering that resulted due to no fault of her own. Narratives, I argue, project and enact ways of being human; they script human rights.

To be sure, issues of human rights are not new in African women's literature; Bessie Head, Ama Ata Aidoo, Grace Ogot, Buchi Emecheta, Mariama Bâ, Flora Nwapa, Ellen Kuzwayo, Zoë Wicomb et cetera, have written stories that address them. Their works were, however, interpreted largely from a postcolonial perspective, which itself was heavily invested in combating the colonial misrepresentation of the African personhood. The theoretical approach to their works therefore blurred their human rights concerns by not highlighting aspects of African cultures that impede rights as much as colonialism had. My interpretive model for African women's literature is in response to the writers' bold embrace of feminist identity, their call on all, especially men, to be fair-minded in relating to them. Feminism, understood within the framework suggested by these writers, functions in the assumption that women want no more than a space in which they can take charge of their minds and bodies as men do theirs, a space where they can exist without the obtrusive intervention of ideologies. This is not an impossible demand, and its moral impetus can best be understood by switching perspectives with women whose lives have been hampered by many ideologies of patriarchal dominance.

Chapter 2, "Feminism as Fairness," interprets Chimamanda Ngozi Adichie's talk, "We Should All Be Feminists," and restates the importance of feminism as ethics. I engage Adichie's ideas with the help of John Rawls's concept of justice as fairness. Rawls suggests the original position, which is a thought experiment that proposes a condition in which people are free, and are able to make choices about the principles that would guide their lives.

Rawls's idea of the original position and works of fiction have one thing in common: they ask people to deploy their imagination and visualize ideal situations in which fairness is the norm. I conclude my discussion by examining Adichie's fictions as instantiations of her ethical call.

Chapter 3, "Diary of Intense Pain: The Postcolonial Trap and Women's Rights," picks up a major strain of the arguments established in the introduction, which is the idea that writing back to the Empire hardly addresses the needs of Africans as individuals; rather it insinuates a postcolonial ideology comparable to the oppressive traditional cosmology that the African women writers are challenging. NoViolet Bulawayo and Chinelo Okparanta have been criticized, by mostly male critics, as serving the imperial needs of Western audiences by indulging in a pornographic display of poverty and misery. But the so-called poverty porn consists of instances of intense pain that the African patriarchal cultures have inflicted on African women's bodies. In this context, I discuss Bulawayo's *We Need New Names* (2013) and Okparanta's *Happiness, Like Water* (2013).

Starting with the idea that the body of a woman who has undergone genital mutilation is disabled, the fourth chapter, "The Body in Pain and the Politics of Culture," engages Warsan Shire's poetry collection, *Teaching my Mother How to Give Birth* (2011) and Nnedi Okorafor's work of magical realism, *Who Fears Death* (2010) as narratives that demonstrate the ethical stance of writing back to the body on the one hand, and on the other, challenge the (mis)use of culture as a means of legitimizing pain.

Chapter 5, "Abstractions as Disablers of Women's Rights," brings to a conclusion the argument posited in Chapters 3 and 4, and which concerns the relation between African cultures and the female body in pain. I read Lola Shoneyin's *The Secret Lives of Baba Segi's Wives* (2010), which is a narrative of polygamy as an institution that inherently incapacitates women's bodies, and Petina Gappah's *An Elegy for Easterly* (2009), a collection of short stories set in Zimbabwe, as expressions of contemporary African women's efforts to challenge the rigidity of African cultural and nationalist paradigms and gender relations in order to enhance the awareness of human rights.

Chapter 6 addresses slavery as a symbol of universal human rights abuse. The discussion of slavery segues into a macro discourse of human rights. Chika Unigwe's novel, *On Black Sisters' Street* (2009) tells the stories of four African women who work as sex slaves in Brussels. The story is a metaphor of the condition of women in Africa because it draws attention to the indignities inflicted on women's bodies directly.

Chapter 7, "Human Rights as Liberatory Social Thought," focuses on the macro instances of human rights abuses in society through the lenses of abuse of women. This chapter engages Atta's *Everything Good Will Come* (2004) and *Swallow* (2010). Through them it examines the breakdown in intersubjectivity between men and women as well as in society as a whole. Atta makes a connection between the patriarchal abuses in the family and the military abuses in society, and pays particular attention to the dignities of children and the rights of women as correlative to those in society.

Chapter 8, "The Obligation to Bear Testimony to Human Rights Abuses," expands the argument of Chapters 6 and 7 by underlining the ethical obligation to bear witness not only to women's sufferings that are specific to cultural ideologies, but also to other forms of human rights abuses, especially during wars. This chapter studies the poems of Patricia Jabbeh Wesley, who details the human rights abuses during the brutal civil war in Liberia. It thus enhances the truth that women's rights are human rights and human rights are women's rights.

Note

1. Admit these distinctions are not clear-cut. Essentially you cannot have a macro instance of pain that does not affect individuals. The reverse is also the case.

Acknowledgements

I am grateful to Northeastern Illinois University for the 2013 Summer Research Stipend that allowed me to work on the initial manuscript of this book. I have been blessed with great students whose critical engagement in class helped me to rethink some of my assumptions. I have also benefitted from my colleagues in the English department. You are the best, friends.

I have drawn much help from friends and colleagues, some of whom have read some parts of this book in raw manuscript. Carli Coetzee, Paul Ugor, Julie Iromuanya, Patricia Jabbeh Wesley, Sangmin Bae, Meg Samuelson, Cris Toffolo, Jeanine Ntihiregeza, Jane Bryce, Tunji Osinubi, Emily Garcia, Alfred Frankowski. Thanks a lot.

Parts of this book appeared in different formats in scholarly journals. I am grateful to these journals for allowing me to reprint them: *Research in African Literature*, for "Feminism With a Big 'F': Ethics and the Rebirth of African Feminism in Chika Unigwe's '*On Black Sisters' Street*'"; *African Studies* (www.tandfonline.com), for "Feminist Empathy: Unsettling African Cultural Norms in *The Secret Lives of Baba Segi's Wives*," and *Interdisciplinary Literary Studies*, "The Open Wounds of Being: The Poetics of Testimony in the Works of Patricia Jabbeh Wesley."

My fellowship at the Stellenbosch Institute for Advanced Studies (STIAS) helped me to prepare this manuscript for publication. STIAS, you really live up to your prestigious reputation.

To Maria. I sincerely appreciate your unwavering support all these years.

Contents

1 Introduction: The Ethical Turn in African Literature   1

2 Feminism as Fairness   43
  Chimamanda Ngozi Adichie

3 Diary of Intense Pain: The Postcolonial Trap
  and Women's Rights   69
  Chinelo Okparanta and NoViolet Bulawayo

4 The Body in Pain and the Politics of Culture   95
  Nnedi Okorafor and Warsan Shire

5 Abstractions as Disablers of Women's Rights   121
  Lola Shoneyin and Petina Gappah

6 The Enslaved Body as a Symbol of Universal Human
  Rights Abuse   145
  Chika Unigwe

7 Human Rights as Liberatory Social Thought   165
  Sefi Atta

8 The Obligation to Bear Testimony to Human
   Rights Abuses   187
   Patricia Jabbeh Wesley

Bibliography   209

Index   227

CHAPTER 1

Introduction: The Ethical Turn in African Literature

Since the late 1980s, African literature has been moving away from the need to confront the West. Bill Ashcroft, Helen Tiffin, and Gareth Griffith suggested the term, "write back" to designate the obsession of the literatures of the former colonized cultures with addressing themselves to the imperial canon.[1] That obsession no longer dominates African writing; African writers increasingly engage the African world per se. Evan Mwangi captures this development in the aptly titled *Africa Writes Back to Self*, in which he discusses the issue of self-reflexivity in contemporary African writing and by women writers in particular.[2] Recent scholarly works on African literature suggest that African literature has not always focused exclusively on meeting the gaze of the West; it has also been concerned with the self. For instance, in examining the phenomenon of pain in African literature, Zoe Norridge suggests that African literature is also a literature of the self.[3] Brenda Cooper's *A New Generation of African Writers*[4] investigates the concept of multiple belonging in a globalized world. Ranka Primorac's *The Place of Tears: The Novel and Politics in Modern Zimbabwe* considers the degree to which Zimbabwean novels address the Zimbabwean condition.[5] Also of importance is Ken Harrow's *Less than One and Double: A Feminist Reading of African Women's Writing*.[6]

The move away from the "write back" ideology asserted itself most vigorously in the new millennium, especially among a group of women writers who secured their positions in African letters between 2000 and

2013 and who have been designated as third-generation writers, that is those who were born in the 1960s and 1970s, and who rose to prominence in the new millennium. Among them are Chimamanda Ngozi Adichie, Sefi Atta, Doreen Baingana, Chika Unigwe, Lola Shoneyin, Petina Gappah, Chinelo Okparanta, NoViolet Bulawayo, Patricia Jabbeh Wesley, Nnedi Okorafor, and Warsan Shire.[7] These writers are more interested in exploring the human condition in their local spheres than in addressing the world from the perspective of the colonized and oppressed. Whereas earlier generations of African writers presented Africa to the world by countering colonial Manichean allegories, these contemporary African writers raise questions of immediate ethical relevance: Who and what are Africans to one another? What exactly does one African body mean to another African body?

Since these women *write back to self*, it is appropriate that they begin with their bodies. They do so in the belief that to be is to be a body. They confront African gender politics and the appalling human rights condition of women, but they do so without the radicalism of certain factions within the feminist movement in the West or of late twentieth-century African alternatives. Rather, having learned from the missteps of both, they make a simple demand from their societies in regard to the relations between men and women; they demand fairness and recognition.

Zoe Norridge states that there is "hesitancy among academics to address questions of pain in African literature" because of the fear of confirming negative stereotypes about Africa.[8] She also argues that "the literary aestheticisation of stories transforms pain into more than a 'memory,' a 'wound' or a 'theory,' instead lending to hurt the immediacy and poignancy of the present." I agree with her idea that "pain is often either a result or a cause of the denial of another person's voice," and I interpret her assertions in ethical terms: (needless) pain is an instance of human rights abuse.[9] I argue that African women writers tell stories of bodies of women in pain primarily to establish their subjectivities in a world that is predominantly controlled by people's uses of abstractions such as heritage, culture, tradition, and religion as justifications for their actions and relations to others.[10] Through a close reading of selected texts, I examine how these writers seek to answer the question of who or what women are, and I invite a reassessment of the conditions of gender relations and human rights in Africa.

African Feminism: Old Wine in a New Wine Bottle?

In the preface, I explained that Chimamanda Ngozi Adichie and many women writers of her generation have revived interest in feminism by drawing attention to the bodies of women in pain. I work with Susan Moller Okin's definition of feminism, which is "the belief that women should not be disadvantaged by their sex, that they should be recognized as having human dignity equally with men, and the opportunity to live as fulfilling and as freely chosen lives as men can."[11] As far as this definition goes, the different generations of African women writers and activists pursue the same goal. The obvious difference between third-generation African women writers and their foremothers is the formers' bold embrace of feminist identity.[12] Whereas, for instance, Buchi Emecheta claimed that she was a feminist with a small "f", Adichie declares herself to be a happy feminist.[13] Susan Z. Andrade has rightly argued that Adichie and others of her generation are indebted to Emecheta, Flora Nwapa, and Mariama Bâ, among others.[14] Unlike the Nwapa-Emecheta generation that was much concerned with the nation as a construct that must be defended against the onslaught of the West, third-generation African women writers are less occupied with concepts of the nation as a space.[15] They are more interested in the woman's body as a violated entity.[16] They see their bodies not as symbols or allegories of something else, but rather as homes to their individual selves. This is the dominant idea that runs through the works of these authors. When they write about polygamy, female genital excision, rape, spousal abuse, or other forms of gender discrimination, they do so because they are acutely aware of these bodies as exclusively theirs, not as belonging to society or their culture. They therefore contest the physical and psychological pain inflicted on them. Most importantly, they draw attention to fundamental ethical questions, one of which is the relation between the African man and the African woman. The contemporary African woman writer therefore understands her feminism to be an ethical statement; it involves people relating to people as individuals and not merely as members of groups.

Ethics, broadly defined, is a science of morality.[17] Morality, in turn, deals with what is good or bad, permissible or forbidden. Whereas morality might be personal, ethics is always about the quality of one's relations with others.[18] Ethics defines right or wrong ways of being or relating to others.[19] Ethics as relationship is intrinsically a recognition of the other. For Judith Butler, the story of how we arrive at the recognition of the other is as important as that recognition itself, for it is the genealogy of the recognition that gives it its ethical character. Underlining the structure of morality as a quality generated among people, she states in an interview that pursuing a moral mode of being is not "something that is exclusively 'mine' and so will have to be a mode of being that is bound up with others with all the difficulty and promise that implies."[20] She uses Adriana Cavarero's idea of recognition; for Cavarero the ultimate question central to recognition of the other is: "Who are you?" Butler interprets Cavarero as suggesting that the subject encounters the other as already essentially "exposed, visible," and as "existing in a bodily way and of necessity in a domain of appearance." This bodily existence is what constitutes the individual's sense of own life and because this corporeality is exposed "it is not that over which I can have control."[21]

Butler's interpretation echoes Alasdair MacIntyre's in *Dependent Rational Animals*.[22] As embodied beings, we are vulnerable, exposed, and therefore are dependent on others, that is, we rely on them for recognition. In Butler's understanding, the recognition of the other takes the singularity and vulnerability of oneself and the other into consideration; this includes the fact that recognition is not an event fixed in time. It is a continuous process that is best captured in the question: "Who are you?" Butler argues that the ethical stance consists in asking that question:

> without any expectation of a full or final answer. This Other to whom I pose this question will not be captured by any answer that might arrive to satisfy the question. So if there is, in the question, a desire for recognition, this will be a desire which is under an obligation to keep itself alive as desire, and not to resolve itself through satisfaction.[23]

To ask "Who are you?" is to indicate interest in relating to the other; it is to invite the other to narrate. Narration assumes an audience, a listener; the narrator/audience sets up the paradigm for relation/recognition. Every individual is a story, which in itself is open-ended, that is, subject to interpretations and discourse. But the narrator tells her story in the knowledge that the act itself is imperfect because it is contingent and relies on the listener to make sense. Listening implies being open and receptive; it also means not settling with whatever answer is given as if it had provided all the information about a person. On the contrary, it establishes a certain degree of dialectical relation between the questioner and the narrator. Butler captures the nature of this dialectical relationship in her suggestion that "the norms by which I seek to make myself recognizable are not fully mine."[24] In other words, I depend on the others to be complete. "So the account of myself that I give in discourse never fully expresses or carries this living self. My words are taken away as I give them, interrupted by the time of a discourse that is not the same as the time of my life."[25]

Lawrence Buell believes that the meeting point of ethics and literature is the relationship "between texts and readers."[26] It is in the texts that readers are asked to imagine the lives of people (characters) they will never meet. As Wolfgang Iser has shown, the act of reading implies a continuous dialogue between the text and the reader.[27] In narrating the stories of women in sexist or patriarchal societies, contemporary African women writers present women who demand that their world asks them the simple question: "Who are you?" instead of providing answers in forms of ideologies.

Ethics as relation and recognition occupies a central place in Emmanuel Levinas's philosophy. Ethics is activated in the presence of the other. For him, it is "the calling into question of my spontaneity by the presence of the Other."[28] Spontaneity means acting as one desires; it implies the activities of self-existent person, a for-itself. When ethics calls my spontaneity into question, it means that I am no longer free to act as I wish. The presence of the other necessarily limits me. But this limitation is not to be understood in a negative sense; it is rather the imposition of responsibility on me. For Levinas, "the strangeness of the Other, his irreducibility to the I, to my thoughts and my possession, is precisely accomplished as a calling into question of my spontaneity, as ethics."[29] In a conversation with Philippe Nemo, he explains that the "face speaks...It is in this that it renders possible and begins all discourse." This discourse is a call which the other's face initiates and which I am obliged to respond to, and in responding, I assume "responsibility which is this authentic relationship."[30] Thus the face is definitively ethical. If ideology totalizes the individual, the face restores her infinity, that is, releases the hold that time and definition have on her. The face prevents us from seeking to capture the being of the other in abstractions such as culture or heritage. Levinas's conception of infinity reflects what Butler means by the desire that keeps itself alive as desire.[31] The notion of the face as ethical expresses my uses of ethics to foreground my discussion of the feminist and human rights concerns of the African women writers in this book. How, for instance, does the face (the body) of the woman in pain urge us to confront the totality (abstraction) that has forced her into that condition? This question is precisely what the writing of contemporary Anglophone African women does. The writers recognize the fact that totality or abstractions disable women's bodies. My project therefore engages the question of how they address women as *disabled bodies* in African patriarchal societies.

By disabled bodies, neither I, nor African women writers suggest that women are inferior by nature or, as Aristotle argued "mutilated males."[32] Any action, condition or system that renders a body or mind incapable of exercising its freedom or realizing its possibilities, disables that body or mind. It is in this sense that I use the term disable, or that I refer to women in patriarchal societies as disabled. As Rosemarie Garland-Thomson states, "more recently, feminist theorists have argued that female embodiment is a disabling condition in sexist cultures."[33] Being a woman is not a disability, but being so in a sexist, patriarchal culture is a handicap. As Iris Marion Young argues, "women in sexist society are physically handicapped."[34] Young argues that women's lives are shaped by society's idea of femininity, which exists as a "set of structures and conditions which delimit the typical situation of being a woman in a particular society."[35] Women are forced into a socially constructed limitation by the roles and expectations their societies place on them. Some of these expectations are packaged in moral or religious languages. They are therefore not living to the tune of their biology, but rather to the tune of social constructs. Within those social constructs, to be feminine is to live as your patriarchal society deems fit, and, given that men establish the paradigms of social existence, they always construct them to their own advantage, to serve their biology. When the socio-cultural apparatuses are designed to serve men's biology, they unavoidably work to the disadvantage of women, by reshaping their comportment to the tune of patriarchal imagination.

Pain is an integral part of being human. To inflict pain gratuitously is inhumane. Unwarranted pain (female genital mutilation, forced marriage, et cetera), which is often legitimized by culture and tradition, disables women's bodies and therefore constitutes an abuse of women's rights. A central argument in this book is that each time a woman is subjected to needless pain, she is violated, and her rights are denied her. The questions, therefore, are: How do African patriarchal and sexist cultures handicap women? What is the morally appropriate response to a culturally handicapped body? How do I relate to the body that has been denied rights? I argue that the easing of the unnecessary pain that the African women experience is a primary concern of contemporary African women writers. These writers demand a response from their readers. How might we understand that response?

I suggest that empathy is a tool by which these women writers draw attention to the condition of women in their societies and elicit responsibility from their readers. I therefore argue that African women writers tell stories about women in pain so that readers can put themselves in the position of those women.[36] This is what I mean by feminist empathy, which I define as the ability to feel oneself in the experience of a woman in suffering because of her gender. The goal of empathy, in this case, is to address the conditions that cause such suffering and therefore impede human flourishing.

AFRICAN FEMINISM: A SHORT HISTORICAL SKETCH

It belabors the obvious to assert that feminism is sometimes loaded with negative connotations, and not only in Africa. Indeed, for most Africans, it is a hot-button term. In Nigeria, for example, it is dismissed as "nonsense." Many there believe that Nigerian women "are all right...no problem."[37] Femi Ojo-Ade is one of the most vocal male critics of the concept in Africa; he suggests that it is little more than a misguided attempt by certain women progressives to strive to be men.[38] Chinweizu, the celebrated Afrocentric scholar and author of the groundbreaking *The West and the Rest of Us*, dismissed it in equally negative terms.[39] Feminism in Africa is generally seen as a Western import and hence part of a colonial paradigm.[40] However, I read the renewed interest in feminism by African women writers as a call for a moral reappraisal of society's relation to the personhood of women who suffer gender discrimination.

Although twenty first-century African women writers are not the first to raise feminist or human-rights issues in Africa, the theory that had guided the interpretation of the works of their predecessors was, like much of African postcolonial discourse, largely driven by the need to respond to the West's attempt to shape the African woman's image. Western feminism,[41] which has been studied and discussed in great detail, had been particularly concerned with the issues of white working-class women.

Thus in the late 1970s and early 1980s, women intellectuals belonging to minority cultures in the West, along with women in Africa, Asia, the Middle East, and Latin America, rightly pointed out the inadequacies of that form of feminism. Western feminism, for instance, ignored the role of racism, colonialism, and imperialism.[42] African feminist theory is part of third-wave feminism, and it highlights, among other things, those same roles in the subjugation of African women.[43] African feminism has therefore been shaped by the combined fear of a backlash in the traditional, patriarchal sectors of African societies and the need to challenge the Western domination of ideas about Africa. In what follows, I discuss some of the authors associated with African feminism.[44] My focus is exclusively on Anglophone writers and scholars.[45] My selection of authors is not exhaustive; it is based on my understanding of the extent to which they influenced the thinking of others.[46]

Carole Boyce Davies specifies ideas that make up a "genuine African feminism." Among them is the recognition of African women's common struggle with African men to remove the "yoke of foreign domination and European/American exploitation." She also urges a recognition of the fact that "certain inequities and limitations existed/exist in traditional societies and that colonialism reinforced them and introduced others." In what can be seen as her preferred feminist theoretical approach, she argues that any future work on African feminist writing must "come to grips with issues such as the treatment of women characters and the growing presence of African women writers."[47] Ifi Amadiume's *Male Daughters, Female Husbands: Gender and Sex in an African Society* did for African feminist discourse what Achebe's *Things Fall Apart* did for African literature. It wrote back to the Western feminist canon by providing a prolonged and profound critique of the Western misrepresentation of the African woman's personhood. As Amadiume argues, Western women, referencing their own history, believed in the "universal social and cultural inferiority of women." For her, "this kind of global presupposition is itself ethnocentric," because Western female scholars were concerned primarily with themselves. Therefore, they viewed all other women in their own image. These ethnocentric biases led them to condemn "other people's customs such as arranged marriage and polygyny as exploitative to women."[48] Amadiume focuses on Igbo culture, and argues that contrary to Western assumptions, third-world women, and Igbo women in particular, have not been helpless; they have always had access to power. She contends that the:

flexibility of Igbo gender construction meant that gender was separate from biological sex. Daughters could become sons and consequently male. Daughters and women in general could be husbands to wives and consequently males in relation to their wives, etc.[49]

Amadiume provides a counter-narrative rooted in culture, one that could be realized sociologically. However, her suggestion that Igbo daughters could become sons and consequently male, that is, that they are not limited by their gender, fails to interrogate the patriarchal epistemologies that undergird the practice of women marrying other women. Oyeronke Oyewumi reaffirms the basic contention of Amadiume's book through examples from Oyo-Yoruba culture. She attacks the Western imposition of gender categories on Yoruba cosmology. For her, the "cultural logic of Western social categories is based on an ideology of biological determinism: the conception that biology provides the rationale for the organization of the social world. Thus the cultural logic is actually bio-logic."[50] For her, "African women and feminism are at odds because despite the adjectives used to qualify feminism, it is Western feminism that inevitably dominates even when it is not explicitly the subject under consideration."[51] Western feminism, she argues, is entangled with the history and practice of European and North American imperialism; those interested in feminism in Africa and other parts of the world outside the West almost always propagate Western interests even without being aware of it.[52] Oyewumi's notion of African feminism is premised on saving the African woman from the imperial gaze. But like Amadiume's, it does not interrogate the African patriarchal gaze, which is equally devastating to the African woman's body.

Chikwenye Okonjo Ogunyemi argues that gender questions in Africa are fundamentally different from those of the West and therefore would be better understood via the concept of womanism, which, for her and others such as Alice Walker, is an ideology designed for African women by African women to come to grips with issues that are specific to women both in Africa and the Diaspora.[53] The life of the African woman is shaped by a "mother-centered ideology, with its focus on caring—familial, communal, national, and international" aspects of human relationships. The operative idea in the concept of womanism is that the African woman is by nature more disposed toward care and mediation than her Western (white) counterpart. She lists other issues that the African woman has to contend with and which define African womanism. Included among these are racism, imperialism, and capitalism.[54] Okonjo Ogunyemi states that African women do not perceive themselves as existing independently of their menfolk. In that regard, any understanding of feminism as womanism must include the African tradition of *palava* (continual negotiation). She praises women who, in their accommodation to polygamy, exhibit true African womanism.[55]

For Mary Kolawole, feminism has always been rooted in African cultures. The idea of "group action by women, based on common welfare in social, cultural, economic, religious and political matter[s]" is nothing more than what feminism demands, and it "is indigenous and familiar to a majority of these women."[56] Catherine Obianuju Acholonu believes that motherism, rather than feminism, should be the central idea guiding African women's lives. For her, motherism is boldly Afrocentric and should "be anchored on the matrix of motherhood which is central to African metaphysics and has been the basis of the survival and unity of the black race through the ages."[57] Molara Ogundipe-Leslie's concept is more social than racial. She believes that the African alternative to Western feminism should be Stiwanism. Stiwanism is an acronym for Social Transformation Including Women of Africa.[58] Obioma Nnaemeka pleads for the recovery of what is indigenous to Africa. For her, "African worldviews and thought are capable of providing the theoretical rack on which to hang African literature."[59] She proposes a term for this recovery: nego-feminism, which is grounded in negotiation. For her, "negotiation has the double meaning of 'give and take/exchange' and 'cope with successfully/go around.'" Specifically, African feminism "challenges through negotiations and compromise, knows when, where, and how to detonate patriarchal landmines; it also knows when, where, and how to go around patriarchal land mines."[60]

In her compelling analysis of the Igbo society, Nkiru Uwechia Nzegwu argues that contemporary appeals to culture as a means to justify men's position and to curtail women's rights are erroneous. She states that "most of this curtailment occurs within the context of the family, specifically under the provisions of family law that rest on customs and traditions as well as on cultural conceptions of the family."[61] Ironically, these customs and traditions, Nzegwu argues, are the inventions of the European colonial policies. Thus the African family that had hitherto made specific provisions for women has now been remodeled on the European Christian nuclear and patriarchal structure in which the man is the center of the family.

If it is true that African women had rights before colonialism, how might those rights be reclaimed and enhanced? What should the contemporary African woman undertake in order to salvage her own body? The important issue raised by African women is: "How do you deal with this pain I am experiencing?"

THE WEAKNESSES OF AFRICAN FEMINIST THEORY

The theoretical approaches to African feminism as articulated by the African women authors thus far discussed are insufficient to explain the place of the African woman in traditional African cosmology. Nor can they explain the contemporary African woman's experience. They are largely Afrocentric abstractions designed to subvert and replace Eurocentric models.[62] The gesture towards abstraction has its own problems. The individual is short-changed. As Elleke Boehmer rightly argues, "women-as-sign buttresses national imagining," and "gender has been, to date, habitual and apparently intrinsic to national imagining."[63] Women-as-sign is, however, a project in which female subjectivity is ignored. Secondly, in the project of nation-building, the African woman is used as a symbol of virtue in the African world, which, as Florence Stratton argues, is not necessarily positive. She contends that the Negritude construct, of Africa as a woman, created and worshipped a mythology that does not further any understanding of the African woman.[64] Meg Samuelson extends Boehmer's arguments and examines how women's subjectivities were authored and performed, especially during the South African transition to post-apartheid democracy. Samuelson is particularly "concerned with questions of who gets to speak and be heard, under what conditions they speak and where their authority of authorship begins and ends."[65]

Of course, I do not wish to diminish the importance of these African feminist conceptions. To the contrary, they form important historical accounts of African women's efforts to interpret their colonized world, and therefore must be read sympathetically, given the urgency at that time to respond to colonialist/Westerners' narratives about Africa. Their ideas, in my reading, should be understood as part of the postcolonial project of identity- and nation-building. Yet, we cannot ignore the fact that the African woman has fallen victim to these meta-projects of nation-building. Pinkie Mekgwe recognizes the importance of African women positing their own understanding of feminism and femininity because "women do not easily fall into neat categories." She insists that "as long as theories of African feminism remain 'reactionary' and definable 'against' Western feminism, they are not likely to go beyond 'hinting the vision of a more liberated future' because they are primarily tied to an elusive notion of a common history of colonialism for definition."[66] She argues further that if Africa continues to define herself against the West, she will remain entangled in "a colonial trap," and will likely never reach "self-definition and total independence."[67] By colonial trap, Mekgwe refers to the need to talk back to the West especially in the same binary language adopted by the West in its othering of Africa.[68] Part of the colonial trap is the inflation of difference as a tool of resistance.[69] Given their attention to nation-building, and their reliance on autochthonous grand narratives, African feminist theories discussed thus far have done very little to highlight the specific issues about women in different African cultures: the being of women as women. The image of the woman as a peace-loving, compromise-seeking person who would sacrifice her own needs for the greater good or for the needs of her children is undercurrent in this thinking. The mother bears her pain in silence for some imagined (and imaginary) greater good.[70] Mekgwe's idea finds support in Sylvia Tamale's advocacy of radical feminism. Rejecting the pretensions of the first-generation African feminists, Tamale argues:

> We must reject the arguments that Africa is not ready for radical feminism. What such arguments are saying in essence is that we are not ready for transformation. In fact, the majority of people who espouse the "women-should-take-it-nice-and-slow" line are those that have never directly experienced gender discrimination.[71]

Tamale identifies radical feminism as a means to reject "all forms of fundamentalisms," such as the idea of virginity tests or the crippling of women's sexual and reproductive rights, all of which "pose a serious threat to the feminist agenda."[72] I agree with Tamale, especially in her observation that those who reject feminism, men in particular, have probably never experienced gender discrimination; they have never been disabled by systems designed to exploit women. These women writers make the same argument through their stories.

Besides the exploitation of the trope of African femininity, what these various theories have in common is that they fall back on abstract group identities. Florence Stratton captures the fate of the African woman in the face of anti-colonial narratives, symbolized by Achebe's *Things Fall Apart*.

She asks: "how could things fall apart for whom they were not together?"[73] Of what use is the idea of African liberation for a woman who has just been divorced and left without means because she did not give birth to a son? How do we assess the condition of a woman who realizes that her brothers have all inherited her father's estates because they are males, and she must be a guest to one of them?

Female Subjectivity and African Feminist Discourse

In *The Nation Writ Small*, Susan Andrade follows a Marxist path of interpretation of African women's writing, and aims to revitalize Fredric Jameson's allegorical reading of postcolonial African literature; she argues that the feminist impulses in works by female African writers in the twentieth century can best be understood within nationalist epistemologies. In such works, and contrary to the interpretive modality that privileged African female subjectivities, Andrade asserts that "nationalism or national politics takes precedence over or usurps women's subjectivity."[74] Even where these writers' narratives center on local spheres such as the family, they do so, in Andrade's view, only when such scenes function as a "unit that looms over and plays out national dramas."[75]

Though Andrade's reading offers valuable insights into African women's writing in the twentieth century, I am attracted to critical works that have interpreted the same writing as a quest for African female subjectivity per se. These scholars understand the female subject not as symbolic; rather it is an end in itself, one that is located in the body of living women. This is not to reduce the value of Andrade's insights. However, it is worth mentioning that as colonized subjects, twentieth-century women writers such as Emecheta, Flora Nwapa, and Mariama Bâ were definitely concerned with the destiny of the nations they inherited from their colonizers. But they were feminists with a small "f" and as such, more interested in the pain of a woman's body than in national issues.[76] Indeed, because the first and second generations of African women writers undertook to right the wrongs done to their bodies, many third-generation African women writers consider them as their foremothers.[77]

I pointed out in the previous section that conventional African feminism largely replaced Eurocentric abstractions with Afrocentric models. Any theoretical approach to women's issues in Africa that fails to dislodge such constructs invariably fails to address how African women's worlds are authored. The only way to negate ideologies is to focus on the individual. In this assertion, I echo Carole Boyce Davies, Salome C. Nnoromele,[78] and Juliana Makuchi Nfah-Abbenyi.

I have already commented on Boyce Davies's idea that any true discussion of African feminist writing must "come to grips with issues such as the treatment of women characters."[79] Pursuing the same line of thinking, Nfah-Abbenyi traces the history of the absence and silencing of women's voices in African literature, and argues that over time, "the African woman was... spoken for; she herself was no speaking subject."[80] African women writers have "therefore posited the African woman as a speaking subject, making their 'self-descriptions' the nucleus to challenge the 'uniform generalizations' by many male authors."[81] These generalization represent patriarchal uses of abstraction in relation to African women. She suggests engaging "women's subjectivity through the critical use of gender as a category of analysis in feminist research grounded in African women's writing."[82] I understand Davies and Nfah-Abbenyi to mean that the experiences and feelings of individual African women, the ways they perceive the world, and their pains and pleasures are integral to an understanding of African women in general. The purposeful focusing on women's subjectivities negates the effects of abstraction. Following in the footsteps of these scholars, I offer a new perspective that acknowledges the African woman for who she is: a person with unique dreams, desires, fears, aspirations, and a consciousness that deserve the total attention of society and those she lives with.[83] If I speak of new perspectives or theories, I do not intend to add to the plethora of neologisms, some of which were mentioned above. Nor am I interested in discovering an undiscovered African essence that would provide answers to African discourses of feminism. My concept of theory follows the succinct definition given by Terry Eagleton in *After Theory*: a "reasonably systematic reflection on our assumptions."[84] In framing my idea of feminist empathy, I ask: what does an African woman mean when she calls on her society to be fair-minded in its thinking about her and about male–female relations? Being male and African, how should I respond to this call? To appreciate the moral impact of this question, I put myself in the position of a fifteen year-old girl about to be married off to a fifty year old man. I put myself in the position of a woman whose clitoris is excised in accordance with the demands of her culture.

My reading of contemporary African women writers via feminist empathy seeks to highlight female subjectivities to the degree that they flourish in the company of others. Whereas the African woman has been *spoken for* and narrated as a bearer of culture, and whereas she has been encouraged to *speak for herself*, it is time to turn our attention to how she seeks to *speak with*. By speaking with her friends, partners, brothers and sisters, uncles and nieces, the African woman draws attention not only to her individual self but also to other people who inhabit her world. She draws attention to her community as a space of *ubuntu*, a space where human life is allowed to flourish.

Empathy: Making Sense of a Concept

In the preface, I defined feminist empathy as the ability to feel oneself into the experience of a woman in unwarranted suffering. Empathy is not the same as pity. It is not sympathy. It transcends both. The *OED* defines empathy as "the power of projecting one's personality (and so fully comprehending) the object of contemplation." Mencius is best known for giving Confucianism its most profound philosophical grounding. He says: "no man is devoid of a heart sensitive to the suffering of others. Suppose a man were, all of a sudden, to see a young child on the verge of falling into a well. He would certainly be moved to compassion."[85] Adam Smith argues that we are fundamentally interested in the fortunes of others; we identify with others by "conceiving what we ourselves should feel in that like situation." This identification requires a conscious effort of imagination. In some measure, we become "the same person with him, and thence form some idea of his sensations, and even feel something which, though weaker in degree, is not altogether unlike them."[86] Smith recognizes the impossibility of feeling exactly what others feel; he therefore stresses the situation that provokes those feelings. Martha Nussbaum acknowledges the same condition in her definition of empathy as the "imaginative reconstruction of the experience of the sufferer." Empathy "involves a participatory enactment of the situation of the sufferer, but always combined with the awareness that one is not oneself the sufferer."[87]

Frans De Waal states that empathy is an instinct that humans have in common with the primates.[88] He traces the contemporary use of empathy to Theodor Lipps (1851–1914), a German psychologist.[89] Lipps notes that we experience suspense when watching a high-wire artist "because we vicariously enter his body and thus share his experience. We're on the rope with him."[90] Lipps describes this interaction as *Einfühlung* (a feeling into). He further offers *empatheia, em* (into), and *pathos* (feeling), "experiencing strong affection or passion" with the other.[91] Therefore empathy is a sentiment that compels one to enter into the feelings of other, different selves.

Simon Baron-Cohen argues that "empathy occurs when we suspend our single-minded focus of attention, and instead adopt a double-minded focus of attention."[92] The single-minded focus of attention considers other people as objects, perhaps to be used for our benefit. Baron-Cohen further argues that:

> Being able to empathize means being able to understand accurately the other person's position, to identify with "where they are at".... Empathy makes the other person feel valued, enabling them to feel their thoughts and feeling have been heard, acknowledged and respected.[93]

Suzanne Keen argues that "empathy, a vicarious, spontaneous sharing of affect, can be provoked by witnessing another's emotional state, by hearing about another's condition, or even by reading."[94] She provides a succinct differentiation between empathy and sympathy. The empathetic person says: "I feel what you feel. *I feel your pain*," whereas in sympathy one says "I feel supportive about your feelings. *I feel pity for your pain*."[95] Empathy is superior to pity and sympathy in the sense that in it, the empathizer and the empathized are seen as equal. The only difference is that one experiences discomfort and the other feels it vicariously. Unlike in pity, there is no feeling of condescension.

Empathy is not an uncontested concept. Keen points out that some feminists and postcolonial critics dismiss empathy as relying on the notion of universal human emotions. For them, empathy "becomes yet another example of the Western imagination's imposition of its own values on cultures and peoples that it scarcely knows, but presumes to 'feel with,' in cultural imperialism of the emotions."[96] There is a palpable concern that empathy might lead to paternalism. But this critique assumes that Western imperialism is concerned with the humanity of the oppressed or exploited peoples of the world. The opposite is indeed the case. As Abdul JanMohamed[97] and Albert Memmi[98] have maintained, imperialism actually seeks to negate the humanity of the oppressed, and it does so by deploying what JanMohamed has called the Manichaean allegory. Indeed, were the colonialists or imperialists to exercise empathy, their project of domination would fall apart because they would have switched perspectives with the exploited people of their colonies. The critique also assumes that the colonized have no capacity or no need for empathy among themselves. Empathy is not passive, and it does not seek to shape the life of the other. The only way to appreciate the importance of empathy is to imagine a world without it, a world in which a great deal of personal interaction is controlled by cold logic and adherence to abstract ideologies.

I am drawn to the concept of empathy because it is the most basic and profound form of relation between individuals. It functions without regard to culture or ideology except, of course, where it has been systematically blocked by upbringing and indoctrination. Nazi Germany, apartheid South Africa, and the Jim Crow American South are the most obvious examples. De Waal argues that:

> We sometimes deliberately shut the portal, such as when we suppress identification with a declared enemy group. We do so by removing their individuality, defining them as an anonymous mass of unpleasant, inferior specimen of a different taxonomic group.[99]

Where empathy is not blocked by indoctrination, it brings people back to the most basic form of bodily identification with others regardless of race, sex, age, religious beliefs, and other forms of group identifications. Colonialism, imperialism, and other forms of exploitation and oppression close the portals of empathy by maintaining narratives that dehumanize different groups. The importance of empathy in cultural, political, and legal institutions cannot be overemphasized. It often means the difference between saving a drowning person and leaving him to die. James D. Johnson et al. have argued that the absence of racial empathy can lead to problems in the American judicial system; it impacts everything from jury selection to verdicts. Thus justice is not always blind.[100] Sophie Trawalter et al. contend that racial bias can also impact doctors' relation to their patients. One study has shown that some medical professionals assume that black people feel less pain than white people. Therefore white people are more likely to receive treatment for pain while black people are left to languish.[101]

What is said of racial relations in America applies to relations between the sexes in Africa. Different ideologies that are packaged in seemingly harmless terms such as culture, tradition, heritage, et cetera, can block people's empathy towards others. Thus a man who has multiple wives or who simply dismisses his first wife because she did not bear him a son can easily explain away his action as merely fulfilling the dictates of his culture. In this regard, therefore, adhering to cultural heritage or even to nation-building as categories for interpreting the African woman's experience is flawed. My conception of feminist empathy undercuts the effects of ideologies by centering on women's subjectivities.[102]

Human Rights and Literature

What are human rights? How different are African and Western notions of human rights? Might they inform one another and thereby create a more robust understanding of the human person in society? How can literature prompt us to read, think, or talk about human rights and other ethical issues? I work provisionally with the definition of human rights as "rights inherent to all human beings, whatever our nationality, place of residence, sex, national or ethnic origin, colour, religion, language, or any other status."[103] Though this definition is fairly incontestable, differences and disagreements emerge in practice. In the introduction to their important collection of essays, An-naim Abdullahi and Francis M. Deng argue that local African cultural values can be used to check human rights abuses especially when leaders seek "shelter behind cultural relativism."[104] Assessing the various contributions to the collection, they, however, admit to the problems of defining the proper roles of various cultural traditions in regard to assuring the rights of individuals. The contributors have mixed feelings about this because "the assertiveness of these traditions acts as a force that casts doubt on the universal validity of international standards."[105] So, then, how do we mediate between universal human rights in theory and the often contradictory demands of different cultures in practice, especially in Africa?

Marie-Bénédicte Dembour has identified four schools of thought in human rights discourse. The natural school understands "human rights as those rights one possesses simply by being a human being." The deliberative school "conceives of human rights as political values that liberal societies *choose* to adopt." The protest school is "concerned first and foremost with redressing injustice." And the discourse school argues that "human rights exist only because people talk about them."[106] To date, the natural school's vision of human rights seems most widespread; it is also the one adopted by the United Nations in their Universal Declaration of Human Rights.[107] Thomas Buergenthal recalls that it is rare to read this declaration without thinking of the American Declaration of Independence, the ensuing Constitution, and the French Declaration of the Rights of Man.[108] Lynn Hunt and Jack Donnelly argue that the conceptions of human rights as they have been formulated and adopted by most countries of the world are the invention of the West; they are therefore historically contingent.[109] The issue, however, is not whether human rights as we know them today are Western inventions; it is whether the ideas inherent in them are universal.[110] Jack Donnelly argues that "if human rights are the rights one has simply because one is a human being as they usually are thought to be, then they are held 'universally,' by all human beings. They also hold 'universally' against all other persons and institutions."[111]

The Universal Declaration of Human Rights has its provenance in the European Enlightenment. As a reference point, I use the Kantian categorical imperative, which states that one should treat oneself and all humanity as an end and never as a means. Immanuel Kant is widely acknowledged as the philosophical father of human rights.[112] He understands humans to be endowed with reason and free will. For him, right consists in individuals exercising their free will in virtuous action. The categorical imperative is a universal principle that will guide people's relations to others: "Act only according to that maxim by which you can at the same time will that it should become a universal law."[113] But the categorical imperative might become problematic when put into practice, because people might consider their own individual actions to be universal and a justification for lording themselves over others. Kant therefore offers another imperative that would check the other in practice. He argues that:

> every other rational being thinks of his existence on the same rational ground which holds also for myself; thus it is at the same time an objective principle from which, as a supreme practical ground, it must be possible to derive all laws of the will. The practical imperative, therefore, is the following: Act so that you treat humanity, whether in your own person or in that of another, always as an end and never as means only.[114]

Kant's ideas are in the tradition of Descartes, who firmly established the duality of mind and body, reason and feeling; his formulation of right and dignity is centered on "I" even while referencing the other. The "I" is always at the center, and it is the "I" that has the capacity for reason. As Elizabeth S. Anker argues, even though the notions of human dignity upon which the Universal Declaration of Human Rights is based are useful, they are ultimately fictions, because of the "contradictory status of the body within" that liberal tradition:

> As liberalism scripts the human, the dignified individual in possession of rights is imagined to inhabit an always already fully integrated and inviolable body: a body that is whole, autonomous, and self-enclosed. This premise turns corporeal integrity into something of a baseline condition that precedes the ascription of dignity and rights to an individual. At the same time, it posits a dangerously purified subject, one purged of the body's assumedly anarchic appetencies: its needs and desires, its vulnerabilities and decay. And when the body cannot be thus ignored, the liberal tradition generally treats it as an entity that must be repressed, quarantined, or otherwise mastered by reason.[115]

At the core of Anker's argument is that the Enlightenment-based formulation of the Universal Declaration of Human Rights fails to locate the human body at the center of consideration. The degree to which the body is removed from consideration of dignity parallels the distance between the individual and community. This is perhaps where the African conceptions of human rights can help.

African conceptions of human rights are codified in the African Commission on Human and Peoples' Rights, also known as the Banjul Charter.[116] As most African scholars of human rights argue, Africa is not averse to the spirit of the Universal Declaration of Human Rights. There are, however, disagreements as to the specificities deriving from its genealogy. Sylvia Tamale argues that the formulation entrenched in the UN's declaration "reflects normative values, inspirations and interests of Western culture of a specific state of historical evolution."[117] In her thinking, African cultures and African feminism are not of necessity incompatible with human rights; indeed, African cultures have mechanisms to enhance women's rights. She cites article 29.7 of the Banjul Charter[118] and argues that any work designed to liberate women's sexuality and grant them their human rights has to address questions such as how cultural processes work and how to seize opportunities within systems that discriminate against women. Based on her research among the Baganda people of Uganda, she argues that African cultures have openings in which advocates of human rights can work. Her work on the sexuality of Baganda women has shown that it is possible for women to discover their agency within the parameters of African cultures. She "discovered how the evolution of *Ssenga* practices has allowed women to negotiate agency, autonomy and self-knowledge and their sexuality. This illuminated the liberatory value of indigenous institutions."[119] At the core of the *Ssenga* ritual is the maximization of female sexual pleasure, that is, a statement about women's ownership of their bodies. Tamale argues:

> At the helm of this elaborate socio-cultural institution is the paternal aunt (or surrogate versions thereof), whose role is to tutor young girls and women in a wide range of sexual matters, including pre-menarche practices, pre-marriage preparation, erotic instruction and reproduction.[120]

For Micere Githae Mugo, the African conception of human rights is closely aligned with the understanding that life does not belong to individuals alone. An individual is part and parcel of community, and whatever happens to this individual happens to the community. As she argues, orature was an important tool for "instilling consciousness pertaining to human rights among the Gikuyu" in *zamani* times. It is through orature that "the community and especially its young were nurtured."[121] For example, the Shona oral culture "includes ritual greetings and laudatory praises, myths, legends, stories, proverbs, riddles, word games and songs,"[122] and in each instance the individual was always embedded in the consciousness of the community. The reverse is also the case. She further notes that "the birth of a Shona child was received with happiness not only by his/her family but also by the whole community. S/he was in fact considered to be the child of every other parent in the community."[123] Mugo introduces the helpful concept of "*ubuntu*, which perceives communalism and collective growth as core aspects of any vision of human rights."[124] Mugo is not advocating a return to ancient collectivism. Rather she draws attention to the inseparability of the individual from community, and, by implication, the idea that rights and life are one and the same.

Mugo's concern, in my understanding, is how to embed the individual or the body in the life of community so that being human and living fully are manifested in the individual in that community. It is to be deduced that the community cannot willfully do harm to the individual because the community considers the individual as an organic part of itself. Tamale and Mugo do not suggest that there is no discrepancy between the ideals of the African notion of human rights and the reality on the ground. It is, however, instructive that both emphasize the body embedded in the community consciousness.

Ubuntu, a concept of African human rights, has experienced a robust revival, especially since Desmond Tutu praised it as an important element in South Africa's peaceful transition to democracy and its successful Truth and Reconciliation Commission. I have discussed *ubuntu* in full elsewhere.[125] I use Tutu's explication of the concept to support a distinctly African idea of human rights. For Tutu, *ubuntu*:

> speaks of the very essence of being human. When we want to give high praise to someone we say, "*Yu, u nobuntu*": "Hey, so-and-so has *ubuntu*." Then you are generous, you are hospitable, you are friendly and caring and compassionate. You share what you have. It is to say, "My humanity is caught up, is inextricably bound up, in yours." We belong in a bundle of life. We say, "A person is a person through other persons." It is not, "I think therefore I am." It says rather: "I am human because I belong. I participate. I share."[126]

In my view, a key to determining whether human rights are, or ought to be universal, lies in applying some of their assumptions to the lives of individuals, especially those suffering oppression, when they manifest in intersubjective relationships. By this, I mean that for every universally held idea to be relevant it must be capable of addressing the body. Indeed, it must consider the body as its locus. Barring the influence of ideologies, every human being, or rather *every body*, wants to be treated with dignity. That body wants to relate to other bodies in total freedom; that body wants to be seen not as a means to some end. These are the moral conditions that lend human rights their universality. I work within the contexts of the normative conception of morality, which stipulates that there are universal codes of conduct that can be justified by a systematic application of reason in all societies. All those who recognize the principles derived from that process can conduct themselves accordingly.[127] It is in this sense that I interpret feminist concerns framed as human rights as moral and universal. One of those concerns is the simple idea that male and female bodies are equal as human beings and should be treated accordingly.

Desmond Tutu contrasts *ubuntu* with Western thinking. "It is not, 'I think therefore I am.' It says rather, 'I am human because I belong. I participate. I share.'"[128] What Tutu and Micere Mugo say in regard to the African understanding of human rights is that the person (the body) is always embedded in the thinking of community. There cannot be an

"I" without a "You" and a "We." The expression, "I am because you are" places the condition of the existence of my body in that of the other. The "you" refers to the singular and the plural forms of the second person. Human flourishing implies the flourishing of the individual in the company of others.

Yet the African conception of human rights as posited above risks subsuming the individual within a collective "we," which might in turn be guided by the abstractions of ideologies. It is fair to argue that the African notion of human rights does not seek to replace the Western view; it makes the latter more palpable by incarnating the body in community. I agree with Elizabeth Anker that literature incarnates "facets of selfhood that liberal human rights obscure," and that writers "reclaim and reanimate registers of corporeal engagement."[129]

Joseph R. Slaughter asks how we can translate the abstract formulations of human rights into palpable forms, how we can render it legible. For him, this legibility is best achieved by the "*Bildungsroman*, whose plot we could provisionally gloss as the didactic story of individuals who are socialized in the process of learning for themselves what everyone else (including the reader) presumably already knows."[130] Slaughter argues that, in effect, the *Bildungsroman* and the liberal formulations of human rights:

> are mutually enabling fictions: each projects an image of the human personality that ratifies the other's idealistic visions of the proper relations between the individual and society and the normative career of free and full human personality and development.[131]

As Slaughter rightly observes, the *Bildungsroman* is exemplary in enabling our reading of human rights because of "its technical capacity to make the convoluted, esoteric, and improbable narrative grammar of citizen-subjectivation not only legible but ordinary, so ordinary that it often goes unremarked, seeming merely to conform to common sense."[132] The *Bildungsroman* is not the only literary form that achieves that goal. Poetry and other novel genres achieve it, although in varying degrees and in different forms. Indeed, narrative aids our comprehension of human rights, not only because it articulates human development or that it provides an idealistic vision of humanity, but also because it simply presents humanity in all its imperfections. As David Palumbo-Liu argues, literature "delivers" the lives of others to us and challenges us to respond and to relate to them.[133] With regard to the African women's writing under discussion here, literature delivers their pain and in so doing privileges those bodies in the community. One of the mechanisms through which literature and orature embed the body in the thinking of community is through empathy.

As Donnelly argues, human rights "should not be confused with the values or aspirations underlying it or with enjoyment of the object of the right."[134] We speak of rights when abstract aspirations or values such as dignity are realized socially in the lives of individuals. As far as abstract values go all peoples believe that every human being has dignity. In matters of rights though, opinions diverge. How then can there be universal rights when cultures and traditions are unique and opinionated? How can we find a justification to grant individuals in different cultures rights to their bodies, that is, the freedom to live their lives as they deem fit? What should we do, for instance, when cultural traditions allow for child marriage?[135] In Chapter 5, "Abstractions as Disablers of Women's Rights," I show that rationalizations based on cultural pluralism that had once been used to fend off the arrogance of Western cultural imperialism no longer suffice, There, I cite Jacob Zuma's recourse to his culture as a justification for having sex with a woman against her will. Indeed, contemporary African women writers reject these rationalizations, and they do so by telling about their bodies.

As I have already noted, women's rights are now widely accepted as human rights. A component of the rights Clinton spoke of is "the right to speak freely and the right to be heard."[136] These specifics recall the Cavarero/Butler question: "Who are you?" To speak is to provide an answer to that question, and to listen is to relate to the speaker. When we listen, we do so because we are morally obliged by the speaker's personhood. Consistent with Levinas's thinking, the speaker's face arrests our spontaneity, and imposes responsibility on us.

In the subsequent section, I discuss how literature enacts the other body's speech, or answers the question, "Who are you?" I seek to answer the question of how literature disposes us toward empathy.

Narratives, Privilege, and the Pain of Other People

Joan Didion underscores the anthropological and moral importance of stories in her assertion that "we tell ourselves stories in order to live."[137] We make sense of our experiences by telling them. This is true for both written and oral cultures. Stories show us how to live by helping us formulate ethical dispositions to the world. Stories make us aware of the dignity of others and the necessity to accord them their rights as humans. Underlining the importance of stories in human rights, James Dawes states that:

> After years spent interacting with human rights and humanitarian fieldworkers, I have come to believe that human rights work is, at its heart, a matter of storytelling... Indeed, for those in need of rescue and care, the hope of being able to tell the story is sometimes the only hope. How do you make your case? Get someone to believe you? Get someone to speak for you?[138]

As I have suggested above in my discussion of Judith Butler, narratives provide us with characters whose mere existence challenges us to ask the important question: Who are you? Their presence on the pages of our book provides answers to that question. These answers urge a recognition, a relation. Stories do not make categorical ethical statements; indeed, stories and their interpretations are not fixed as are rules of logic.[139] Stories do not tell one what to do in any given circumstance. However, as Arthur W. Frank argues, they:

> get under people's skin. Once stories are under people's skin, they affect the terms in which people think, know, and perceive. Stories teach people what to look for and what can be ignored; they teach what to value and what to hold in contempt.[140]

Frank talks specifically about how stories impart values. They do this effectively because they operate without our being conscious of their action. It is obvious that much of what we know about the world is received and shaped by our culture, and stories are one of the most fundamental ways that cultures function. We are literally what we tell ourselves about ourselves. Stories impart knowledge and shape people's views of the world. One of the ways that narratives appeal to us is by placing other people's vulnerabilities squarely before us and having them challenge us. Stories were central to the evolution of human rights in eighteenth-century European thought.[141] Even before Immanuel Kant formulated his famous conceptions of human rights, philosophers and writers such as Voltaire, Jean-Jacques Rousseau, and Samuel Richardson revealed instances of others in pain, and these revelations challenged people's sense of common decency. Narratives in general and those of eighteenth-century writers in particular encouraged introspection and respect toward one's fellow humans. In their most private moments, people began to reflect that others, after all, felt pain just as they, the readers, did. Lynn Hunt lays particular emphasis on the role of co-feeling in the formulation of human rights. Might this be what the contemporary African women writers hope to achieve with their narratives of women's pain? In telling stories of specific women, do they seek to shed light on the patriarchal privileges that made such pain possible in the hope that fellow members of their *ubuntu* community would respond?

Male privilege in most patriarchal societies in Africa is comparable to that of whites in racist Western societies. To fully understand this parallel, I use Shannon Sullivan's discussion of white privilege.[142] Sullivan describes white privilege as the "mental and physical patterns of engagement with the world that operate without conscious attention or reflection."[143] White privilege is manifested in the ways in which a white person thinks and occupies the world in the presence of others of disadvantaged ethnic background. Being white is a privilege to the extent that the difference in phenotypes and socio-cultural backgrounds grants the white person certain advantages over those others. With regard to whites in South Africa, who occupy privileged positions because of their race, Samantha Vice argues that an appropriate emotion for them to experience in the face of massive social and economic inequality in that country is one of agent-regret. By agent-regret she refers to the moral agency of the individual who acknowledges his guilt for having participated in, or benefited from, the unfairness of a system. Having acknowledged his guilt, the person feels shame. The feeling of shame, in turn, urges that person to action.[144] Agent-regret is therefore an active moral stance in the world.

Men enjoy certain privileges that derive solely from their gender, the most obvious of which is the unquestioned control over their own bodies, especially with regard to sexual functions. Ideas articulated by Sullivan and Vice express the positions of male members of African patriarchal cultures about which the contemporary African women writers write. When presented in narratives, the inequities in their traditional societies should awaken a sense of moral conscience in men so that they acquire a capacity for shame and agent-regret regarding their unmerited advantage over the female members of their society.

The foregoing reflection raises important questions for our inquiry about human rights. Why do sexist and patriarchal societies refuse to recognize the rights of women, that is, the right to own their bodies as men do theirs? Why do men in such societies not relate to women on the basis dictated by the question, "Who are you?" but rather on the basis of cultural and traditional ideologies? Why are women not allowed to play active roles in human flourishing in most African societies? Human flourishing is an extension of the Greek notion of *Eudaimonia*, "eu" ("good") and *daimōn* ("spirit"). It occupies a central place in Aristotle's philosophy and refers to the highest human virtue, a condition for living a life of enduring happiness and fulfillment. It also refers to the condition in which every individual achieves optimal well-being in freedom. It equates to a happy life. Human flourishing is also a condition of belonging to communities, helping others, and benefiting from others.[145]

Adam Newton argues that ethics, transmitted through literature, "signifies recursive, contingent, and interactive drama of encounter and recognition, the sort which prose fiction both crystallizes and recirculates in acts of interpretive engagement."[146] Of particular importance in Newton's discussion is his phrase, "drama of encounter and recognition." This is in alignment with Judith Butler's fruitful interpretation of Adriana Cavarero's question: Who are you? Narrative as ethics traces its provenance to Aristotle's *Poetics*. There are certain elements in Aristotle's definition of tragedy to which every understanding of narrative as ethics returns directly or indirectly: "imitation of an action" that "arouses pity and fear" affecting through that a "*katharsis* of such emotions."[147] Thus stories, which are recreations of people's actions or encounters, are told to arouse emotional responses in the listener/reader. Aristotle suggests that the need for stories is born of the need to imitate.[148] Humans raise imitation to the level of culture, to a thing that can be made (*poesis*), and that can be orchestrated for leisure and educational (moral) purposes. This is where he places tragedy, defined as:

> an imitation of an action that is admirable, complete and possesses magnitude; in language made pleasurable, each of its species separated in different parts, performed by actors, not through narration; effecting through pity and fear the purification of such emotions.[149]

Narrative involves individuals (characters) to whom we relate. Stephen Halliwell states that pity and fear refer specifically to the "capacity to sympathize with the sufferer." He emphasizes that "Aristotle does not derive this sympathy from an undifferentiated sense of humanity: instead, he takes it to be rooted in a felt or perceived affinity between the subject and the object of the emotion." In that regard, tragic characters "have to be within the reach of an audience's compassion."[150] What Halliwell calls sympathy, Suzanne Keen identifies as empathy. She describes the factors that might evoke a reader's empathy. These include dispositional or existential experience, or simply literary taste. She argues that the link between feelings for fictional characters and acting on behalf of real people is tenuous.[151] It is difficult to measure how literature produces empathy. It is also not a given that readers will identify or empathize with characters. Indeed, some will resist identification. What is undeniable is the contact, the meeting between the reader and text. In that meeting, something happens in the reader's imagination. I assume that the reader's world is influenced in part because they have identified with (or rejected), fully or partially, the aspects of the narrated world.

One central idea connects Aristotle, Adam Smith, and Martha Nussbaum: their emphasis on situations that cause discomfort. Our feelings of pity (Aristotle), sympathy (Smith), or empathy (Nussbaum) are possible because we imagine ourselves experiencing (the same) *like situations* as the agents (characters). Aristotle is emphatic that imitation is not of agents, but of actions. Fiction, to the degree that it causes us to suspend disbelief, presents those like situations to us.

Paul Ricoeur elaborates on Aristotle's notion of imitation in his concept of emplotment, which is a recreation of *like situations*.[152] For him, narrative understanding is the most basic form of understanding; people make sense of their lives through narration. We narrate in order to relate to what we have been and what we ought to become; we narrate in order to relate to others, and we do so by experiencing what others have experienced via *like situations*. The point of narrative as ethics is to make explicit the Socratic idea that only an examined life is worth living.[153] Ricoeur distinguishes between two forms of understanding of human nature: the Greek, *phronesis* (*prudentia* in Latin, wisdom in English) and the Latin, *scientia*, meaning scientific understanding. Narratives provide the former, while the various disciplines in science provide the latter.[154] The understanding provided by narrative is rooted in our imaginative reconstruction of people's experiences. Ethics is activated at the moment the reader puts himself in the situation the character is experiencing. Without this perspective-switching, literature would be less effective as an ethical tool. Literature is about relations; the relation of the reader to the text, and by implication, the reader's relation to people. Literature is also, and chiefly, about the reader's relation to themselves.

While literature delivers others to us, it also presents us to ourselves; as we relate to the characters in the text, we reflexively interrogate ourselves. I consider thoughts about human (women's) rights as a product of our intensive engagement with the pain of the other. As Lynn Hunt makes clear in her discussion of the evolution of human rights in the West, people began to articulate ideas of human rights in eighteenth-century Europe when they read stories of others in pain.[155]

What does one African body mean to other Africans in general, and in particular, what does the female African body mean to African males? Feminism, which, for these women writers, equals fairness, necessarily calls for the adoption of attitudes that urge people, men especially, to see those of the opposite sex not as objects or as means to society's (men's) ends, but as ends in themselves. Another way to understand the issue is to consider the difference between seeing women, in a relational way, as people and seeing them as instrumental. Feminist concepts motivate a person (man) to treat every woman as he would like to be treated: with respect and dignity. Seen as such, feminism is not only useful to women; it also benefits those men who are conscious of the moral quality of their relationship to other people, especially women. Feminism is ethics.[156] To the degree that it is ethics, it is about the rights and dignities of female members of society; it is about human rights.

African Women's Narratives and Feminist Empathy

James Dawes raises an important issue about "the paradox of representing suffering, namely that speaking for others is both a way of rescuing and usurping the other's voice."[157] I admit that there can be some form of epistemic violence in claiming to represent other people's stories. However, not representing stories at all might be a worse option.[158] Chantal Zabus argues that the idea of looking at women's experiential narratives "has the merit of breaking down the insider/outsider debate and dwarfing the clash of Titans such as 'universalism' and 'relativism' by forcing us to address the ethics of conflict."[159] I agree with her and read "ethics of conflict" as focusing on the parties involved in any encounter rather than judging them abstractly. Indeed, treating people's narratives as abstract formulations, or as lifeless visions of humans, to paraphrase Elizabeth S. Anker, underwrites "liberal articulations of human rights.[160] Zabus rightly claims that "African women writers are indeed keen to wrest their flesh and bodies back from various nexuses of power and to partake of the contemporary feminocentric urge to perceive the lived body as a source of experiential narrative."[161] Of course, what Zabus says about African women's biographical narratives applies to works of fiction and poetry.[162] Indeed, in Zabus's understanding, the contemporary African women writers take the words of Hélène Cixous seriously; they write, and in writing take back what rightly belongs to them: their bodies.[163] When African women writers reclaim their bodies from society's (male) narratives, when they write about their bodies that had been misrepresented, abused, or objectified by their cultures, they invite the readers to consider their pain not from an abstract, impersonal perspective, but rather to pay close attention to what that says about them and about their culture. They invite us to switch perspectives with them. They ask us to engage in feminist empathy.

By feminist empathy, I do not suggest that there are modes of empathy that are exclusively feminine. Empathy does not assume that people should suddenly, automatically begin to like one another or that readers will like the characters in a book. Literature, of course, is not about whether a particular character is likable or not; rather, it is the means through which authors interrogate the human condition. I thus restate my definition of feminist empathy as the ability to feel oneself enter into, or imagine, the experience of a woman in pain caused by society's construction of femininity. It is realized when we switch perspectives with a woman suffering oppression or privation because of her gender. Suzanne Keen's definition of narrative empathy is relevant to my idea of feminist empathy with regard to the selected works of contemporary African women writers. For her, it is "the sharing of feeling and perspective-taking induced by reading, viewing, hearing, or imagining narratives of another's situation and condition."[164] In my engagement with the narratives that explore the condition of African women in African societies, I do not seek to provoke sympathy or pity for women as victims. Rather, I imagine a male African reader putting himself in the position of a woman and then realizing that her pain was caused by a system that is inherently unfair. Thus, I argue that contemporary African women writers produce stories that challenge us to share the pain that African women are forced to endure in African worlds, and that they do so by creating the *like situations* that these women experienced.

The bulk of my analysis will rest on how characters relate to themselves and to others, and on what those relationships imply for our understanding of ethics and human rights in Africa. Do the characters see themselves and others as ends or means to ends? How are the characters' facets of selfhood narrated?

Notes

1. Bill Ashcroft, Helen Tiffin, and Gareth Griffith, *The Empire Writes Back: Theory and Practice in Post-Colonial Literatures*. London: Routledge, 1989 (Ashcroft et al. 1989). There are, of course, important exceptions to the writeback ideology exemplified by *Things Fall Apart*. These include writers such as Wole Soyinka, Yambo Ouologuem. See especially Chapter 8 of Kwame Anthony Appiah, *In My Father's House: Africa in the Philosophy of Culture*. New York: Oxford University Press, 1992 (Appiah 1992).
2. Evan Mwangi, *Africa Writes Back to Self: Metafiction, Gender, Sexuality*. New York: State University of New York Press, 2009 (Mwangi 2009).
3. Zoe Norridge, *Perceiving Pain in African Literature*. New York: Palgrave Macmillan, 2012 (Norridge 2012).
4. Brenda Cooper, *A New Generation of African Writers: Migration, Material Culture & Language*. Suffolk, UK: James Currey, 2008 (Cooper 2008).
5. Ranka Primorac, *The Place of Tears: The Novel and Politics in Modern Zimbabwe*. London: Taurus Academic Studies, 2006 (Primorac 2006).
6. Ken Harrow, *Less than One and Double: A Feminist Reading of African Women's Writing*. Portsmouth, NH: Heinemann, 2002) (Harrow 2002). See also Marie Kruger, *Women's Literature in Kenya and Uganda: The Trouble with Modernity*. New York: Palgrave, 2011 (Kruger 2011).
7. My book centers exclusively on Anglophone African writers. This is not a statement on Francophone African writing. South Africa presents unique challenges. For more on South African feminism see Pumla Dineo Gqola, *Rape: A South African Nightmare*. Johannesburg, SA: Jacana Media, 2015 (Dineo Gqola 2015). Missing in the list of works I have discussed here is Doreen Baingana's book, *Tropical Fish: Stories Out of Entebbe*. Amherst: University of Massachusetts, 2003 (Baingana 2003). I have discussed it exhaustively in my other work. See Chielozona Eze, *Postcolonial Imagination and Moral Representations in African Literature and Culture*. Lanham: Lexington Books, 2011 (Eze 2011) See also Chielozona Eze, "Rethinking African Culture and Identity: The Afropolitan Model," *Journal of African Cultural Studies*, 26.2 (2014): 234–247. (Eze 2014).
8. Norridge, *Perceiving*, 4. (Norridge 2012).
9. Ibid., 1–2. It is also true that the literary aestheticization of pain could lead to voyeuristic pleasure.
10. My uses of the word "pain" in this book refer specifically to those instances of privation, injustice, displeasure, or indeed, bodily trauma that are directly or indirectly occasioned by culture or tradition. Such instances of pain, of course, refer more to conditions rather than to a specific experience of ache or displeasure such as migraine, backache, et cetera.

11. Susan Moller Okin, *Is Multiculturalism Bad for Women?* New Jersey: Princeton University Press, 1999, 10–23 (Moller Okin 1999).
12. As I hope to make clear in my discussions, contemporary African women writers, building upon the efforts of their predecessors, stress the need to go beyond the Africa/West dichotomy of the conventional discourse. When Lola Shoneyin, for instance, tells the stories of four women forced to share a common man, and later fleshes out the queer sexual orientation of one of them in a piece of drama, she follows the admirable footsteps of Ama Ata Aidoo in *Changes*, Buchi Emecheta in *The Joys of Motherhood*, and Flora Nwapa in *Efuru* and directly addresses her community in view of enhancing human flourishing there.
13. Chimamanda Ngozi Adichie, We Should All Be Feminists, 2013 (Ngozi Adichie 2013). http://tedxtalks.ted.com/video/We-should-all-be-feminists-Chim. This difference is not qualitative. Indeed, Emecheta's *The Joys of Motherhood* is a profound feminist text that lends itself to the model of interpretation I suggest here. If Emecheta and the writers of her time were interpreted predominantly in the nationalist paradigm, it is because of the political mood of the period, which downplayed the needs of individuals for the benefit of the nation.
14. Susan Andrade, *The Nation Writ Small: African Fictions and Feminisms, 1958–1988*. Durham: Duke University Press Books, 2011 (Andrade 2011).
15. A reviewer has pointed out that Chimamanda Ngozi Adichie could be said to be concerned with the (Biafran) nation in *Half of a Yellow Sun*. I am not sure that she laments the loss of Biafra as a nation as much as she highlights man's inhumanity to man. It is conceivable that she uses the historical context of the Nigerian civil war to examine the human condition.
16. There has been an explosion of studies on the African woman's body. These studies include the image of the body, the African woman's body image, et cetera. See for instance, Pumla Dineo Gqola, "Editorial: Yindaba kaban' u'ba ndilahl' umlenze? Sexuality and Body Image," *Agenda: Empowering Women for Gender Equity* 63, African Feminisms, 2.2: Sexuality and Body Image (2005): 3–9 (Dineo Gqola 2005).
17. For more on this definition see Robert Attfield and Susnne Gibson, "Ethics," in *A Dictionary of Cultural and Critical Theory*, ed. Michael Payne. Oxford, UK: Blackwell Publishers, 1996 (Attfield and Gibson 1996).
18. Of course one can also have a relation to oneself, as Foucault implies in the care of the self. Michel Foucault, *Ethics: Subjectivity and Truth: The Essential Works of Michel Foucault, 1954–1984*, ed. Paul Rabinow. New York: The New Press, 1997 (Foucault 1997).
19. See Jacques Rancière, "The Ethical Turn of Aesthetics and Politics," *Critical Horizons*, 7.1 (2006): 1–20 (Rancière 2006).

20. Butler in interview, cited in Carolyn Culbertson, "The Ethics of Relationality: Judith Butler and Social Critique," *Continental Philosophy Review*, 46 (2013): 449–463 (Culbertson 2013).
21. Judith Butler, "Giving an Account of Oneself," *Diacritics*, 31.4 (2001): 25 (Butler 2001). See also Judith Butler, *Giving an Account of Oneself*. New York: Fordham University Press, 2005. (Butler 2005).
22. Alasdair MacIntyre, *Dependent Rational Animals: Why Human Beings Need the Virtues*. Peru, Illinois: Open Court, 1999 (MacIntyre 1999).
23. Butler, "Giving an Account," 28 (Butler 2005).
24. Ibid., 35.
25. Ibid., 36.
26. Lawrence Buell, "What We Talk About When We Talk About Ethics," in *The Turn To Ethics*, ed. Marjorie Garber et al. New York: Routledge, 2000, 6 (Buell 2000).
27. Wolfgang Iser, *The Act of Reading: A Theory of Aesthetic Response*. Baltimore: Johns Hopkins University Press, 1980 (Iser 1978).
28. Emmanuel Levinas, Totality and Infinity, trans. Alphonso Lingis. Pittsburgh: Duquesne University Press, 1969, 43 (Levinas 1969).
29. Levinas, *Totality*, 43. (Levinas 1969).
30. Emmanuel Levinas, *Ethics and Infinity: Conversations with Phillip Nemo*, trans. Richard Cohen. Pittsburgh, Duquesne University Press, 1985, 87–88 (Levinas 1985).
31. Levinas, *Totality*, 50 (Levinas 1969).
32. Cited in Rosemarie Garland-Thomson, "Integrating Disability, Transforming Feminist Theory," *NWSA Journal*, 14.3 (2002): 1–32 (Thomson 2002).
33. Rosemarie Garland-Thomson, "Integrating," 6. See also Rosemarie Garland-Thomson, *Extraordinary Bodies: Figuring Physical Disability in American Culture and Literature*. New York: Columbia University Press, 1997 (Thomson 1997).
34. Iris Marion Young, "Throwing Like a Girl: A Phenomenology of Feminine Body Comportment Motility and Spatiality," Human Studies 3.2 (1980): 152 (Young 1980). See also, Iris Marion Young, *Throwing Like a Girl and Other Essays in Feminist Philosophy and Social Theory*. Bloomington: Indiana University Press, 1990 (Young 1990). Chimamanda Ngozi Adichie alludes to the fact that sexist and patriarchal societies disable women's bodies in her talk, "We Should all be Feminists." I will return to this idea in Chapter 2. See also Susan Archer Mann, Ashly Suzanne Patterson, eds, *Reading Feminist Theory: From Modernity to Postmodernity*. New York: Oxford University Press, 2015 (Archer Mann 2015).
35. Young, "Throwing Like a Girl," 140 (Young 1990).
36. As I will make clear in my discussion of empathy, it is obvious that some readers resist identification.

37. Glo Chukukere, "An Appraisal of Feminism in the Socio-Political Development of Nigeria," in *Sisterhood, Feminism and Power: From Africa to the Diaspora*, ed. Obioma Nnaemeka. Trenton, NJ: Africa World Press, 1998, 134 (Chukukere 1998).
38. Femi Ojo-Ade, "Female Writers, Male Critics," *African Literature Today*, 13 (London: Heinemann, (1983): 158–179 (Ojo-Ade 1983).
39. See Chinweizu, *Anatomy of Female Power: A Masculinist Dissection of Matriarchy*. Lagos, Nigeria: Pero Press, 1990 (Chinweizu 1990).
40. It is not always unambiguous what a feminist interpretation would be. Furthermore, when positions and causes are claimed by academics who live and work in the Northern Hemisphere, or those who position themselves as defenders of Africa, these interpretations often become even more complexly contradictory.
41. I do not imply that there is a monolithic form of Western feminism. Nor can one make the same claim about African feminism, or African culture. I merely seek to capture the differences between the practices of feminism in the West and in Africa.
42. See Chandra Mohanty Talpade, Ann Russo, and Lourde Torres, eds, *Third World Women and the Politics of Feminism*. Bloomington: Indiana University Press, 1991 (Mohanty Talpade et al. 1991).
43. As I pointed out above, African feminism has, of course, gone beyond the initial demands of third-wave feminism. There are now many works that increasingly concentrate on the African woman's body image. Evan Mwangi's *Africa Writes Back to Self* also deals with the attention to African women's queer bodies as part of African self-reflexivity.
44. I present the works of these authors more as a literature review in order to establish the need for my theoretical intervention. My overall contention is that the theory most of them pursued was aimed at writing back to the colonial assault on Africa, not to critically explore Africa's complex condition. In so doing the theorists failed to engage the ethical dimension of African writing.
45. I do not ignore important works that engage with feminism in the Francophone areas of Africa: example, works of writers such as Irène d'Almeida, *Francophone African Women: Destroying the Emptiness of Silence*. Gainesville: University of Florida Press, 1994 (Almeida 1994). Also of importance is Ayo A. Coly, *The Pull of Postcolonial Nationhood: Gender and Migration in Francophone African Literatures*. Lanham: Lexington Books, 2010 (Coly 2010).
46. See Obioma Nnaemeka, ed., *Sisterhood, Feminism and Power: From Africa to the Diaspora*. Trenton, NJ: Africa World Press, 1998 (Nnaemeka 1998) and Tejumola Olaniyan and Ato Quayson, eds, *African Literature: An*

Anthology of Criticism and Theory. Malden, MA: Wiley-Blackwell, 2007 (Olaniyan and Quayson 2007). See also Susan Arndt, *The Dynamics of African Feminism: Defining and Classifying African-Feminist Literatures*. Trenton, NJ: Africa World Press, 2001 (Arndt 2001). Gloria Chukukere, *Gender Voices and Choices: Redefining Women in Contemporary African Fiction*. Enugu: Fourth Dimension, 1995 (Chukukere 1995). Stephanie Newell, ed., *Writing African Women: Gender, Popular Culture and Literature in West Africa*. London: Zed, 1997 (Newell 1997). See also Phanuel A. Egejuru and Ketu H. Katrak, eds, *Nwanyibu: Womanbeing and African Literature*. Trenton: Africa World, 1997 (Egejuru and Katrak 1997).

47. Carole Boyce Davies, "Introduction: Feminist Consciousness and African Literary Criticism," in *Ngambika: Studies of Women in African Literature*, ed. Carole Boyce Davies and Anne Adams Graves. Trenton, NJ: Africa World Press, 1986, 8–12 (Davies 1986).
48. Ifi Amadiume, *Male Daughters, Female Husbands: Gender and Sex in an African Society*. London: Zed Books Ltd, 1987, 4–6 (Amadiume 1987).
49. Ibid., 15.
50. Oyeronke Oyewumi, *The Invention of Women: Making an African Sense of Western Gender Discourses*. University of Minnesota Press, 1997, xii (Oyewumi 1997). See also Nkiru Uwechia Nzegwu, *Family Matters: Feminist Concepts in African Philosophy of Culture*. New York: State University of New York, 2006 (Nzegwu 2006).
51. Oyeronke Oyewumi, ed., *African Women and Feminism: Reflecting on the Politics of Sisterhood* (Trenton, NJ: Africa World Press, Inc., 2003), 1 (Oyewumi 2003a)
52. Ibid., 2.
53. Chikwenye Okonjo Ogunyemi, "Womanism: The Dynamics of the Contemporary Black Female Novel in English," in *The Womanist Reader*, ed. Layli Phillips. New York: Routledge, 2006, 28 (Ogunyemi 2006). Layli Phillips highlights the relationship between Walker and Okonjo-Ogunyemi by providing their original texts, and the contexts of their ideas.
54. Chikwenye Okonjo Ogunyemi, *Africa Wo/Man Palava: The Nigerian Novel by Women* (Chicago: University of Chicago Press, 1996), 114 (Ogunyemi 1996).
55. For a critical assessment of this position, see Chapter 5 of this book.
56. Mary E. Modupe Kolawole, *Womanism and African Consciousness*. Trenton, NJ; Asmara: Africa World Press, 1997, 27 (Kolawole 1997).
57. Catherine Obianuju Acholonu, *Motherism: The Afrocentric Alternative*. Owerri, Nigeria: Afa Publications, 2002, 110 (Acholonu 2002).

58. Morala Ogundipe-Leslie, *Re-creating Ourselves: African Women and Critical Transformations.* Trenton, NJ: African World Press, 1994, 207–238 (Ogundipe-Leslie 1994).
59. Obioma Nnaemeka, "Nego-Feminism: Theorizing, Practicing, and Pruning Africa's Way," *Signs: Journal of Women in Culture and Society*, 29.2 (2003): 369 (Nnaemeka 2003).
60. Ibid., 377–378.
61. Nzegwu, *Family Matters*, 2 (Nzegwu 2006).
62. One particular example in which Afrocentric abstraction replaced a Eurocentric model is in Okonjo Ogunyemi's discussion of Mariama Bâ 's novella about polygamy. I have discussed it in Chapter 5.
63. Elleke Boehmer, *Gender and Narrative in Postcolonial Nation.* Manchester University Press, 2005, 4–5 (Boehmer 2005).
64. Florence Stratton, *Contemporary African Literature and the Politics of Gender.* New York: Routledge, 1994 (Stratton 1994).
65. Meg Samuelson, *Remembering the Nation Dismembering Women? Stories of the South African Transition.* University of Kwazulu Natal Press, 2007, 7 (Samuelson 2007).
66. Pinkie Mekgwe, "Theorizing African Feminism(s): The 'Colonial' Question," *QUEST: An African Journal of Philosophy/Revue Africaine de Philosophie*, XX (2008): 21–22 (Mekgwe 2008).
67. Ibid.
68. For more on the pitfalls of postcolonial thinking see Denis Ekpo, "Introduction: From Negritude to Post-Africanism," *Third Text*, 24.2 (2010): 182. (Ekpo 2010).
69. Sarah Nuttal has critiqued postcolonial theory as ineffectual in explaining the complex nature of present-day reality. Postcolonialism has erred in its exaggeration of difference between the West and others. See Sarah Nuttall, *Entanglement: Literary and Cultural Reflections on Post-apartheid.* Johannesburg: Wits University Press, 2009, 31 (Nuttall 2009).
70. Buchi Emecheta exposes the poverty of this attitude towards women in *The Joys of Motherhood.* London: George Braziller Inc., 1980 (Emecheta 1980).
71. Sylvia Tamale, "African Feminism: How Should We Change?" *Development: Supplement: Women's Rights and Development; Association for Women's*, 49.1 (2006): 38–41. (Tamale 2006).
72. Ibid., 2.
73. Stratton, *Contemporary African Literature*, 22 (Stratton 1994).
74. Andrade, *The Nation Writ Small*, 30 (Andrade 2011).
75. Ibid., 34.
76. Buchi Emecheta, "Feminism with a Small 'f!," in *Criticism and Ideology. Second African Writers' Conference*, ed. Kirsten Holst Petersen. Uppsala: Scandinavian Institute of African Studies, 1988, 173–185 (Emecheta 1988).

1 INTRODUCTION: THE ETHICAL TURN IN AFRICAN LITERATURE 37

77. See for instance Chika Unigwe, *In the Shadow of Ala. Igbo Women Writing as an Act of Righting*. Thesis (Ph.D.) Leiden University, 2004 (Unigwe 2004).
78. Salome C. Nnoromele, "Representing the African Woman: Subjectivity and Self in *The Joys of Motherhood*," *Critique: Studies in Contemporary Fiction*, 43.2. (2002) (Nnoromele 2002).
79. Carol Boyce Davies, "Introduction: Feminist Consciousness," 8–12 (Davies 1986).
80. Juliana Makuchi Nfah-Abbenyi, *Gender in African Women's Writing*. Bloomington: Indiana University Press, 1997, 5 (Nfah-Abbenyi 1997).
81. Ibid., 6.
82. Ibid., 14.
83. Nancy Topping Bazin, "Venturing into Feminist Consciousness: Two Protagonists from the Fiction of Buchi Emecheta and Bessie Head," *Sage II* (Spring 1985), 32–36 (Bazin 1985).
84. Terry Eagleton, *After Theory*. New York: Basic Books, 2003, 2 (Eagleton 2003).
85. *Mencius*. Translated by D.C. Lau. London: Penguin Classics, 1970, 82 (Lau 1970).
86. Adam Smith, *The Theory of Moral Sentiments*. Edited by Knud Haakonssen. Cambridge University Press, 2002, 11–12 (Smith 2002).
87. Martha Nussbaum, *Upheavals of Thought: The Intelligence of Emotions*. Cambridge, UK: Cambridge University Press, 2001, 327 (Nussbaum 2001a).
88. Frans De Waal, *The Age of Empathy: Nature's Lessons for a Kinder Society*. New York: Harmony Books, 2009, 115 (De Waal 2009).
89. Theodor Lipps, *Zur Einfühlung*. Leipzig: Engleman, 1913 (Lipps 1913).
90. De Waal, *The Age of Empathy*, 65 (De Waal 2009).
91. Ibid., 65.
92. Simon Baron-Cohen, *Zero Degrees of Empathy*. London: Allen Lane, 2011, 10 (Baron-Cohen 2011).
93. Ibid., 12.
94. Suzanne Keen, "A Theory of Narrative Empathy," *Narrative*, 14.3 (2006): 208 (Keen 2006).
95. Ibid., 209 (Original emphasis).
96. Suzanne Keen, *Empathy and the Novel*. New York: Oxford University Press, 2007, 147–148 (Keen 2007).
97. Abdul R. JanMohamed, "The Economy of Manichean Allegory: The Function of Racial Difference in Colonialist Literature," *Critical Inquiry*, *"Race," Writing, and Difference*, 12.1 (1985): 59–87 (JanMohamed 1985).
98. Albert Memmi, *The Colonizer, the Colonized*. Boston, MA: Beacon Press, 1990 (Original, 1965) (Memmi 1990).
99. De Waal, *The Age of Empathy*, 214 (De Waal 2009).

100. James D. Johnson, Carolyn H. Simmons, Amanda Jordav, Leslie Maclean, Jeffrey Taddei, Duane Thomas, John F. Dovidio, and William Reed, "Rodney King and O.J. Revisited: The Impact of Race and Defendant Empathy Induction on Judicial Decisions," *Journal of Applied Social Psychology*, 32.6 (2002): 1208–1223 (Johnson et al. 2002).
101. Sophie Trawalter, Kelly M. Hoffman, and Adam Waytz, "Racial Bias in Perceptions of Others' Pain." http://www.plosone.org/article/info:doi/10.1371/journal.pone.0048546 (Accessed March 24, 2014) (Trawalter et al. 2014).
102. When I identify the works of contemporary African women writers in terms of feminist empathy, I do not imply that the writers of previous generations were never similarly engaged. They were. However, given the time period in which they wrote, most scholars of their time were more interested in addressing what they perceived as the larger threat to Africa's existence: Western imperialism. They therefore did not pay adequate attention to the pain that African sociocultural institutions inflicted on women's bodies. It is also not surprising that even in our time, scholars such as Susan Andrade insist that the feminist works of these earlier writers be read as attempts to frame the nation.
103. United Nations. "What Are Human Rights?" http://www.ohchr.org/EN/Issues/Pages/WhatareHumanRights.aspx (Accessed March 2, 2015). (United Nations 2015).
104. An-naim Abdullahi and Francis M. Deng, eds, *Human Rights in Africa: Cross-Cultural Perspectives*. Washington, DC: The Brookings Institute, 1990, 1 (Abdullahi and Deng 1990).
105. Ibid., 1–2
106. Marie-Bénédicte Dembour, "What Are Human Rights? Four Schools of Thought," *Human Rights Quarterly*, 32.1 (2010): 2–4 (Dembour 2010).
107. For details on the Universal Declaration of Human Rights, see. The United Nations, "The Universal Declaration of Human Rights," http://www.un.org/en/documents/udhr/ (Accessed March 2, 2015) (United Nations 2015).
108. Thomas Buergenthal, "International Human Rights in an Historical Perspective," in *Human Rights: Concept and Standards*, ed. Janusz Symonides. Aldershot, UK: Dartmouth Publishing Company Ltd, 2000, 3 (Buergenthal 2000).
109. Lynn Hunt, *Inventing Human Rights: A History*. New York: W.W. Norton & Company, 2008 (Hunt 2008); Jack Donnelly, *Universal Human Rights in Theory and Practice* (2nd edition). Ithaca: Cornell University Press, 2003 (Donnelly 2003).
110. See also, Sangmin Bae, *When the State No Longer Kills: International Human Rights Norms and Abolition of Capital Punishment*. New York: State University of New York Press, 2007 (Bae 2007).

111. Donnelly, *Universal Human Rights*, 1 (Donnelly 2003).
112. See also Jerome J. Shestack, "The Philosophical Foundations of Human Rights," in *Human Rights: Concept and Standards*, ed. Janusz Symonides. Aldershot, UK: Dartmouth Publishing Company Ltd, 2000, 54 (Shestack 2000).
113. Immanuel Kant, *Foundations of the Metaphysics of Morals*. Translated with an Introduction by Lewis White Beck. Upper Saddle River, NJ, 1997, 38 (Kant 1997).
114. Ibid., 46.
115. Elizabeth S. Anker, *Fictions of Dignity: Embodying Human Rights in World Literature*. Ithaca: Cornell University Press, 2012, 4 (Anker 2012).
116. African Commission on Human and Peoples' Rights, "African Charter on Human and Peoples' Rights." http://www.achpr.org/instruments/achpr/#a29 (Accessed May 20, 2015). (African Commission on Human and Peoples 2015).
117. Sylvia Tamale, "The Right to Culture and the Culture of Rights: A Critical Perspective on Women's Sexual Rights in Africa," *Feminist Legal Studies*, 16.1 (2008): 47–69, 50 (Tamale 2008).
118. African Commission on Human and People's Rights, "African Charter" (African Commission on Human and People's Rights 2015)
119. Tamale, "The Right to Culture," 61. (Tamale 2008).
120. Sylvia Tamale, "Eroticism, Sensuality and 'Women's Secrets' Among the Baganda: A Critical Analysis," *Feminist Africa Issue: Sexual Cultures*, 5 (2005): 9 (Tamale 2005).
121. Micere Githae Mugo, *African Orature and Human Rights in Gikuyu, Shona and Ndebele Zimani Cultures*. Harare, Zimbabwe: Sapes Book, 2004, 7 (Githae Mugo 2004).
122. Ibid., 24.
123. Ibid., 24.
124. Ibid., 8.
125. Chielozona Eze, "Transcultural Affinity: Thoughts on the Emergent Cosmopolitan Imagination in South Africa," *Journal of African Cultural Studies*, 17.2 (2015): 216–228 (Eze 2015).
126. Desmond Tutu, *No Future Without Forgiveness*. New York: Image Doubleday, 1999, 31 (Tutu 1999).
127. Bernard Gert, "The Definition of Morality", *The Stanford Encyclopedia of Philosophy* (Fall 2012 edition), Edward N. Zalta, ed. http://plato.stanford.edu/archives/fall2012/entries/morality-definition/ (Accessed May 20, 2013). (Gert 2012).
128. Tutu, *No Future Without Forgiveness*, 31 (Tutu 1999).
129. Anker, Ibid., 2–3.

130. Joseph R. Slaughter, *Human Rights, Inc: The World Novel, Narrative Form, and International Law*. New York: Fordham University Press, 2007, 3 (Slaughter 2007).
131. Ibid., 4.
132. Ibid., 252–253.
133. David Palumbo-Liu, *The Deliverance of Others: Reading Literature in a Global Age*. Durham: Duke University Press, 2012, 3–9 (Palumbo-Liu 2012).
134. Donnelly, *Universal Human Rights*, 11 (Donnelly 2003).
135. Though child marriage is defined as marriage before age 18, in most cases it is girls under the age of 15 who have been married away against their will. See http://www.unfpa.org/child-marriage See also, "Early Marriage in Nigeria," http://nigeria.unfpa.org/nigeirachild.html.
136. Hillary Rodham Clinton, "Women's Rights Are Human Rights." http://gos.sbc.edu/c/clinton.html (Accessed May 15, 2013) (Clinton 2013). See also Hillary Clinton, Helping Women Isn't Just a 'Nice' Thing to Do." http://www.thedailybeast.com/witw/articles/2013/04/05/hillary-clinton-helping-women-isn-t-just-a-nice-thing-to-do.html (Accessed May 15, 2013) (Clinton 2013).
137. Joan Didion, *We Tell Ourselves Stories in Order to Live: Collected Nonfiction*. New York: Alfred Knopf, 2006 (Didion 2006). See also Margaret Atwood, "Why We Tell Stories." 2010. www.bigthink.com/ideas/24259 (Accessed June 3, 2012) (Atwood 2012).
138. James Dawes, "Human Rights in Literary Studies," *Human Rights Quarterly*, 31.2 (2009): 395 (Dawes 2009). See also James Dawes, *That the World May Know: Bearing Witness to Atrocity*. Cambridge, MA: Harvard University Press, 2007 (Dawes 2007).
139. I fully embrace the emotional impact that stories make on us even as I step back to critically interrogate those impacts. Jesus Christ is recognized not only as a religious figure, but also as an unquestionable moral leader. He fully utilized the power of narratives to impart moral values. For example, when he was asked a simple question of who one should consider one's neighbor, he told the story of the Good Samaritan.
140. Arthur W. Frank, *Letting Stories Breathe*. Chicago: The University of Chicago Press, 2010, 46 (Frank 2010).
141. Hunt, *Inventing Human Rights*, 82 (Hunt 2008). See especially Chapter 3 of the same book.
142. Shannon Sullivan, *Revealing Whiteness: The Unconscious Habits of Racial Privilege*. Bloomington: Indiana University Press, 2006. (Sullivan 2006).
143. Sullivan, Cited in Samantha Vice, "How Do I Live in This Strange Place?" *Journal of Social Philosophy*, 42.3 (2010): 325 (Vice 2010).
144. Ibid., 331.

145. See Aristotle, *Nicomachean Ethics*. Trans. Terence Irwin. Indianapolis: Hackett Publishing Co, 1999, 1–8 (Aristotle 1999). See especially Book 1 Chapter 5. §2. Aristotle underlines the importance of people pursuing happiness for its own sake. This has to be conducted in freedom. So it is imperative that people freely embrace virtue and responsibility in order to protect the lives of every individual in community. Freedom and responsibility are therefore necessary for human life to flourish. Alasdair MacIntyre is one of the most important contemporary philosophers to have fruitfully interpreted Aristotle's idea of human flourishing. See especially Chapter 8 Alasdair MacIntyre, *Dependent Rational Animals: Why Human Beings Need the Virtues*. Peru, IL: Open Court, 1999 (MacIntyre 1999).
146. Adam Zachary Newton, *Narrative Ethics*. Cambridge, MA: Harvard University Press, 1995, 12(Zachary Newton 1995).
147. Aristotle, *Poetics*. Trans. Malcolm Heath. London: Penguin Books, 1996 (Aristotle 1996).
148. Ibid., 6.
149. Ibid., 10.
150. Stephen Halliwell, *Aristotle's Poetics*. Chicago: University of Chicago Press, 1998, 175–179 (Halliwell 1998).
151. Keen, *Empathy and the Novel*, 146 (Keen 2007).
152. Paul Ricoeur, *Time and Narrative*, Trans. Kathleen McLaughlin and David Pellauer. Chicago: The University of Chicago Press, 1984 (Ricoeur 1984). I will return to this especially in Chapter 3, "Diary of Intense Pain: The Postcolonial Trap and Women's Rights."
153. Narratives do not prescribe a set of rules or norms. Indeed, as Tony E. Adams argues, a preformed set of principles runs the risk of doing violence to a story. Tony E. Adams, "A Review of Narrative Ethics." *Qualitative Inquiry*, 14.2 (2008): 179 (Adams 2008).
154. Paul Ricoeur, "Life in Quest of Narrative," in *On Paul Ricoeur: Narrative and Interpretation*, ed. David Wood. London: Routledge, 1991, 23 (Ricoeur 1991).
155. Hunt, *Inventing Human Rights* (Hunt 2008).
156. Feminism as ethics is different from feminist ethics. The latter seeks to "rethink traditional ethics to the extent it depreciates or devalues women's moral experience." See Rosemarie Tong and Nancy Williams, "Feminist Ethics", *The Stanford Encyclopedia of Philosophy* (2014) (Tong and Williams 2014). Edward N. Zalta, ed. http://plato.stanford.edu/archives/fall2014/entries/feminism-ethics/.
157. Dawes, "Human Rights in Literary Studies" (Dawes 2009).
158. I will return to this issue in Chapter 8, in my discussion of the moral obligation of bearing witness to suffering.

159. Chantal Zabus, *Between Rites and Rights: Excision in Women's Experiential Texts and Human Contexts*. Stanford, CA: Stanford University Press, 2007, 3 (Zabus 2007).
160. Anker, *Fictions of Dignity*, 8 (Anker 2012).
161. Zabus, *Between Rites and Rights*, 8–9 (Zabus 2007).
162. Françoise Lionnet makes the same argument about women's self-representation. See Françoise Lionnet, *Postcolonial Representations: Women, Literature, Identity*. Ithaca: Cornell University Press, 1995 (Lionnet 1995).
163. Hélène Cixous, "The Laugh of the Medusa," Translated by Keith Cohen and Paula Cohen, *Signs*, 1.4 (1976): 875–893 (Cixous 1976).
164. Suzanne Keen, "Narrative Empathy," in *The Living Handbook of Narratology*, ed. Peter Hühn et al. Hamburg: Hamburg University Press, 2014. hup.sub.uni-hamburg.de/lhn/index.php?title=NarrativeEmpathy&oldid=2044 (Accessed April 20, 2014) (Keen 2014).

CHAPTER 2

Feminism as Fairness

Chimamanda Ngozi Adichie

In the introduction, I pointed out that the first and second generations of African women scholars and writers maintained a cautious distance from feminism, especially given its heavily white, Western origins and influence. On the contrary, their third-generation counterparts conceive of their feminism not in opposition to the West, but in relation to it. They understand feminism as a moral issue that transcends cultural differences precisely because it seeks to enhance the dignity of individuals without disrupting community cohesion. In this chapter, I seek to reestablish the thesis that African feminism, which is not conceived as essentialist or exclusive to Africa, is about fairness in the relation between men and women in Africa; it does not seek to establish an ideology, or set up an ideal of how African women should be. It rather urges a reevaluation of the cultural and moral assumptions that undergird the lives of African women, assumptions that, in the words of Iris Marion Young, define and handicap women. In the first part of this chapter, I attempt a restatement of Chimamanda Ngozi Adichie's thesis that all fair-minded people should be feminists.[1] In the later part, I discuss her novel, *Purple Hibiscus* and her short story, "Tomorrow is too Far," as parts of her effort to highlight the system that denies women recognition on the one hand and, on the other, maintains technologies that disable women's bodies in African societies.

© The Author(s) 2016
C. Eze, *Ethics and Human Rights in Anglophone African Women's Literature*, Comparative Feminist Studies,
DOI 10.1007/978-3-319-40922-1_2

In regard to feminism, Adichie is the most vocal of contemporary African women writers. In an interview with R. Krithika, she stated: "I am a happy feminist. I think all fair-minded people should be."[2] She expanded this conception of feminism in a 2012 TEDx talk titled, "We Should All Be Feminists," underlining the moral and social challenges of feminism for all. It is instructive that she equates fairness and feminism, especially considering how deeply suspicious her African audience is of that idea. It is the conflation of feminism and fairness that has attracted my intellectual curiosity. This fusion of two seemingly distinct terms will constitute the central idea of my discussion. Why is feminism all about fairness? Fairness for whom? I locate Adichie's understanding of feminism in the intellectual tradition that takes the moral equality of men and women as a starting point. Moral equality requires that men and women be held accountable for their actions as adults. If one is to be judged as a responsible adult, one has to act without coercion, an idea prevalent in works by Mary Wollstonecraft, and more recently, bell hooks.

In her letter to M. Talleyrand-Perigord, Bishop of Autun, Mary Wollstonecraft reinforces the Aristotelian idea that virtue can only flourish in the face of freedom:

> Let there be then no coercion *established* in society, and the common law of gravity prevailing, the sexes will fall into their proper places. And, now that the more equitable laws are forming your citizens, marriage may become more sacred: your young men may choose wives from motives of affection, and your maidens allow love to root out vanity.[3]

In a society where women are not free to pursue their dreams or to control their bodies as men do theirs, women cannot be expected to be virtuous. They may comply with the law, social and cultural norms, but that compliance cannot be judged as virtuous, for, as Wollstonecraft states, virtue can flourish only in a society in which freedom and equality are taken as a given: "the more equality there is established among men, the more virtue and happiness will reign in society."[4]

The prominent African American feminist author, bell hooks, acknowledges the complex nature of feminism, especially among third-world women and women in minority cultures in the West. She argues that "women from exploited and oppressed ethnic groups dismiss the term because they do not wish to be perceived as supporting a racist movement; feminism is often equated with white women's rights effort."[5] For her, however, feminism is the struggle to end sexist oppression. Its aim is not to benefit any specific group, race, or class of women, nor does it privilege women over men. It has the power to transform our lives in meaningful ways.[6] Ending sexist oppression is for the greater good of all. She further argues that:

> Feminist thinking and practice emphasize the value of mutual growth and self-actualization in partnerships and in parenting. This vision of relationships where everyone's needs are respected, where everyone has rights, where no one need fear subordination or abuse, runs counter to everything patriarchy upholds about the structure of relationships.[7]

Essentially, hooks argues for a fair-minded society, and one of the ways to achieve it is to reassess the moral grounds for human relationships. She talks about a society in which relationships are not controlled by ideologies, but rather by a simple idea of fairness. Her idea, I think, expresses in a more theoretically grounded way what Adichie has sought to do in her interview and in her TEDx talk. Indeed, the title of Adichie's talk, "We Should All Be Feminists" echoes bell hook's book, *Feminism Is for Everybody*. What these two women have in common is their passion for social justice, fairness, and the enabling of bodies that had been disabled by patriarchal and sexist constructs.

WE SHOULD ALL BE FEMINISTS

In one of the many important episodes of the TEDx talk, Adichie alludes to an article she wrote about what it means to be young and a female in Nigeria. People told her that her piece was angry, and she agreed with their judgment: "Of course it was angry. I am angry. Gender as it functions today is a grave injustice as fairness. We should all be angry."[8] Her anger is rooted in her belief in a universal moral principle: justice. Based on this conviction, she believes that, all things being equal, she should not be the only person expressing anger. Every person should be angry. It is important to note that she does not indict people. To the contrary, she indicts the system which she has already identified. It is the system that supports gender as it functions today. She thus expresses hope that the condition she is about to describe would arouse people to indignation and to seek to change the unfair paradigms of relation between men and women: "And I would like today to ask that we begin to dream about and plan for a different world. A fairer world. A world of happier men and happier women who are truer to themselves."[9] Adichie is not afraid of making reference to universal ideals such as the belief in a fairer world and people's capacity to dream for that. When she dreams of a world of happier men and happier women, she seeks no more than what we have already identified as human flourishing, a world devoid of needless pain.

Adichie's simple demand that people dream of, or imagine a fairer world is not different from what Martha Nussbaum and Simon Baron-Cohen had already said about empathy being rooted in the power of the imagination. It is the power of one person to put him- or herself in the position of the other. In asking her audience to dream with her, she prepares them to imaginatively reconstruct the pain of the women she is going to talk about. Nussbaum has pointed out that to imagine the pain of the sufferer, one has to be constantly aware that one is oneself not the sufferer of pain. Imagining the pain of others, we know, can be a very difficult affair. Yet there seems to be no easier or even better way for people to envisage a fairer society unless, of course, one simply obeys society's norms and rules in strict Kantian deontological format. Dreaming of a better world, or imagining a fair society also recalls John Rawls's notion of the veil of ignorance. I will return to this later.

Adichie seeks to expose the foundations of unfair structures of society in regard to women. Women are taught from childhood that their position in society is inferior to that of men. They are conditioned not to desire. The degree to which they are taught to accommodate themselves to inferior positions equals the degree to which men perceive themselves as superior, lords:

> We teach girls to shrink themselves, to make themselves smaller. We say to girls, "You can have ambition, but not too much. You should aim to be successful, but not too successful, otherwise you would threaten the man. If you are the bread winner in your relationship with a man, you have to pretend that you're not. Especially in public. Otherwise you will emasculate him."[10]

Iris Marion Young has written about how society's unjust constraints limit women's freedom and opportunity.[11] She argues that feminine bodies are made to repress or withhold their motile energy, and in that way:

> feminine bodily existence frequently projects "I can" and an "I cannot" with respect to the very same end. When the woman enters a task with inhibited intentionality, she projects the possibilities of that task—thus projects an "I *can*"–but projects them merely as the possibilities of "someone," and not truly *her* possibilities—and thus projects an "I *cannot*".[12]

Young's ideas were reaffirmed by a popular video commercial that ran during the 2015 Super Bowl, titled "Throw Like a Girl."[13] In the commercial, people are asked to show how girls run, fight and throw. The actors perform inferior versions of each of these acts. We learn that they are merely acting out society's sexist images of women. A different version of the same acts are performed, but without sexist connotations. The result is totally different. Girls run, fight, and throw not like girls but like human beings: the way each individual can throw, run, or fight. Adichie expresses the same idea as Young and the Super Bowl commercial with her observation that the African society she speaks of teaches "girls to shrink themselves." Those societies disable the girls when the girls learn to make themselves smaller and not to have ambition.

To enunciate the inferior roles of girls, society raises them to compete "not for jobs, or for accomplishments" but "for the attention of men. We teach girls that they cannot be sexual beings in the way that boys are."[14] In teaching girls not to desire, society indirectly lets them feel they are to be desired and that they cannot be masters of their world. Ideally, only masters desire. Objects are desired. Adichie's ideas on the upbringing of boys and girls tap into the understanding that people could be brought up to hate one another by conditioning, that is, by subjecting them to the ideology of tradition. As I have pointed out in the introduction with reference to De Waal, empathy can be blocked in people by conditioning.[15] Fear readily leads to the demonization of others, thus freezing their being in abstractions; it is no surprise that women are feared as sources of temptations and evil—at least judging from mythologies. De Waal's ideas support Gabriel Marcel's views on abstractions (patriarchy, culture, tradition, heritage) that hinder us from being fraternal to others.[16] Abstractions not only block our empathy towards others because these concepts have already prejudged and packaged them in simplistic categories; they also constrain our thinking and feeling within extremely localized, ethnocentric modules. Empathy, on the other hand, expands our thinking and feeling, and allows us to imagine reality as all-encompassing and all-embracing.

Adichie points to the incontestable fact that the disparity and the unfairness in the upbringing of boys and girls have immediate and lasting impacts on their lives:

> We teach girls shame. "Close your legs!" "Cover yourself!" We make them feel as though by being born female, they are already guilty of something. And so, girls grow up to be women who cannot say they have desire. They grow up to be women who silence themselves. They grow up to be women who cannot say what they truly think. Adichie, "We Should All Be Feminists" (Adichie 2013)

Adichie just falls short of stating that these girls grow up disabled. In her understanding, fairness can defuse the empathy-blockage brought about by patriarchal upbringing. The *OED* defines fairness as "the quality or condition of being fair." Being fair is identified as acting "equitably, honestly, impartially, justly." Being fair also means being free from bias. I admit that it is in the human constitution to think and act in ways that would often benefit our narrower interests: our race, our ethnic group, tribe, family, gender, color, and so on. The demands of community, however, put some checks on that primal instinct of bias. Living together with others of different ethnic or religious abstractions demands that we put ourselves in other people's positions and then judge our actions and thoughts from that particular point; it implies that we act in such a way that if we were to consider our actions from other people's viewpoints, we would be able to find those actions permissible, justified, and fair. When Adichie demands that we should all be feminists, she projects a system that enables the African woman to raise her daughter in virtuous ways. But first, that system has to be fair to those daughters; it has to first of all recognize them as individuals with distinct wishes and dreams that ought to be taken seriously just as it does those of boys. She suggests that girls cannot be policed more than boys are. How can we restructure that system in order to assure that individual boys and girls get fair treatment from their societies?

JOHN RAWLS AND THE ORIGINAL POSITION

The political philosopher John Rawls[17] provides an explanation of what it means to be just and fair in our relation to others in society. At the core of his explanation is what he calls the original position, which is a thought experiment that proposes a condition in which people are free, equal, rational, and are able to make choices about the principles that would guide their lives. The central feature of the original position is the veil of ignorance. Rawls seeks to establish a society guided by "a fair system of cooperation between free and equal persons."[18] The goal of the idea of the original position can be understood in the following question: How can different racial, ethnic, cultural or religious groups approach their society in order to ensure that they and others have a fair access to its material and intangible resources? Rawls argues that those who speak on behalf of such groups, when engaging in deliberations about their society, should operate behind a veil of ignorance of the "social positions or the particular comprehensive doctrines of the persons they represent." The veil of ignorance should prevent them from knowing people's "race and ethnic group, sex or various native endowments such as strength and intelligence, all within the normal range."[19] The veil of ignorance effectively removes any bargaining advantage between different parties. When this becomes the case, Rawls argues, ideas of justice taken from all traditions of philosophy, when presented to citizens, will enhance the interest of their parties, and would impel them by reason to opt for "equal basic rights" and "equal opportunities for all," thus making any social contract possible.

Rawls's conditions are, of course, hypothetical and have been criticized as far-fetched. Moller Okin argues that he takes for granted the sexism inherent in societies in which he intends his contract to apply.[20] She wonders whether his theory of justice applies to women. Martha Nussbaum suspects that Rawls's idea ignores a community's duty to encourage different human capabilities, which are best demonstrated in the workings of the family. Rawls's theory tends to take the parochial nature of the Western nuclear family as the norm of social interactions. In other societies, the family is more community-oriented and functions more on principles of mutual support than on those of contracts.[21] Alasdair MacIntyre raises questions about the place and needs of the community in Rawls's world.[22] Like Kant, Rawls privileges reason, which, as we have already seen, is disembodied.

It is true that Rawls operates on a hypothetical basis. For instance, how can whites in America, who have been in positions of political, cultural, and economic power, ever pretend not to know the social situations of the people they represent in the struggle for the resources of the country? How can blacks not bring in the facts of history? How can men in Igbo society pretend not to know the interests of the group they represent in matters of purely patriarchal importance? As Nkiru Uwechua Nzegwu aptly argues:

> the weakness of this abstract experience is that the others whose bodies have been the target of stigmatization and are given to monthly hormonal cycles cannot easily imagine away features that are constitutive of their body. The mere idea of a removal of these stigmas does not mean that the individual automatically enters a prestigmatization phase.[23]

In my view, the importance of Rawls's thought lies precisely in its hypothetical nature. The original position invites us to imagine an ideal situation "that is fair to the parties as free and equal, and as properly informed and rational. Thus any agreement made by the parties as citizens' representatives is fair."[24] Applied to patriarchal systems, it invites men and women to imagine a situation in which every member of society is treated equally and fairly regardless of gender.

A further thought experiment helps elucidate Rawls's point. If, as zygotes in the womb, ignorant of the conditions of our future lives, we were asked to imagine a society in which we all would be born, what would that society be? We would most likely imagine an equitable society where justice, fairness, love, and consideration for the weak would reign. This is largely because human beings tend to think of their own interests. But these interests are tempered if they, through a simple act of switching perspectives, imagine themselves in the position of the weak. We would most likely opt for a society of fair-minded people free of bias, because we might be in disadvantaged positions. We might be born blind, crippled or deaf. In her feminist writings and in her utterance that all fair-minded people should be feminists, Adichie demands such a simple act of perspective-switching; she demands that we don a veil of ignorance.

My interest in the original position has less to do with its implication for Rawls's social contract theory than with its social and moral implications. The degree of an individual's feeling of fairness is proportional to one's relation to others in general. The original position evokes Adam Smith's "impartial spectator," who arrived at his impartiality by an act of sympathy, imagining himself in the position of others.[25] Putting ourselves in the position of others allows us to judge their actions as if we were those persons, yet we retain the knowledge that we are not those persons. The advantage of these dual perspectives allows us to weigh situations critically and in a much more balanced way than we could have done from our perspective alone. In other words, we enter into a contract with others, and that contract is moral more than it is social or political.

In many ways, Martha Nussbaum's notion of empathy, Rawls's hypothetical world, and works of fiction have one thing in common: they engage the imagination. Following Aristotle's explanation, tragedy is different from, and even richer than, history because it imagines what is possible based on what is real.[26] This, I think, is what Adichie seeks to capture with her injunction on her audience to dream, and to imagine a fairer world. Of course, we acknowledge the gap between ideal and reality. But it is precisely this gap that the imagination seeks to bridge.

Why Does Society Hate My Body?

In Adichie's short story, "Tomorrow Is Too Far" from the collection, *The Thing Around Your Neck*, a young woman accuses her society of having disabled her body. She also indicts herself for physically doing to her brother's body what her society did to hers through the modules of ideology. An unnamed female protagonist who had a Nigerian father and an African American mother, and who is a resident of the USA, gets a call from Nigeria, informing her that her grandmother has died. The call initiates a remembrance of a past incident that she had suppressed.

The story's second-person-singular narrative point of view lends it a Freudian air. The voice is that of the protagonist's superego, her conscience, which reminds her, in a therapeutic manner, of her missteps. "It was the last summer you spent in Nigeria, the summer before your parents' divorce, before your mother swore you would never again set foot in Nigeria to see your father's family, especially Grandmama."[27] The temporal and spatial situating of her wrongdoing makes the protagonist's guilt more pronounced. She was about 10 years old when, overcome by a powerful sense of unfairness against her and in favor of her brother, she consciously caused his death. Eight years later, she has to face her nemesis. She is no longer in the fiercely agitated mode that marked her actions then; she is now haunted by guilt following the full realization of her wrongful deed. This is most visible in her reaction at receiving the call from Nigeria:

> you leaned on your office desk, your legs turning molten, a lifetime of silence collapsing, and it was not Grandmama you thought of, it was Nonso, and it was him, Dozie, and it was the avocado tree and it was that humid summer in the amoral kingdom of your childhood and it was all the things you had not allowed yourself to think about, that you had flattened to a thin sheet and tucked away.[28]

The amoral kingdom of her childhood refers to her quasi-sexual games with her cousin, but more specifically to her hatred of her own brother, Nonso. With the advantage of hindsight, and aided by the voice of her conscience, she now judges her past in unmixed terms. But at the same time she invites the reader to adopt her perspective and to understand what led her to cause her brother's death. This is where Adichie asserts her demand on the reader to imagine fairness. Why was the protagonist agitated? Why did she cause her brother's death? The protagonist's sense of guilt endears her to us, and thus, we begin to empathize with her. She is just like any of us. But she was offended. What offended her sense of justice was Grandmama's preference of her brother, because of his gender. Grandmama worshipped the male in Nonso, and consequently began to teach the boy the technologies of survival in their harsh patriarchal and parochial world. She remembers exactly what Grandmama did: "Grandmama let only your brother Nonso climb the trees to shake a loaded branch, although you were a better climber than he was... it was the summer Grandmama taught Nonso how to pluck coconuts."[29] The narrator emphasizes the fact that the protagonist was a better tree climber than her brother in order to draw our attention to a breach of fairness. Grandmama did not act according to principles of merit but according to the privileges that the patriarchal order granted Nonso as a male. The protagonist herself saw Grandmama's actions as unfair; she interpreted that as Grandmama not wanting her to thrive as a human being. Indeed Grandmama had disabled the girl's body with the help of the system that she was promoting. Why could Grandmama not sense the pain she was inflicting on the girl's body by her failure to recognize the girl? But the truth is that Grandmama had been conditioned to block her empathy against the protagonist. Yet, one still wonders why she would act against her own interest. I will return to this question further on.

Thus far in the story, two things become obvious, none of which contributes to human flourishing. Firstly, Grandmama works against her own gender. Secondly, there was an unspoken enmity between the siblings due to the imbalance in the way their sexes were constructed and enacted in society. This chasm between the two siblings ultimately led the protagonist to begin to think of the elimination of her brother. Her anger is, of course, misdirected because she blamed her brother for her own misery. But there did not seem to be any other way for her to interpret the anomaly of her world. To underline the unfairness in the system, we are reminded again that the protagonist knew that her brother was not superior to her. "You were better at things that did not need to be taught, the things that Grandmama could not teach him."[30] Adichie draws our attention to the source of inequality between men and women. It is not in their bodies as such, but in society's interpretations and definitions of these bodies, in tradition, heritage, patriarchy, or other abstractions that society has invented in the name of order. These abstract categories harm the individual because they overlook their specific histories, their stories; they deny women their rights as humans.

As Adichie states in her talk, women are taught from childhood that their positions in society are inferior to those of men. The degree to which they are taught to accommodate themselves to inferior positions equals the degree to which men perceive themselves as superior.[31] It is then no surprise that Nonso effortlessly occupied the space created for him by his world. He began to enjoy male privileges, and to the detriment of his sister. He was to his sister what a white person is to a black person in a racist Western society. Strictly speaking, what troubled the protagonist was not specifically Nonso's body; it was not superior to hers. What troubled her was the ontological status that his body occupied in that culture. But part of the tragedy of their situation was that the protagonist was not in the position to realize that it was the system that made Nonso's body a direct threat to hers. The boy's exercise of male privilege made the difference between his body and hers. It was what made him lovable to Grandmama, and consequently what infuriated the protagonist, made her the evil one. Knowing that the problem was not with her own body, but with that of her brother, she wanted to mar the supposed perfection of her brother's body, "to make him less lovable."[32] That was why, when Nonso began to exercise the art he learned from Grandmama by climbing the avocado tree, she, the protagonist, frightened him by telling him that he was close to a poisonous snake called "tomorrow is too far." Nonso lost his grip on the tree branches and fell.

I mentioned earlier that Grandmama was not aware of the workings of the ideology that demeaned her own body. It is telling that Grandmama, who is of the same gender as the protagonist, was the one to demonstrate to the protagonist the supposed inferiority of their gender. Why then did Grandmama work against her own self-interest? Judith Butler wonders why subordinated individuals become attached to their subordination, and thereby willful instruments of their own subjection. She observes that "power that at first appears external pressed upon the subject, pressing the subject into subordination, assumes a psychic form that constitutes the subject's self-identity"[33] She suggests that "the subject is effect of power in recoil."[34] The subordinated is created by the power it is resisting, and in so doing becomes dependent on that power relation. Might this also be the case of Stockholm syndrome, in which hostages develop some bonds with their captors? Interpreting Nietzsche, Butler argues that "the peculiar turning of a subject against itself…takes place in acts of self-reproach, conscience."[35] As Althusser argues:

> ideology "acts" or "functions" in such a way that it "recruits" subjects among the individuals (it recruits them all), or "transforms" the individuals into subjects (it transforms them all) by the very precise operation which I have called interpellation or hailing, and which can be imagined along the lines of the most commonplace everyday police (or other) hailing: "Hey you there."[36]

Echoing Althusser, Butler states that "there is no formation of the subject without a passionate attachment to subjection."[37] In defending the institution that subjugated her, the individual believes that she is asserting her importance.[38] One of the sad aspects of the narrative, "Tomorrow Is Too Far" is that the protagonist, Grandmama, and Nonso were trapped in a tragic situation that was not of their own making. Grandmama relied on tradition for the justification of her actions. "Girls never plucked coconuts."[39] Grandmama, to be sure, did not privilege boys for just being boys; she did so to perpetuate the Father's name, or as Butler would argue, to sustain the source of her subjugation. Her conscience has trapped her in a condition that disables her. This is evident in the rigorous distinctions between the ways she treated her granddaughter and the ways she treated Nonso and Dozie, her other grandson, obviously from her other daughter not mentioned in the story. In Igbo tradition, men have no right of inheritance in their mother's natal homes. Right of inheritance is handed down through male lineages, through the fathers of families. Patriarchy functions in the name of the father, effectively dispossessing all mothers and daughters.

Adichie's choice of the name of the protagonist's father reveals the overarching patriarchal epistemologies that undergird the system she is addressing. Nnabuisi in Igbo means "Father is the figurehead." The choice of this name reveals her sardonic attitude towards patriarchy, especially given that Nnabuisi is absent. He is not a resident of Nigeria; he is a US resident, and he visited Nigeria as a tourist. He is no longer bound to Igbo traditions. Given his absence, that is, the absence of the man in whose name Grandmama operates, it is absurd that Grandmama would subject her granddaughter to the pain of unfairness that results from her obvious preference of her grandson. Why exactly would Nnabuisi still control and disrupt the relationship between Grandmama and her granddaughter? Hélène Cixous suggests that this is not exceptional; it is precisely how men have succeeded in destroying women. She argues that "Men have committed the greatest crime against women. Insidiously, violently, they have led them to hate women, to be their own enemies, to mobilize their immense strength against themselves, to be the executants of their virile needs."[40]

Adichie suggests that all the parties in this system were controlled by a blindness they were not aware of. As Althusser argues, ideologies function precisely because of the physical absence of the direct beneficiaries of the system they sustain. How could they and society become aware of the forces that rob them of their humanity? Could Grandmama have realized the unfairness of her position if she were to put on a veil of ignorance? Would she actually prefer a society in which her gender was ontologically fixed in an inferior position? Would she willfully inflict pain on her granddaughter if she knew that there were better alternatives?

As much as "Tomorrow is Too Far" centers on challenging the patriarchal ideology in Igbo society, it is also about empowering women. The story involves the narrator's self-discovery and self-affirmation. It is her heightened sense of self that alerts her to the deep-rooted unfairness of the patriarchal system, a system that a priori had condemned her body as inferior, unworthy of being protected and nourished by Grandmama, the bearer of the light of tradition. The degree to which the protagonist loves herself equals the degree to which she abhors the condition that condemns her to an inferior position in society.

Susan Andrade has discussed Tsitsi Dangarembga as one of Adichie's genealogies.[41] In Dangarembga's novel, *Nervous Conditions*, Tambudzai, the sharp-witted narrator, declares in the novel's first sentence that she was not sad that her elder brother, Nhamo, died. Indeed, she was relieved to learn of his death. It literally opened doors of opportunities for her.[42] Part of Dangarembga's triumph is in showing how Nhamo and his uncle Babamukuru embodied the unfairness of patriarchy. Nhamo's death becomes figurative of the possibilities available to women if patriarchy were overthrown. Andrade is correct in identifying Dangarembga as Adichie's foremother in this respect. Both writers have in common a search for fairness in a world that is inherently unfair because of the privileges that men enjoy in their societies. However, Adichie tempers the perceived rawness of the female character by having her nameless protagonist fall in love with Dozie, her cousin. Her love for Dozie is simultaneous with her hatred of Nonso, thus reminding us of her major concern: the love of self, not the hatred of men. Her love of self can only flourish in an atmosphere of fairness. It is no accident that the penultimate section, in which we learn of her evil deed, begins with her reference to the period of her "first self-realization." The pain of Grandmama's preference for Nnabuisi's son was also inflicted on Dozie. When the protagonist developed a crush on him, she developed a love for yet another neglected person. Her love for Dozie is a cry for solidarity with her fellow victims of the patriarchal unfairness. If Dozie had been a girl, the narrator would still have developed a deep love for her because of their shared experience of unfairness. In this context, feminism becomes, for Adichie, a means to create solidarity among men and women. Fairness to all is the foundation of that solidarity.

Another important distinction between Tambudzai and Adichie's protagonist is the latter's realization of guilt. To be sure, Tambudzai never caused the death of her brother; therefore, she has no reason to feel guilty. Yet the reader feels closer to Adichie's protagonist because of her (protagonist's) realization of her guilt; we see her "weeping standing alone under the avocado tree."[43] Her admission of guilt allows us to understand the degree to which she has been victimized by the patriarchal order. We empathize with her given that her guilt makes her more vulnerable and human.

In the subsequent section, I discuss what her realization of guilt implies to her understanding of fairness. I will first establish a thematic link between the short story and Adichie's novel *Purple Hibiscus*, which also treats patriarchy as a hurdle to social justice and human flourishing.

Narrating Justice and Fairness

In its conceptions of justice, fairness, freedom, and equality in society, *Purple Hibiscus* bears a remarkable resemblance to "Tomorrow is Too Far." The novel dramatizes the ugliness of systems that allow for absolute patriarchal control over reality, where the male agent determines right and wrong, fairness and unfairness. This observation is in line with Cheryl Stobie's remarks that patriarchy is one of the infallible systems that Adichie sets out to dethrone in *Purple Hibiscus*.[44] The first section, "Breaking Gods" sets the stage for the confrontation in the narrative, a confrontation that attempts to destroy the concept of patriarchal infallibility. "Things started to fall apart at home when my brother, Jaja, did not go to communion and Papa flung his heavy missal across the room and broke the figurines on the étagère."[45] The allusion to *Things Fall Apart* not only situates *Purple Hibiscus* in an easily recognizable canon, but also allows us to see the correlation between the patriarchal order in the world of Okonkwo (*Things Fall Apart*) during colonial times, and that of Eugene (*Purple Hibiscus*), decades after independence. The confrontation itself is between individuals and the ideology that conceives of power and right as issuing from the paterfamilias. The very existence of family members is contingent upon that of the paterfamilias; their rights, if they have any, issue from his. The typical patriarchal order stands in contrast to the conception of marriage as a union of loving partners who enter into a relationship that presupposes equal rights and mutual respect. It is no accident that things start to fall apart at home and not, for example, in the church or at work. Deji Toye suggests that Eugene is a recreation of Okonkwo.[46] Just as Okonkwo brought about the disintegration of his family, so does Eugene cause his family to fall apart. The figurines on the étagère are symbolic of the members of the family breaking under the unbearable patriarchal pressure of his presence. Patriarchy literally breaks things up.

Eugene's adherence to patriarchal thinking is further complicated by his religious fundamentalism. Adichie seems to suggest that these two ideologies destroy the basis for recognition and a meaningful gender relationship in Africa, relationships based on equality and mutual respect between men and women, Cynthia R. Wallace argues that *Purple Hibiscus*:

> certainly participates in a critique of Christian religion, aligning colonial whiteness, conservative Catholicism, and the rule of the father, and exposing their destructive power in the psyche (and body) of the novel's young narrator Kambili as well as her brother, Jaja and mother Beatrice.[47]

Wallace's observation is true, especially when seen from the perspectives of Beatrice and her children. Patriarchy incapacitates the psyche and the body of the subordinates. Kambili feels stifled and disabled by the system that grants her father absolute power over his family. She is horrified to see her father abuse her mother, whose swollen eye is often like the "black-purple color of an overripe avocado."[48] It is not accidental that the figurines are Beatrice's special possessions and that she is devoted to them just as she is devoted to her children, Kambili and Jaja, who are little more than ordinary statuettes in the eyes of Eugene, the patriarch.

In a touching scene suggestive of the solidarity between mother and daughter, Kambili addresses her mother shortly after her father has thrown his missal at Jaja: "I'm sorry your figurines broke, Mama."[49] This immediate identification with the oppressed is both an invitation to the reader to empathize with her mother and an indication of Kambili's growing self-awareness. She too might be condemned to the same fate as her mother. Her suspicions are realized soon enough. When Beatrice tells Kambili that she is expecting another child, she also reveals that she has had some miscarriages in her efforts to give birth to another male heir. The Igbo have a proverb in that regard: *Ofu anya ji ishi ugwo*—having just one eye is close to blindness. The more male heirs the more secure a woman is in her husband's home. Given that only males can be the legitimate heirs to their fathers, any woman who does not give birth to a son is considered a guest in her own home. She can be "sent back to her parents," meaning that she can be divorced any time, and left without means. Indeed, Eugene's relatives have urged him to marry other wives or to have concubines, which would assure him more male heirs. The story thus far explains Adichie's call for a revaluation of the moral fabric of African societies in "We Should All Be Feminists." A simple switching of perspectives could bring men, who had never imagined themselves in such situations, to question that system.

Adichie paints a sarcastic picture when Beatrice highlights Eugene's good-heartedness in not marrying another woman.[50] It is ironic that she would show such respect for the man who has abused her; this is in line with what Butler describes as a subjects' psychic identification with their subjection. The irony in this relationship exposes Beatrice's weakness and allows us to interrogate the system that would tolerate such a situation. Kambili, in a moment of epiphany, following her mother's disclosure of her efforts to secure legitimate heirs to her father, realizes that she, like her mother, is living a tenuous life created by that culture. Strictly speaking, she has no place in it. It is the awareness of the fragility of the lives of women in Igbo culture that links the narratives of "Tomorrow Is Too Far" and *Purple Hibiscus* and lends them their most powerful feminist and ethical tenor. Like the protagonist in "Tomorrow Is Too Far," Kambili accuses her culture, and asks: Why do you hate my body?

In a further feminist emphasis, Eugene leads Kambili and Jaja to believe that his wife is guilty of her own miscarriage and of the beating that preceded it.[51] He asks them to pray that God will forgive her. He not only disables his wife physically, he seeks to do so morally. Kambili, perceptive, but still timid, wonders about this: "I did not even think to think what Mama needed to be forgiven for."[52] This narrative suggests that Eugene believes his wife should be forgiven for being a woman because to be a woman is to be in the wrong. Eugene's train of thought is consistent with the Christian belief that sin came into the world through a woman, Eve, whereas salvation came through a man, Christ. For Eugene, Beatrice's world is stuck in the image of women derived from his religious faith. In Eugene's world, conservative Catholic teaching and the Igbo patriarchal tradition are mutually reinforcing.

Besides highlighting the pain inflicted on women, *Purple Hibiscus* achieves its ethical authority indirectly through the disempowerment of its characters, their silences. We are drawn into the family circle and are allowed to see that Eugene beats his wife badly enough to cause a miscarriage. Then, in the belief that he is keeping Kambili safe from sin, he pours hot water on her feet.[53] We feel compelled to challenge the wife to do something, to fight back, to run away, to resist this abuse, to do anything to defy Eugene's violence. Beatrice's annoying lethargy compels us to step in to defend her. Her defenselessness confronts our moral world because we have empathized with her and her children as victims of patriarchal violence. In the introductory chapter, I asked a Levinasian question that might aid our reading of these feminist texts: How does the face (the body) of the woman in pain urge us to confront the totality (abstraction) that put her in that condition? This question helps us to appreciate Adichie's vision in this text. We come face to face with Beatrice and our spontaneity is arrested by her fragility. Would Rawls's concept of the original position enable Eugene to reexamine the moral consequences of his violent actions toward his wife and children? Could he change his ways if he were to fully confront the needless pain he had inflicted on his wife? If he were to "dream" and imagine himself in the position of his wife and children? Could a switching of perspectives have led him to be fair-minded? These questions are as much for Eugene as they are for the reader (society) whom Adichie invites to think of feminism as fairness.

Guilt and the Search for Justice

The protagonist in "Tomorrow Is Too Far" felt guilt not only for bringing about the death of her brother, but also for sowing the seed of enmity between the two elder women in her life: her mother and her grandmother. The *Chambers Dictionary* defines guilt as "the state of having done wrong: sin, sinfulness, or consciousness of it; the painful or uncomfortable emotion or state of mind caused by the awareness or feeling of having done wrong; the state of having broken a law; liability to a penalty (legal)." The operative idea in this definition is the awareness of having done wrong and feeling pain as a result. This pain creates a state of isolation from community, the feeling of no longer being an active member who contributes to the common good. P.S. Greenspan argues that "guilt ascribes something negative to the self and is itself a negative state of feeling. It is not itself a virtue—nor is feeling it or having a tendency to feel it—but rather a requirement of *imperfect* virtue and a goad to future virtuous action."[54] By imperfect virtue, Greenspan means one that allows subjects to admit room for improvement in their lives. Imperfect virtue has its own moral merit; it is a necessary condition for virtue. The necessity of the feeling of guilt is an ideal, not a practical matter.

In "Tomorrow Is Too Far," the protagonist's voice of conscience recalls for her the absence of moral ideals in her life; it recalls how she lied to her mother when she said that it was Grandmama who urged Nonso to climb "to the highest branch of the avocado tree to show her how much of a man he was. Then she frightened him—it was a joke, you assured your mother – by telling him that there was a snake."[55] The immediate effect of the lie was that her mother accused Grandmama of killing Nonso, calling her a "stupid fetish African woman."[56] The protagonist, it might be argued, avenged herself on the "fetish African" tradition that did not consider her body worthy of being taken seriously. Through her own mother—the African American woman—she condemns Grandmama, the guardian of the African tradition that failed to accord her rights. But her action symbolizes the lack of solidarity between these generations of women. She ultimately acted against her own self-interest by destroying the possibility of solidarity between them. The appreciation of the seriousness of her moral lapse is, in line with Greenspan's thinking, an imperfect virtue; it might lead to a better life. More importantly, it reveals the nobility of her character as Greenspan argues about guilt:

> The notion of a noble character seems to include a kind of heightened sensitivity to one's own moral wrongs. We sometimes think of this as a nobler ideal than moral purity, for that matter—so that imperfect comes out as better in a way than perfect virtue.[57]

The protagonist's recognition of guilt is at the same time a recognition of her failure to pursue a perfect life. Guilt plays an important role in our self-estimation. Guilt reveals our concerns about people, society, and the common good; it is a compass that seeks to redirect us to our sense of community and fairness, and it reveals our scale of values. According to William Neblett:

> our capacity to feel guilt is also intimately tied, not only to respect for others, but also to self-respect: Self-respect, in the presence of moral transgression, yields self-disapprobation [and] self-disapprobation, as a feeling, is felt as guilt. In other words, the feeling of guilt is genuinely moral to the extent to which it is self-reflexive.[58]

Given that the awareness of guilt reveals the degree to which we think about ourselves especially in relation to others, it is arguably correlative to our feelings of empathy for others and our responsibility to our world. We reflexively put ourselves in the position of others and imagine the pain that our action might have caused them. For Neblett:

> morality makes it incumbent upon us to feel guilt, and morality provides warranted ways for our feelings of guilt to be "discharged," i.e., provides for and permits us to *redeem* ourselves. Moreover, it not only *provides* for redemption, it *demands* it.[59]

In "Tomorrow Is Too Far," the guilt felt by the protagonist leads her toward self-reflexivity and ultimately to seek redemption by making a visit to the place of her transgression in Nigeria. She seeks to realign her relationship to society and thus redeem herself. Although her brother's death makes her direct appeal to him impossible, we understand that she can still make amends by forgiving herself, and she does so because she has adopted the position of others; she has understood the anger and disappointment and pain they would likely feel, and has implicitly asked for forgiveness. The self-reflexive nature of guilt makes it possible for us to forgive ourselves. We do so on behalf of society, and we feel that our fractured relationship with society has been realigned. The idea of fairness asks us to be self-reflexive, to think about ourselves in relation to others, or others in relation to us. The protagonist shows us the lead in this regard; she shows society the way to fairness and human flourishing.

Agent-Regret as Necessary for Fairness

In the introductory chapter, I discussed the idea of male privilege as analogous to white privilege in South Africa. Samantha Vice suggests agent-regret as the appropriate feeling for a privileged white South African. The same could be said of men in patriarchal societies. In *Purple Hibiscus*, Jaja knows that he is a member of the privileged gender: male. This is so irrespective of the fact that he, too, is a victim of his father's abuse. Being male, he knows he will grow past that abuse when he becomes a man. The same cannot be said of his mother and his sister. They are stuck in their condition given the ontological status of their gender in that society. He therefore feels agent-regret, and consequently undertakes a redemptive act.

While Kambili and Jaja are spending time in Aunt Ifeoma's house at the University of Nigeria in Nsukka, Jaja learns of his namesake, King Jaja of Opobo, who defied the colonial masters, and "refused to let them control all the trade."[60] The boy was given the nickname Jaja as a child; the name struck Aunty Ifeoma as appropriate in her prediction of the boy's character. The idea of Aunty Ifeoma linking him with the great King Jaja of Opobo could not have come at a more appropriate place than at Aunt Ifeoma's house, where he and Kambili have their awakening. One of the lessons he learns is that "the British won the war, but they lost many battles."[61] The ease with which Jaja utters his observation stuns Kambili. But Jaja is no longer the person he used to be. He has realized that expressing defiance is the right thing to do in the face of tyranny. His father is to his family what the colonial lords had been to African societies. His ultimate redemption comes when his mother eventually confesses to her children that she poisoned his father. Jaja feels that he would have done what his mother did. When the police come to interrogate the family, Jaja "did not wait for their questions; he told them he had used rat poison, that he put it in Papa's tea."[62] Some readers might question Jaja's logic, but in Jaja's world, it has its own justification. King Jaja of Opobo would have defied his own oppressors. His feelings of guilt arises from his perceived failure to protect his mother.

Jaja's awareness of guilt is not lost on Kambili. She visits him in prison and observes that: "His eyes are too full of guilt to really see me, to see his reflection in my eyes, the reflection of my hero, the brother who tried always to protect me the best he could. He will never think that he did enough."[63] The narrative thus portrays him as having realized the need for solidarity long before the police came to interrogate the family. Shortly after their mother confesses, he "wrapped his arms around (Kambili) and turned to include [their mother] but she moved away.[64]" His action is undoubtedly a product of agent-regret. It is possible that Jaja might have put himself in the position of Kambili and their mother. He is redeemed by his effort to make amends for the lapse of his gender in fairness. The cry for fairness and solidarity is another thread that links "Tomorrow Is Too Far" and *Purple Hibiscus*. This is a cry for solidarity between women, the victims of patriarchal excesses, but also between men and women. It is a plea for men to extend the hand of solidarity to women in order to form a community in which fairness is a given in people's relation to one another.

IMAGINING HUMAN RIGHTS

Like the other women writers of her generation, Adichie is more interested in telling stories, especially those of the bodies in pain than in accusing men of having oppressed women. She would most likely declare with Ovid that she tells of bodies that have been transformed into different shapes and forms.[65] The bodies in Adichie's narratives are those of women who have been transformed into unwholesome shapes by the patriarchal order of their societies. Adichie does not seek to overthrow fathers. Nor does she seek to relieve them of their responsibilities as fathers; she seeks to make them even more like fathers, real fathers.

Interrogating patriarchal ideology is not the same as rejecting men. Nor is it about women striving to be men. It is about people being fair-minded in their relation to others. Feminism is also about daughters having fulfilling relations with their fathers, relationships in which they feel happy and affirmed as human beings worthy of respect and esteem. Feminism is about fathers being protective, caring fathers. In an incident that recalls Nwoye's acceptance of the new religion in *Things Fall Apart*, Eugene's daughter falls in love with a man who possesses the exact opposite of her father's qualities, a Catholic priest: Father Amadi. Kambili tells: "I wished I were alone with him. I wished I could tell him how warm I felt that he was here, how my favorite color was now the same fire-clay shade of his skin."[66] Father Amadi successfully foils the ugly image of "the Father" created by Eugene. In falling in love with him, Kambili expresses everything her mother's generation would have wished for from the men in their lives. Father Amadi is an ideal; he is the crystallization of Kambili's wishes for a more fulfilling, enabling relationship with her father. Her falling in love with Father Amadi is the same as the protagonist of "Tomorrow Is Too Far" falling in love with her cousin. These two young women hunger for affirmation from the men of their world. They know no other way to express this wish to be seen as human beings than in sexual language. Joseph R. Slaughter writes that the:

> *Bildungsroman* posits as the culmination of modern subjectivation the cultivation of a democratic, humanitarian sensibility—a profound fellow-feeling that enables the *Bildungsheld* to recognize the equal humanity and fundamental dignity of the human personality in both self and others.[67]

Purple Hibiscus exemplifies Slaughter's assessment of the *Bildungsroman* as cultivating humanitarian sensibility. Kambili, the *Bildungsheld* projects the wishes for equal humanity and dignity for all. Adichie uses purple hibiscus (the flower) as a metaphor of Kambili's wishes for dignity. The flower, the narrator tells us, does not need too much care. "The stalks might take root and grow if they were watered regularly... hibiscuses didn't like too much water, but they didn't like to be too dry, either."[68] Aunt Ifeoma, Kambili's father's younger sister, helps her niece in that regard. Aunt Ifeoma is educated and teaches at the university; she sees herself as equal to men and acts accordingly. She is liberal and forward-looking. Kambili admires her because she sees in her the possibility of what she could be. "It was the fearlessness about her, about the way she gestured as she spoke, the way she smiled to show that wide gap."[69] Kambili sees in Aunt Ifeoma a body that is not disabled; or rather, one that has successfully defied the disability that society had foreseen for her. In her aunt, there is no inhibited intentionality. Aunt Ifeoma even once prods Kambili to put on trousers, a symbol of emancipation. In her father's thinking, however, it is sinful for women to wear trousers because it makes them look like men.[70] In another moment of inspiration, Kambili hears about the importance of defiance from Aunt Ifeoma. "Defiance is like marijuana—it is not a bad thing when it is used right."[71] To underline the positive traits in Aunt Ifeoma and underscore her own dreams, another feminist thrust of the narrative, she begins to imitate Aunt Ifeoma in her dreams. "That night, I dreamed that I was laughing, but it did not sound like my laughter, although I was not sure what my laughter sounded like. It was cackling and throaty and enthusiastic, like Aunt Ifeoma's."[72] Her dream is not a complicated one; it is merely her wish to feel comfortable in her own body, her wish to flourish. Aunt Ifeoma can laugh freely because she has already defied the boundaries set for her body by patriarchy; she has discovered the beauty of being oneself. Kambili is on the road to doing so. That is why it features in her dream. We note that she does not dream of doing away with the men in her life; she just dreams of being happy the way she is. Aunt Ifeoma is presented as a possibility for Kambili. Now that she firmly occupies a space in Kambili's psyche as a female member of her society, one who has reached the admirable goal of self-determination, Kambili knows that such a goal is not far-fetched for her.

When Adichie declared in an interview that every fair-minded person should be a feminist, she was imagining a society in which people's thoughts and actions are conducted as if from behind a veil of ignorance. In a society of fair-minded people, no gender would be granted an a priori ontological status. People would be judged by the content of their character, not by their gender. Adichie's more humane society might be no more than one in which a young woman can issue "cackling and throaty and enthusiastic" laughter without fear of a patriarchal censure of these happy expressions of her body. It is one in which men and women can regard one another as equals, as ends in themselves, not as means to other people's ends.

Notes

1. Chimmanda Ngozi Adichie, "We Should All Be Feminists." April 29, 2013 (Adichie 2013). http://tedxtalks.ted.com/video/We-should-all-be-feminists-Chim.
2. R. Krithika, "I Am a Happy Feminist" (Krithika 2013). www.hindu.com/mag/2009/08/09/stories/2009080950020200.htm (Accessed January 25, 2013).
3. Mary Wollstonecraft, "To M. Talleyrand-Perigord, Late Bishop of Autun," in *Masters of British Literature*, ed. David Damrosch and Kevin J.H. Dettmar. New York: Pearson, Longman, 2008, 147–148 (Wollstonecraft 2008).

4. Mary Wollstonecraft, "Vindication of the Rights of Women," in *Masters of British Literature*, ed. David Damrosch and Kevin J.H. Dettmar. New York: Pearson, Longman, 2008, 152 (Wollstonecraft 2008).
5. bell hooks, "Feminism: A Movement to End Sexist Oppression," in *Readings in Feminist Rhetorical Theory*, ed. Cindy L. Griffin, Karen A. Foss, and Sonja K. Foss. Thousand Oaks: Sage Publications, 2004, 51 (hooks 2004).
6. Ibid., 53.
7. bell hooks, *Feminism is for Everybody*. Cambridge, MA: South End Press, 2000, 103 (hooks 2000).
8. Adichie, "We Should All Be Feminists" (Adichie 2013).
9. Ibid.
10. Ibid.
11. Iris Marion Young, *Throwing Like a Girl and Other Essays in Feminist Philosophy and Social Theory*. Bloomington: Indiana University Press, 1990 (Young 1990).
12. Young, "Throwing Like a Girl: A Phenomenology of Feminine Body Comportment Motility and Spatiality." *Human Studies*, 3.2 (1980): 147 (Young 1980).
13. Maura Judkis, "Always Super Bowl 2015 Commercial: Redefining 'throw like a girl.'" *Washington Post* (Judkis 2015) http://www.washingtonpost.com/blogs/style-blog/wp/2015/02/01/always-super-bowl-2015-commercial-redefining-throw-like-a-girl/.
14. Ibid.
15. Frans De Waal, *The Age of Empathy: Nature's Lessons for a Kinder Society*. New York: Harmony Books, 2009, 214 (Waal 2009).
16. Gabriel Marcel, *The Existential Background of Human Dignity*. Harvard University Press, 1963, 123 (Marcel 1963).
17. I am aware that many Africanists are suspicious of such liberal philosophers as Kant and Rawls. I do not suggest that African women writers subscribe to their liberal understanding of society. I do believe, though, that some of their ideas could enhance our understanding of society.
18. John Rawls, *Justice as Fairness: A Restatement*. Edited by Erin Kelly. Cambridge, MA: Harvard University Press, 2001, 14 (Rawls 2001).
19. Ibid., 15.
20. Susan Moller Okin, *Justice, Gender and the Family*. New York: Basic Books, 1989, 2 (Moller Okin 1989).
21. Martha Nussbaum, *Women and Human Development: The Capabilities Approach*. Cambridge University Press, 2001. (Nussbaum 2001).
22. Alasdair MacIntyre, *After Virtue*. University of Notre Dame Press, 1984 (MacIntyre 1984).

23. Nkiru Uwechia Nzegwu, *Family Matters: Feminist Concepts in African Philosophy of Culture*. New York: State University of New York, 2006, 276 (Nzegwu 2006).
24. Rawls, *Justice as Fairness*, 16 (Rawls 2001).
25. Adam Smith, *The Theory of Moral Sentiments*. Edited by Knud Haakonssen. Cambridge University Press, 2002, 11–12 (Smith 2002).
26. Aristotle. *Poetics*. Trans. Malcolm Heath. London: Penguin Books 1996 (Aristotle 1996).
27. Chimamanda Ngozi Adichie, *The Thing Around Your Neck*. Lagos: Farafina Books, 2009 (Adichie 2009).
28. Ibid., 192.
29. Ibid., 187.
30. Ibid., 195.
31. Adichie, "We Should All Be Feminists" (Adichie 2013).
32. Adichie, *The Thing*, 195 (Adichie 2009).
33. Judith Butler, *The Psychic Life of Power: Theories in Subjection*. Stanford, CA: Stanford University Press, 1997, 3 (Butler 1997).
34. Ibid, 6.
35. Ibid., 18.
36. Louis Althusser, *Lenin and Philosophy*. Trans. Ben Brewster. New York: Monthly Review Press, 1971, 163 (Althusser 1971).
37. Butler, *The Psychic Life*, 67 (Butler 1997).
38. For a better understanding of Butler's concept of psychic dependency, see Amy Allen *The Politics of Our Selves: Power, Autonomy, and Gender in Contemporary Critical Theory*. New York: University of Columbia Press, 2008 (Allen 2008).
39. Butler, *The Psychic Life*, 188 (Butler 1997).
40. Hélène Cixous, "The Laugh of the Medusa," translated by Keith Cohen and Paula Cohen. *Signs*, 1.4 (1976): 878 (Cixous 1976).
41. Susan Andrade, "Adichie's Genealogies: National and Feminine Novels," *Research in African Literature* 43.3 (2011), 96–99 (Andrade 2011).
42. Tsitsi Dangarembga, *Nervous Condition*. New York: Seal Press, 1988, 16–20. (Dangarembga 1988).
43. Adichie, *The Thing*, 197 (Adichie 2009).
44. Cheryl Stobie, "Gendered Bodies in Chimamanda Ngozi Adichie's Purple Hibiscus," in *Literature of Our Times: Postcolonial Studies in the Twenty-First Century*, ed. Bill Ashcroft, Ranjini Mendis, Julie McGonegal, and Arun Mukherjee. Amsterdam and New York: Rodopi, 2012, 421–435 (Stobie 2012).
45. Chimamanda Ngozi Adichie, *Purple Hibiscus*. New York: Anchor Books, 2003, 3 (Adichie 2003).
46. Deji Toye, "Unmasking the Okonkwo Complex in Purple Hibiscus," *Nigerian Guardian* 24 January 2005 (Toye 2005).

47. Cynthia R. Wallace, "Chimamanda Ngozi Adichie's Purple Hibiscus and the Paradoxes of Postcolonial Redemption," *Christianity and Literature*, 61.3 (2012): 467 (Wallace 2012).
48. Adichie, *Purple Hibiscus*, 11 (Adichie 2003).
49. Ibid., 10.
50. Ibid., 20.
51. Ibid., 32–34.
52. Ibid., 36.
53. Ibid., 194.
54. P.S. Greenspan, "Guilt and Virtue," *The Journal of Philosophy*, 92.2 (1994): 58 (Greenspan 1994).
55. Adichie, *The Thing*, 194 (Adichie 2009).
56. Ibid., 194
57. Greenspan, "Guilt and Virtue," 61 (Greenspan 1994).
58. William Neblett, "The Ethics of Guilt," *The Journal of Philosophy*, 71.18 (1974): 655. (Neblett 1974).
59. Ibid.
60. Adichie, *Purple Hibiscus*, 144 (Adichie 2003).
61. Ibid., 145.
62. Ibid., 291.
63. Ibid., 305.
64. Ibid., 291.
65. Ovid, *Metamorphosis*. Trans. Mary M. Innes. London: Penguin Books, 1955, 29 (Ovid 1955).
66. Adichie, *Purple Hibiscus*, 221 (Adichie 2003).
67. Joseph R. Slaughter, *Human Rights, Inc: The World Novel, Narrative Form, and International Law*. New York: Fordham University Press, 2007, 253 (Slaughter 2007)
68. Adichie, *Purple Hibiscus*, 197 (Adichie 2003).
69. Ibid., 76.
70. Ibid., 80.
71. Ibid., 144.
72. Ibid., 88.

CHAPTER 3

Diary of Intense Pain: The Postcolonial Trap and Women's Rights

Chinelo Okparanta and NoViolet Bulawayo

In the introductory chapter, I discussed Pinkie Mekgwe's notion of the colonial trap, which is the need to talk or write back to the West, especially in the same binary language adopted by the West while othering Africa. To what degree, if ever, does the obsession with the gaze of the West affect women's rights in Africa? How does Africa's ideological need to talk back to the West affect people's awareness of, and sensibility towards, fairness?

The Caine Prize for African writing, established in 2001, brought many talented African writers to the attention of the Western publishing world; it gave them exposure and publicity they would not have readily found in Africa because of problems unique to Africa's book publishing industry. However, critics of the prize point out that most of the new writers appear to be obsessed with the underbelly of African existence. They allege that these writers are merely replicating the colonial image of Africa by indulging in pornographic portrayals of violence and misery. Is there truth in the criticism, or is it that the fixation with the gaze of the West is making a comeback in the twenty-first century, and to the detriment of women? In this chapter, I return to the issue I raised in the introduction: the "writeback" ideology of the Achebe era ignores the pain that some sectors of the African populace are subjected to. Based on analyses of NoViolet

Bulawayo's *We Need New Names*[1] and Chinelo Okparanta's *Happiness, Like Water*,[2] I argue that while many of the new narratives focus on violence and misery in Africa, the writers do not engage such instances of misery for their own sake. Quite to the contrary, they bring to our moral awareness the pain that the victims of Africa's patriarchal and sexist structures suffer, and they do so in view of initiating a reappraisal of the moral foundations of Africa's gender relations. They thus enhance the core thesis posited in Chapter 2, which is that feminism is about fairness in dealing with women's bodies. I see the preliminary ethical import of these works in light of Zachary Adam Newton's observation about stories. For him, "the story is its own lesson."[3] Newton proposes a triadic structure of narrative ethics that enables this. His structure involves:

> (1) a narrational ethics (in this case, signifying the exigent conditions and consequences of the narrative act itself); (2) a representational ethics (the costs incurred in fictionalizing oneself or others by exchanging "person" for "character"); and (3) a hermeneutic ethics (the ethico-critical accountability that acts of reading hold their readers to).[4]

With regard to the authors I discuss here, and given the suffering in Africa, much of which is structural, it is fair to claim that storytelling itself is an ethical act. The representation of people's suffering is not a neutral act. On the contrary, it requires a serious engagement and responsibility on the part of writers and readers. I understand a part of the writers' responsibility as exposing the structures that hinder human flourishing in Africa. In so doing the writer performs human rights.

The Limits of Postcolonial Criticism

I suggested earlier in this book that one of the flaws of late twentieth-century African feminism was its provenance in the anti-colonial intellectual movement. It was designed to respond to colonialist/Western narratives about Africa. Its weakness was indulgence of postcoloniality. I have shown elsewhere, with reference to Simon Gikandi,[5] how Chinua Achebe set the African postcolonial discourse in the write-back trajectory that challenged the misrepresentation of the African image in Western narratives.[6] His famous critique of Joseph Conrad is a permanent feature in most cultural studies and discussions of postcolonial literature.[7] There is a peculiar twenty-first-century resurgence of this preoccupation with Western representation of Africa. When NoViolet Bulawayo's short story, "Hitting Budapest" won the prestigious Caine Prize in 2011, most African bloggers responded with astonishment that her story, set in the slums of Zimbabwe, was chosen at all.[8] Even as a shortlisted story, it attracted much negative reaction. Critics dismissed it and others like it as exercises in "Africa-poverty-pornography."[9] Bulawayo's novel, *We Need New Names*, which was shortlisted for the 2013 Booker Prize, and which was built on the experiences of characters in "Hitting Budapest," met with similar eviscerations by reviewers, most of whom were African. Writing in *The Guardian*, the Nigerian novelist Helon Habila asks whether the jury had not succeeded in imposing an aesthetic of violence on Africa. He laments what he calls "poverty-porn": stories that dwell mainly on child soldiers, genocide, child prostitution, female genital mutilation, political violence, police brutality, dictatorships, predatory preachers, dead bodies on the roadside. He asks whether:

> [the] new writing is a fair representation of the existential realities of Africa, or if it is just a "Caine-prize aesthetic" that has emerged in a vacuum created by the judges and the publishers and agents over the years, and which has begun to perpetuate itself.[10]

Habila argues that the award itself is infusing poverty porn into the African imagination because "writing is an incestuous business: style feeds on style, especially if that particular style has proven itself capable of winning prizes and book deals and celebrity."[11] This is a surprising review from Habila, given that he, too, is a product of the Caine Prize tradition, and that two years earlier he had praised the new generation of writers nurtured by the Caine Prize organization as "post-nationalist," meaning that the writers look beyond the nation and national politics.[12] Might one suspect that he was swayed by Dobrota Pucherová's sarcastic assessment of the Caine Prize's short stories, in which she suggests that African writers are now engaging in self-anthropologizing?[13]

Writing in *NEXT*, once an influential Nigerian newspaper, Ikhide Ikheloa laments that "the creation of a Prize for 'African writing' may have created the unintended effect of breeding writers willing to stereotype Africa for glory."[14] In what appears to be a page from Robert Mugabe's anti-imperialist rhetoric, the Zimbabwean critic Stanley Mushava takes Habila's criticism further by alleging that Bulawayo is merely pandering to Western readers:

> The Western media is in consensus that Africa is a dark continent and Zimbabwe is a troubled spot. Stories about local achievements and authentic African aspirations always get overlooked while Africa is only a synonym of war, poverty and civil unrest going by the lenses of Fox, CNN and BBC.[15]

Another Zimbabwean writer and academic, Dr Tinashe Mushakavanhu, lamented in an interview with Stanley Mushava that African writing was "being produced more as a commodity than as a value" because those who control the institutions responsible for the production of African narratives "possess fixed ideas about what African literature should and should not be, and what authentic African characters can or cannot do"; their ideas about Africa are not different from the one represented in "Joseph Conrad's 'heart of darkness' [sic]."[16]

The criticism leveled by Habila and others plays into the ideological premises of Binyavanga Wainana's "How to Write About Africa,"[17] and Chimamanda Ngozi Adichie's "The Danger of a Single Story."[18] These premises can be traced back to Chinua Achebe and other postcolonial theorists, who challenged the West's representation of non-Westerners in order to contest the power relation between the West and colonized nations. This construct has become a staple of postcolonial theory. Resistance to the West was, and still is, a necessary act of survival in Africa. Sadly, one of the consequences of such an act has been an instinctive reaction to defend Africa as it is.[19] The critics of Bulawayo, who operate from the perspective of postcoloniality, assume that the writer is merely promoting the cause of imperialism in Africa. As Lizzy Attree argues, such critics "presume the motives of African writers themselves, which is a dangerous critical tendency."[20]

Okparanta's writing shows similar characteristics to that of Bulawayo with regard to the alleged creation of a pornography of poverty. However, most reviews of *Happiness, Like Water* have been written by Westerners in Western media outlets, and are overwhelmingly positive. Of course, that would not surprise critics such as Habila and Mushava because Westerners, in their minds, have merely discovered stories that confirm their yearning for African poverty narratives. Is it really true that these writers merely write to please the Western audience? How about the human rights of the individuals represented in the story? Is it accidental that most of the critics are male?

The writers in question have not let the criticism of their works go unanswered. Bulawayo has argued that her interest is in "the real stories on the ground."[21] What does she mean by that? My concern in this chapter is not to judge the merits or failures of African narratives, nor to judge the merits of Bulawayo's aesthetics based on her stated goals. I am interested in examining the grammar of motives in her narrative and that of her contemporary, Okparanta. What do their narratives reveal about women's rights in the societies they write about? When I speak of a grammar of motives, I am not suggesting a knowledge of the intentions of the authors. Rather, I return to the second element in Adam Zachary Newton's triadic structure of narrative ethics, that is, "the costs incurred in fictionalizing oneself or others by exchanging 'person' for 'character.'"[22] What are the ethical implications of their project? By examining the world of the characters, I intend to discuss the ethical burdens that the authors have accepted and the demands that their narratives place on readers. "Grammar of motives" is a term introduced by Kenneth Burke, and one of its assumptions is that the only way we can understand why people do what they do is to impute motives arrived at by interpreting their actions. Burke identifies act, scene, agent, agency, and purpose as keys to the understanding of motives in literary works.[23] In this regard, it is important to consider Lizzy Attree's intervention in the debates about the authentic representation of African reality in contemporary African writing. She argues that:

> It is so much more interesting to look at a writer's work outside and beyond the limits of postcolony as modern subject and agent, which is where they should be, rather than as objects to be critiqued using postcolonial theories, such as those espoused by Said, Spivak, and Bhabha...Moving beyond the limits of the postcolony opens up the realm of possibilities and lays bare the plethora of subjects about which African writers can choose to write.[24]

I agree with Attree, and submit that Bulawayo and Okparanta write about the suffering of women in African societies not because African men are worse than the men in other parts of the world, but because the patriarchal systems in African societies subject women to needless suffering and hinder their facets of selfhood. As Ricoeur argues, the representation of such suffering in literary works must be understood in the Aristotelian sense of mimesis, of "imitation of action."[25] Storytelling is not a neutral act; it always comes packaged with the storyteller's assumptions. Nor are interpretations without bias. Yet there is a common ground between telling and listening. At some point, the listener feels that she has understood something in the story; the story touches her. As Newton argues, listening is also an ethical act; it calls for "response as responsibility."[26] To understand what Okparanta and Bulawayo are doing, in hearing their stories, we need to understand their characters (agents) by imaginatively reconstructing the world the authors create and by feeling, to the extent we can, what the characters feel.

Pain and the Challenge of Being an African Woman in the Twenty-first Century

Okparanta's short story "Runs Girl" occupies a central position in her aesthetics and ethics. It is constructed around the lives of three women: Ada, her terminally ill mother, and Ada's friend Njideka. The specific nature of Ada's mother's illness is unknown; the family lives in poverty and cannot afford adequate medical care. Ada is at a desperate dead end when Njideka suggests a way out: Ada can become a runs girl—a Nigerian name for a female escort. Njideka, who is a runs girl herself, can show Ada how it is done.

In describing the impasse faced by Ada's family, Okparanta creates a synecdoche for society's regard to women. Her attention is on the social structures that hinder women's rights by turning them into objects in the hands of men. The family's misfortune is that of society writ small. The poor get by only by luck or by wringing out every drop of their sweat in bone-crushing labor. They enter into Faustian bargains in order simply to exist. We do not know why Njideka became a runs girl. But the narrator suggests that she is not comfortable with the task, and she masks her pain and discomfort; she wears a shiny wig. Ada, somewhat still a conventional girl, contrasts herself with Njideka. In order to maintain her perception of Njideka's humanity, she forces herself to imagine Njideka's "head under all that artificial hair," envisioning "bald patches and a thinning hairline." It is comforting to Ada "to think that deep down, under all that perfection was a version of her that was just as imperfect as me."[27] Through Ada's search for the real Njideka underneath the mask, Okparanta alerts the reader to differences between perception and reality. Underneath the hairpiece is a *patch of pain*. We assume that Njideka would not have been playing that game if she lived in better economic conditions. Perhaps she is just masking some inner agony. Thus the narrative questions whether women are in control of their destiny in that world. Why does Ada have to make herself an object of men's carnal desire in order for her mother to survive? Why can she not relate to men on equal grounds, and in dignity?

The ethical core of the narrative is the relationship between Ada and her mother, especially in regard to how it has been shaped by the socio-cultural structures of their world. They can no longer shape their destiny. To the contrary, they are shaped by forces outside their control. It is important to consider how their family came to be poor. Ada's father has died, and Ada was witness to the physical and psychological collapse of her mother soon after her father's death. Ada and her mother, without a man in their lives, are left to fend for themselves "in a world where it was hard for a woman to do so honestly."[28] By acknowledging such a world, the narrator establishes a pronounced connection between Ada's family and the larger society; she points to the patriarchal and socially dysfunctional system that militates against women's rights. Moreover, it is Ada's mother who most completely embodies the condition of women in that society, and in this way, her experiences become figurative of those of women. That condition is one of pain: "Mama was in pain, and the doctors did not know the cause."[29] The fact that the illness is not named is not accidental; it insinuates a more encompassing malady in society, a malady that disables women's bodies. Is the illness in society to be understood as the system and its ideologies? The invocation of religious devotion strengthens the grip that ideology has on mother and daughter alike, and mollifies its pain: "We prayed again that night and Mama read again from Job: *Despise not though the chastening of the Almighty: For He maketh sore, and bindeth up: He woundeth, and His hands make whole.*"[30] Like Job, mother and daughter accept their condition as a given and probably as ordained by God. In situations in which ideologies oppress people, it is always difficult for the victims to put their finger on the exact cause of their suffering.

Ada yields to Njideka's suggestion that she too become a runs girl: "To get the money for Mama. To get the money so that I could take her to a specialist, one that Njideka would recommend."[31] Ada does not know what she is getting herself into; she has no idea that being a runs girl means having sex with men. She is raped on the first encounter.[32] In this encounter, Okparanta hints at the paradigm of male–female relationships under the conditions that have already been established as ordained by God. In focusing on the situations that Ada and her mother experience, Okparanta prevents the reader's relation to the individuals in pain from lapsing into diffuse sympathy. Rather we empathize with Ada, and we do so because of her innocence and her helplessness. She suffers undeservingly. Could she have helped her mother in any other way? Was there no other way to survive? But then we are reminded that they live *in a world where it was hard for a woman to do so honestly*. Okparanta suggests that patriarchy makes it impossible for women to be honest. Mary Wollstonecraft had made the same argument. Patriarchy makes both men and women insincere. Within the contexts of the systemic constraints under which women suffer, the rape of Ada is symbolic of the condition of women in that society, one in which it is hard for them to provide for themselves. Thus the mother's unnamed pain becomes that of the daughter, and their discomfort mirrors that of women. In its ability to call attention to the suffering of women in sexist societies, "Runs Girl" exhibits similar narrative attitudes to those found in NoViolet Bulawayo's *We Need New Names*.

The story of *We Need New Names* takes place in an unnamed African country that we assume to be Zimbabwe. It is narrated by a witty girl named Darling, and begins with a group of urchins on their way to a place called Budapest. Their former home has been razed by their government. Now they live in a makeshift settlement called Paradise. They go to Budapest, an up-scale, largely white neighborhood, for the guava growing there. One of the many crucial scenes in the novel portrays the miraculous spiritual healing at one of the many Pentecostal churches in the country. Darling and her companions come across one of these healings conducted by Prophet Revelations Bitchington Mborro. There are seven sinners—all women—in need of purification. The prophet goes around touching each of them "on the forehead with his stick, and then sprinkles them with holy water before they confess."[33]

A closer consideration of the scene raises several issues that can help us understand Bulawayo's ethical inquiry. Seven is an important number in religious circles. The Catholic Church has seven sacraments. Jesus cleansed Mary Magdalene of her seven demons. The Book of Revelations describes the scroll whose back was "sealed with seven seals."[34] Could the prophet's name—Prophet Revelations Bitchington Mborro—have been derived from the book of Revelations? Is he himself an instrument of divine patriarchal revelation? The more disturbing question has to do with those being cleansed. Why are only women the ones in need of cleansing? Why is it only men who do the cleansing? One answer may lie in the fact that one of the women, Simangele, confesses that she has quarreled with her cousin, whom she suspects of planning to take her husband from her. In that confession, men are presented as worth fighting for. Women are therefore set against one another in their pursuit of this precious commodity. That is their sin, and that is what they have to be forgiven for. Their society has created a system in which they need men in order to be validated, and when they fight to retain the very thing that validates them, they are accused of having sinned. They are therefore trapped in a vicious circle, in a world in which they exhaust their energy trying to prove how good they are. Of course, they will never succeed in demonstrating their value because that value is thought to be extrinsic to them; the patriarch confers it. Secondly, they cannot be thought to be good because the source of their evil is in them: their gender. Like Okparanta, Bulawayo explores the setting against whose backdrop women's agony can be understood. It is fair to argue that her primary concern is simply to expose the structural underpinnings of societies and to have them confront our sense of common decency. Setting is a character in each of these stories, and we are urged to examine how it impacts facets of women's selfhood. We are challenged to ask more questions about these women's rights.

In another scene, Bulawayo sharpens her narrative to reflect the scorn of men and society for women who take pride in their bodies. A woman is brought into the scene by a group of men. She is portrayed as beautiful, as she has "smooth flawless skin like maybe she is an angel." She is fashion-conscious and she is wearing a "purple dress that's riding up her thighs."[35] The narrative tone suggests that the woman's crime is self-confidence, or just the simple awareness of her body as belonging to her; but this is readily interpreted as pride in those religious circles. She is therefore a perfect candidate for exorcism. The men carry her forward to be healed, that is, humiliated, and taught her position in society. She should not care for her body.

The symbolic relevance of exorcism, a ritual carried out by men in most religions, helps Bulawayo to frame the moral argument of her story. Why do many religions see women's bodies as defiled and as a source of evil? This is as true for the three Abrahamic religions as it is for most African indigenous religions. Just as the illness that afflicts Ada's mother in "Runs Girl" is not named, so the woman being exorcised is nameless. She is identified only as "the woman," and in that respect stands for all women in that patriarchal society. This explains why Darling promptly identifies with her. The woman resists the men's assault on her, crying, "Leave me alone, leave me alone, you sons of bitches. You don't know me!"[36] Darling repeats the woman's words: "Leave her alone, leave her alone, you sons of bitches! You don't know her!"[37] The repetition is a mirror image of the woman's words, and it is portrayed as an instance of empathy. Darling has put herself in the position of the woman and says to her: "I feel what you feel. *I feel your pain.*"[38] The scene provides a clear instance of characters displaying empathy towards one another. Of relevance here is that Bulawayo exposes the experience of particular women by recreating what we have already identified as Adam Smith's *like situation*. These situations are products of socio-cultural structure. Juliana Makuchi Nfah-Abbenyi has advocated focusing on women's subjectivities via the category of gender in order to truly understand the condition of African women.[39] Her suggestion proves useful in appreciating why Bulawayo sheds light on a woman who has taken interest in her body, and men who despise her for doing so. Following the patriarchal logic, men would like to see women as disembodied beings, as those who do not (and should not) take pleasure in their bodies. This explains the exorcism in the narrative. Indeed, Prophet Revelations Bitchington Mborro is symbolic of the systemic oppression against which women define themselves. The moment the woman begins to resist and to assert ownership of her body, he feels personally affronted; he perceives her defiance as his personal failure and as a rejection of his authority as the leading patriarch. The woman's resistance prompts an immediate reaction (a backlash), one which reminds her in a unique way that she is a woman, and that she has a defined place in society. He leaps on the woman and:

> prays for the woman like that, pinning her down and calling to Jesus and screaming Bible verses. He places his hands on her stomach, on her thighs, then he puts his hands on her thing and starts rubbing and praying hard for it, like there's something wrong with it.[40]

Prayer is an ideological tool that helps the prophet trick people into accepting the violence of his act. Patriarchal societies generally see women's "thing" as the source of evil in society.[41] The narrator contrasts the Prophet's orgasmic state ("his face is alight, glowing") with the woman's agony: "the pretty woman just looks like a rag now, the prettiness gone, her strength gone."[42] Is rape an act of exorcism? The ethical thrust of the narrative asserts itself the moment we begin to question the men's actions, the moment we interrogate the Prophet's authority. Equally important is what is additionally revealed in this rape scene. The narrator describes the fate of one of the urchins: "Chipo is just waking up and she is looking around like she was lost but has found herself."[43] Chipo is traumatized by what she has seen. But the true source of her trauma lies elsewhere: her own experience of rape by her grandfather, who had forced her down and pinned her like the pretty woman in the story had been: "he clamped a hand over my mouth and was heavy like a mountain, Chipo says, words coming out all at once like she is Mother of Bones. I watch her and she has this look I have never seen before, this look of pain."[44] This incident establishes a parallel between the woman's experience and that of the girl. It serves an important narrative purpose, for it reveals the precarious conditions under which women live.

I noted in the introductory part of this chapter that Bulawayo and Okparanta are interested in the pain that women experience in societies whose systems do not allow them to flourish as responsible human beings. The authors' motives are an ethical choice, and they make it evident in their characters. The scene described above is an example. One thing that troubles Darling is the look of pain on Chipo's face. Her pain, we recall, was provoked by that of the beautiful woman being exorcised of her demons. So, here we have three women connected by pain that does not arise from their bodies as women, but from the attitude of society to those bodies. The women suffer because society subjects them to suffering simply on account of their gender. I referred to Sylvia Tamale's argument that the majority of those who are against feminism in Africa are precisely those who "have never directly experienced gender discrimination."[45] This is true in Africa and in the West. Those who never experience any form of discrimination are more likely to remain passive in the face of discrimination against others. This is largely because they have difficulty relating to the victims' experiences. Empathy seeks to bring the pain of the victims closer to the awareness of the privileged, and dispose the latter to respond.

Of Pain and the Demand for Empathy

Contemporary Western ethical theories have been largely influenced and dominated by utilitarianism and the Kantian deontological approaches. What they have in common is their positivistic ideal of scientific knowledge. They assume that human nature can be understood only by reason. The human person is conceived rationally, and therefore the rules that guide people's interrelationships are grounded in reason. But the Neo-Aristotelians or virtue ethicists argue that rule-oriented ethicists ignore a very important aspect of our moral lives; they ignore the fact that the human person does not live in conditions of pure reason as Descartes had believed, and that moral insights are not acquired through reason alone. Insight can also be gained through literature. In *The Ethics of Cultural Studies*, Joanna Zylinska suggests that the logical applications of ethical rules to specific individuals are ineffective. Ethics, she argues, "emerges from the lived experience of corporeal, sexual beings."[46] Richard Rorty has noted that the modern world has derived more moral progress from "descriptions of particular varieties of pain and humiliation (in, e.g., novels or ethnographies) rather than philosophical or religious treatises."[47] Stories therefore are agents of morality not only because of their impact on us, but also for what they reveal about others through portrayals of their struggle. The situations described in the narratives, Rorty argues, urge us to engage the individual (the literary character) not by way of abstract, cosmic terms, but on her own terms, or on the terms that the pain she experiences as a human being has dictated.[48] Examining the relationship between life and literary fiction, Paul Ricoeur argues that "the plot serves to make *one* story out of the multiple incidents or, if you prefer, transforms the many incidents *into one* story."[49] Through emplotment, the disparate incidents in a particular life are organized into a distinct meaning-making narrative. The meaning of the story is arrived at when we follow the story from one incident to another. To become engaged in the narrated details of the human life is an ethical act. We bring our understanding to bear upon that life. Ricoeur identifies this as the narrative understanding of human life. By this he refers to the understanding that takes into account various aspects of the life of that individual as parts of a comprehensive whole. Narrative understanding is the knowledge resulting from fruitful engagements with narratives, or with a person's life stories.[50] Meaningful links between different and often contradictory events are made in ways that lead to insight. This is a special domain of the hermeneutic circle, where we move from part to whole and back again.[51]

Ricoeur argues that:

> It is the function of poetry in its narrative and dramatic form, to propose to the imagination and to its mediation various figures that constitute so many thought experiments by which we learn to link together the ethical aspects of human conduct and happiness and misfortune. By means of poetry we learn how reversals and fortune result from this or that conduct, as this is constructed by the plot in the narrative.[52]

Narrative understanding is a necessity if ethical relationships are to exist. The ethical content of comprehension is manifested when we cease making judgments about individuals based on abstract rules or ideologies, and instead begin to judge them through the insight gained from their individual stories. Racist or patriarchal ideologies establish abstract modes of judging individuals. Narratives, to the degree that they explore individual lives, are opposed to these ideologies.[53]

Bulawayo and Okparanta advocate a narrative understanding of the African lives they write about. They are not fixated on the pain of their characters per se; rather they highlight that as a part of the individual's stories and as an expression of the anomalies of a given system. Thus the different forms of women's pain embody instances of the system that obstructs the exercise of women's rights. This is where I locate the ethical imperative of their narratives. According to Ricoeur, when the full extent of the incidents of an individual person's life are organized, a phronetic understanding emerges, one that allows us to relate to characters in realistic narratives as if they were real persons.[54] In this case therefore what should occupy a morally conscious person is how to change the systems that necessitate the abuse of rights, rather than save Africa's image.

In Okparanta's story, "Fairness," Uzoamaka's light-skinned mother regularly reminds Uzoamaka of her dark skin. She reads American magazines and buys into the American notion of beauty, which she holds up to her daughter for emulation. The narrator uses the word, "fairness" as a double entendre: "Our skin is the colour not of ripe pawpaw peels, but of its seeds. We are thirsty for fairness."[55] Though the narrator speaks of the color of their skin, she makes a subtle reference to the condition of women in that world, one that cries for *fairness*. In a remarkably self-destructive act that reminds us of Butler's idea on subjection, Uzoamaka's mother prods her daughter to bleach her skin by comparing her to one of the family's maids, Ekaite, who has successfully bleached her own skin. She speaks glowingly of Ekaite as being beautiful in every way.[56] At the same time she despises her other maid, Eno, who has not yet lightened her dark skin, waving her away as if she were a fly.[57] After hearing of the success of lightening skin using bleach, Uzoamaka convinces Eno to dip her face in a bucket filled with laundry bleach. The consequences are obvious: Eno's face is mutilated. She is literally disabled. The descriptive details give the story its narrative-ethical force. Eno screams as the bleach eats into her face:

> Ekaite rushes towards us, sees that it is Eno who is in pain. She reaches her hands out to Eno, holds Eno's face in her palms. Eno screams, twists her

face. Her cheeks contort as if she is sucking in air. She screams and screams. I feel the pain in my own face. Ekaite looks as if she feels it too, and for a moment I think I see tears forming in her eyes.[58]

The description highlights three instances of pain, linked by the author's yearning to bring together three human beings of inherent dignity: Eno, Ekaite, and the narrator. The narrative raises the question: Why must women literally disfigure themselves in order to please society (men)? Why does society subject them to such unnecessary pain? Dave Beech has argued that ideals of beauty have to be understood as part of "the Ideological State Apparatuses of art... Beauty is ideological because it is a cherished term for a specific interpellated subject within art's apparatus. It is because beauty is related to being good that it must be controversial."[59]

"Fairness" could be read as a story of how ideologies lead women to turn against one another in society, and incapacitate one another. These ideologies are woven into society's social and cultural institutions. Consistent with Ricoeur's assertions regarding narrative, Okparanta provides us with incidents in the lives of her female characters that allow us to understand why they seek to destroy one another. We understand that Uzoamaka's mother is not in control of her destiny; she has fallen victim to forces beyond her. She had become psychically attached to her subjection. Fairness towards women consists in first understanding the source of their pain. It is therefore not just a fair complexion that these women want in "Fairness"; they want to be treated with decency. With fairness. But so do the characters in *We Need New Names*. The chapter in the latter titled "Real Change" provides a sarcastic view of history and conditions in post-independence Zimbabwe.

The death of a child named Freedom is of central importance, and it is told in the form of a recollection inserted between narratives about national elections. Election is, of course, a ritual that captures the condition of the new country as a free state, one that is no longer ruled by a white minority. Freedom is exactly what their leader fought for, and won for them. The narrator is haunted by the remembrance of how she and her family were rendered homeless, and how Freedom, their freedom, was killed.[60] When the bulldozers demolish their shanties, they also crush the child of Nomviyo, one of the residents of the slum. Nomviyo had gone shopping, and when she returns and sees that her shanty is no longer there, she screams: "I left my Freedom sleeping in there!... Nomviyo looks at the thing that is also her son and throws herself on the ground."[61] Freedom is therefore a real person and a trope. The display of pun and irony reveals Bulawayo's grasp of the complex African postcolonial condition, and her intention to trouble the simplistic moral imagination of evil white people and good Africans implicit in much of conventional postcolonial thoughts. In ordering the shanties crushed, the leader, who fought against the white regime for independence, indirectly crushes his justification for being. The death of freedom is a signifier of the constraints that the slum dwellers experience, and this is crystallized in the detailed description of Nomviyo's experience of pain. Her suffering elicits empathy from readers, who are made to see the larger forces that conspire against the shanty dwellers. Martha Nussbaum's succinct definition of empathy as the "imaginative reconstruction of the experience of the sufferer,"[62] aids our understanding of the scene. The narrator draws our attention to the pain that these women should not be made to suffer.

"Wahala" in Okparanta's *Happiness, Like Water* describes the troubles in the life of a woman, Ezinne, who is thought to be barren. She is made to go to a medicine woman to remove a curse placed on her by the spirits. She then endures a painful sex act in order to provide her husband with a child that would earn him respect in the community. The *Urban Dictionary* defines *wahala* as "a pidgin English word used mostly by Nigerians, meaning trouble." The story is a commentary on the fate of married women who cannot have children. The husband of such a woman can, without being challenged, "cast her away" and take "another wife."[63] She cannot challenge her husband because she has no right to do so; she has no right because she is a woman.

The issue of childless women has been at the center of African women's writing ever since the pioneer African author Flora Nwapa wrote about it in her novel, *Efuru*.[64] Women writers have been unduly criticized, especially by male critics, for what seems to them to be an excessive focus on barrenness.[65] Yet, the issue of female barrenness is central to the existence of women in a typical African patriarchal context, where women derive rights not only to own property, but also to be able to live in their husbands' home, only through their male offspring. Given the cultural context in that world, few people ask if the imperfection could lie elsewhere; very few question the man's fertility. The narrator confronts this paradigm: "And what if the imperfection was not really even in her? What if it was in *him*?" Of course, the question seeks to challenge the cultural assumptions that made Ezinne's suffering possible. But Ezinne could not dare voice this thought because "it was generally understood that such things were the fault of the woman."[66] By remarking that imperfections such as infertility are generally understood to be the fault of women in the family, the narrator insinuates an association with the biblical narrative of the origin of imperfection in the world. Sin came into the world through Adam and Eve, but more specifically through Eve. In Greek mythology, Pandora's curiosity was responsible for spreading evil in the world. Given the assumption that women are the source of evil, society is disposed to believe that their pain is atonement for their crime. No one in Ezinne's world is genuinely interested in the pain she suffers in intercourse. Each time her husband "made to enter her, she stiffened, and there was pain. Or rather, she said, it was hard to tell which one came first—the stiffening or the pain."[67] Like the pain that Ada's mother experienced in "Runs Girl," Ezinne's pain has no specific source. How then can that pain be stopped? The first step is to listen to her. Her condition requires that she be allowed to tell her own story; it requires that her world ask her: "Who are you?" But no one in her world seems interested.

The failure to listen to Ezinne has obvious ethical implications: it blocks those around her from entering into an empathic relationship with her or to relate to her in any significant way. This failure leads her people to prescribe a generalized and abstract form of healing; they take her to the medicine woman, who comes up with a magical diagnosis of the *wahala*. Ezinne then learns that she had been cursed by the spirits, and for no specific reason. The medicine woman tells her: "They curse us sometimes for no reason at all. Or sometimes they curse us because something or someone has inadvertently angered them. Or sometimes simply because they are in a bad mood."[68] By locating the cause of Ezinne's purported barrenness in the spiritual world, the medicine woman, who represents the traditional attitudes of that world, denies Ezinne a role in the resolution of her *wahala*; Ezinne therefore becomes a mere spectator in her own world. The medicine woman is the very tool with which society imprisons Ezinne, another woman, and thus becomes an agent of society's ideological apparatus.[69] True to her role as a patriarchal functionary, the medicine woman goes on to perform her ritualistic magical healing on Ezinne, who receives it all passively. The medicine woman performs the same function that Grandmama did in Adichie's "Tomorrow is too Far." At this point in the story, the reader has been sufficiently confronted with the absurdity of Ada's condition. Why is she silent and passive? Her silence is designed to confront the reader. Thus her silence becomes a statement on how social structures rob women of their voice and reduce them to the status of slaves in their relations to men.

Having established the backdrop against which we can understand women's concerns, the narrator focuses on a particular instance of Ezinne's pain. When her husband wants to make love to her she allows him. But:

> as he enters her, there is the pain, sharp and as wilful as ever before. She moans, but he enters her anyway. He thrusts himself into and out of her, and she continues to moan, louder and louder. "Please" she finally screams, but he doesn't seem to hear. She tries again. "Chibuzo, please stop."[70]

It is emblematic of society's attitude to women that Chibuzo hears in Ezinne's cry of pain only "gentle sounds of pleasure."[71] Given that Ezinne's mother has also become part of the ideological apparatus, she too hears what Ezinne's husband hears when she eavesdrops on the couple to learn whether they are doing what the medicine woman had prescribed.[72] The narrator paints a picture of a sadistic society with regard to women's *wahalas,* one that reveals the gulf between women and society within patriarchal systems. The system makes people act as if they were sadistic and thus women find no willing ear for their stories. They are therefore silent and silenced; they are further objectified. As Hillary Clinton says in the already cited speech: "human rights are women's rights—and women's rights are human rights. Let us not forget that among those rights are the right to speak freely—and the right to be heard."[73]

Ezinne has been denied her human rights because the system of her society has no place for her to speak freely, and to tell her story. The system could be challenged. The chasm between women and society might be bridged when people begin to be attentive to women's cries and their narratives or when society understands that a woman's cry of pain is, in fact just that, a cry of pain. Indeed, Okparanta suggests that the cure of Ezinne's problem would have begun with listening to her story. "Wahala" and the other stories in the collection could be read as the diary of the "intense pain" that women are forced to endure in patriarchal societies. They raise questions whose answers are in no way obvious in African contexts: Why do women experience pain that others interpret as pleasure? Is it possible for a woman not to enjoy sex with men? Could Ezinne have undergone female genital excision? Could it be that she has a different sexual orientation? None of these questions are likely to be examined closely in an environment in which *wahalas* are given abstract, generalized diagnoses. This is the ethical import of narrated life. We ask questions targeted specifically at the individual as an embodied being.

Pain, Solidarity, and Search for Community

Narration is a search for solidarity with our fellow humans, and when the narrative is a diary of intense pain, it is all the more incumbent on us to respond to the person suffering. As Elaine Scarry argues, pain destroys the basis of community; it kills language and forces humans back to prelinguistic stages of development, to stages in which we express ourselves with only cries or laughter. She states that physical pain is difficult to express. This difficulty has political consequences "by making overt precisely what is at stake in 'inexpressibility' [and it] begin(s) to expose by inversion the essential character of 'expressibility' whether verbal or material."[74] In "Wahala," Ezinne's inability to bear the pain that her world has inflicted on her causes her to regress to a prelinguistic stage of human development. I understand her cry to be the author's plea for us to acknowledge her humanity and to ask relevant questions about the source of her suffering. If it is true that pain takes away language, could it be argued that needless pain takes away women's rights, one of which is the freedom to speak freely? Asking questions in this regard implies a willingness to negotiate with systems that inflict undeserved pain. Above all, it implies the readiness to listen.

The call for the reassessment of such systems as a way to enter into solidarity with people also undergirds the narrative of *We Need New Names*. Chipo is pregnant by her grandfather. Her fellow pre-teenagers are concerned that her belly does not allow her to play with them. They want to help her and they massage her stomach. When they bend a wire clothes hanger to insert into her body, a woman, MotherLove, walks up on them. Forgiveness explains their intention: "we were trying to remove Chipo's stomach."[75] MotherLove's reaction is a shock to the children, who had feared she would beat them. The narrator relays her surprise, and just like the narrator in the scene in "Fairness," this narrator underscores the pain that shows on the face of a woman other than the sufferer:

> I look at her face and see the terrible face of someone I have never seen before, and on the stranger's face is the look of pain, this look that adults have when somebody dies. There are tears in the eyes and she is clutching her chest like there's a fire inside it. The MotherLove reaches out and holds Chipo.[76]

MotherLove and the children have one thing in common: they have seen themselves in Chipo; they know that Chipo's fate could be theirs. The scene is a strong display of solidarity arising from feminist empathy. This solidarity prefigures the author's anticipated response to the *like situations* she portrays. In another instance of such solidarity, while Darling and her companions are in Budapest stealing guava from a white couple's compound, a gang of freedom fighters arrives, chanting:

> Kill the Boer, the farmer, the khiwa!
> Strike fear in the heart of the white man!
> White man, you have no place here, go back, go home!
> Africa for Africans, Africa for Africans!
> Kill the Boer, the farmer, the khiwa![77]

The slogan "Africa for Africans" leads to violence because its fundamental premise is the exclusion of the other. Solidarity is defined by blood and soil. The gang implements Robert Mugabe's vision of the Third Chimurenga,[78] in which white farmers are harassed, evicted from their property, or murdered. The thugs refer to themselves as the "Sons of the soil."[79] Their nativist conception of identity blocks out any feeling for the pain of the white couple. It is at this point that one of the kids, still in the guava tree, asks: "What is exactly an African?"[80] It is relevant in this context that the question was asked by one displaced person about another in the same condition. That question, asked at this point, is an important moral interjection in the narrative; it challenges the nationalist's definition of identity and moral trajectory. We realize that the question is not gratuitous when Sbho, unable to contain the humiliation meted out to the white couple by the Sons of the Soil, begins to cry. Bastard challenges her: "What, are you crying for the white people? Are they your relatives?" The question assumes that empathy and solidarity belong only within one's family. However, Sbho's answer undercuts Bastard's assumption simply and abruptly: "They are people, you asshole."[81] Her answer is rooted in the principle of *ubuntu* and also in the Kantian moral imperative: "Act so that you treat humanity, whether in your own person or in that of another, always as an end and never as means only."[82] It is informed by the conviction that we cannot exist as humans by excluding others because of their race, ancestry, or gender. Sbho's recognition of the humanity of the white couple is designed as a reminder of her own humanity as a female. In her answer are the roots of solidarity based on empathy. She has attained her solidarity through what Martha Nussbaum has identified as the "community of human beings."[83] Her answer is cosmopolitan because she sees in the white couple not color, but human beings who deserve her empathy.

Through Darling and her companions, the dispossessed members of that society highlight not only their miserable human rights conditions; they also speak in a clear moral language which takes the dignities of others seriously. So, while NoViolet Bulawayo sheds light on Budapest as a visible reminder of the past injustices, she also underlines the ugly side of violence and nativism as a means to achieve fairness in the characters' society. In the pain these women suffer, Bulawayo and Okparanta ask us to question the nature of the communities we wish for in African societies. This is perhaps the most profound political aspect of their narratives.

Mugabe Syndrome and the Challenges of Postcoloniality

In this chapter's introduction, I discussed the harsh and dismissive criticisms leveled at the new African writing that directly engages Africa's misery. It would be unfair to the critics mentioned above to dismiss their concerns entirely. Indeed, it is justified to wonder—at least at first glance—why certain African writers, and in particular, the two under consideration, are fixated on the seamy and violent aspects of the African existence. Do they seek to present African women only as victims? Some writers may, in fact, attempt to exploit those conditions. I would not defend such writers, but I would point out that critiques such as those by Habila and Mushava risk becoming mired in the rhetoric of postcoloniality, or in the "colonial trap,"[84] and what Denis Ekpo has characterized as "Africanism."[85] Again, the colonial trap is the condition in which the colonized reject self-reflection and become hypersensitive about criticism in general. In many cases, it blocks the colonized person's empathy towards others.

It is true that Chinua Achebe heavily influenced the trajectory of postcolonial African culture.[86] He rightly challenged Westerners' efforts to shape African destiny in their narratives. However, African politicians have seized on Achebean postcolonial discourse and have transformed it into fierce anti-imperialist rhetoric that resonates among Africans because of their experience of colonialism. In some aspects of African politics and cultural discourses, memory of the colonial past is effectively translated into political capital. Such discourses presume the gaze of the West. The presence of the West, especially its colonial powers, is a constant reminder of the humiliation of the African people by the West. Chinua Achebe calls this humiliation the "wound in the soul."[87] No African politician embodies the uses and abuses of anti-imperialist rhetoric as much as Robert Mugabe, who occupies a special place in African history. For example, during a 2007 failed

European and African Union summit, friction over human rights reached a high point between the two continents. German Chancellor Angela Merkel criticized Mugabe for human rights abuses in Zimbabwe.[88] Mugabe responded that "the colonial power continually manipulates us and wants to change the government, but we say no, we have the right to determine our own future. We will never be a colony again!"[89] His government interpreted the 2008 cholera outbreaks in Zimbabwe as a "genocidal onslaught" conducted by Zimbabwe's former colonial ruler, Great Britain, and supported by its American and Western allies.[90]

Mugabe has mastered the art of inflaming nativist feeling among black Africans to serve as a bulwark against any criticism of his dictatorship. He gives the impression that the African's primary responsibility is to oppose the white man, to reject all manifestations of colonialism and the flaws, real or perceived, that the white man might have observed in the African world. In Mugabe's world, the true African rejects introspection and self-critique. This rejection of self-criticism and the attendant delusion of moral excellence is part of what I call the Mugabe syndrome. Another identifying characteristic of the Mugabe syndrome is the assumption of the white man's gaze. The presence of the white man is presumed to inhabit the consciousness of Africans, resulting in the belief that Africa's problems begin and end with colonialism and its aftermath, imperialism. Consequently, critical examinations of aspects of African culture are viewed with suspicion from the outset. In this regard postcoloniality becomes a means through which society censures women's claim to rights.

Perhaps it is accidental that all the critics above are male. What is not accidental is their failure to consider the pain that women are subjected to. It is possible that their failure to factor women's pain into their criticism is because of their need to defend Africa, which is, strictly speaking, an abstract compared to the bodies of individual African women in pain. In this unproductive self-censure, or worse, the freezing of the imagination, the human condition in Africa is left unexamined and un-narrated.

Notes

1. Chinelo Okparanta, *Happiness, Like Water*. London: Granta, 2013 (Okparanta 2013).
2. NoViolet Bulawayo, *We Need New Names*. New York: Little Brown, 2013 (Bulawayo 2013).

3. Adam Zachary Newton, *Narrative Ethics*. Cambridge, MA: Harvard University Press, 1995, 17 (Newton 1995).
4. Ibid., 17–18.
5. Simon Gikandi, "Chinua Achebe and the Invention of African Culture," *Research in African Literature*, 32.3 (2001): 4–8 (Gikandi 2001).
6. Chielozona Eze, "Transcultural Affinity: Thoughts on the Emergent Cosmopolitan Imagination in South Africa," *Journal of African Cultural Studies*, 27.2 (2015): 1–13 (Eze 2015).
7. Chinua Achebe, *Hopes and Impediments*. New York: Doubleday, 1988 (Achebe 1988).
8. Ikhide Ikheloa, "The 2011 Caine Prize: How Not to Write About Africa" www.xokigbo.wordpress.com (Accessed February 5, 2014) (Ikheloa 2011).
9. Aaron Bady, "Blogging the Caine Prize," *Zungu Zungu,* May 30, 2001. http://zunguzungu.wordpress.com/2011/06/03/blogging-the-caine-hitting-budapest-by-noviolet-bulawayo/ June 3, 2011 (Accessed December 7, 2013) (Bady 2001).
10. Helon Habila, "We Need New Names by NoViolet Bulawayo – Review," 2013 (Habila 2013). http://www.theguardian.com/books/2013/jun/20/need-new-names-bulawayo-review
11. Ibid.
12. Helon Habila, ed. *The Granta Book of the African Short Story*. London: Granta Books, 2011, xiii (Habila 2011).
13. Dobrota Pucherová, "'A Continent Learns to Tell Its Story at Last': Notes on the Caine Prize," *Journal of Postcolonial Writing*, 48.1 (2012): 1–13 (Pucherová 2012).
14. Ikheloa, "The 2011 Caine Prize."(Ikheloa 2011).
15. Stanley Mushava, "Is NoViolet a Victim of West's Propaganda?" *The Herald*. 2013. http://www.herald.co.zw/is-noviolet-a-victim-of-wests-propaganda/ (Mushava 2013)
16. Stanley Mushava, "Zimbabwe: African Literature Reduced to a Commodity," 2013. http://allafrica.com/stories/201312300593.html?viewall=1 (Mushava 2013).
17. Binyavanga Wainaina, "How to Write About Africa," *Granta 92: The View from Africa*. www.granta.com/Archive/92 (Accessed January 2, 2012) (Wainaina 2012).
18. Chimamanda Ngozi Adichie, "The Danger of a Single Story." www.ted.com/talks/chimamanda_adichie_the_danger_of_a_single_story.html (Accessed 8 June 2011) (Adichie 2011).
19. One such defense is the expression "that is my culture," which we have already analyzed in the introductory part of Chapter 2.
20. Lizzy Attree, "The Caine Prize and Contemporary African Writing," *Research in African Literatures*, 44.2 (2013): 40 (Attree 2013).

21. Liesl Jobson, "Author Interview: A Love Letter to All Zimbabweans," 2013 (Jobson 2013). http://www.bdlive.co.za/life/books/2013/10/22/author-interview-a-love-letter-to-all-zimbabweans.
22. Newton, *Narrative Ethics*, 18 (Newton 1995).
23. Kenneth Burke, *Grammar of Motives*. Berkeley: University of California Press, 1945 (Burke 1945).
24. Attree, "The Caine Prize and Contemporary African Writing," 40 (Attree 2013).
25. Paul Ricoeur, *Time and Narrative*. Vol. 1. Trans. Kathleen McLaughlin and David Pellauer. Chicago: The University of Chicago Press, 1984 (Ricoeur 1984). See especially Chapter 3, "Emplotment: A Reading of Aristotle's *Poetics*."
26. Newton, Ibid., 21.
27. Chinelo Okparanta, *Happiness Like Water*. London: Granta, 2013, 73 (Okparanta 2013).
28. Ibid., 70.
29. Ibid., 73.
30. Ibid., 78.
31. Ibid., 79.
32. Ibid., 81.
33. Bulawayo, *We Need New Names*, 39 (Bulawayo 2013).
34. Revelations 5: 1–7.
35. Bulawayo, *We Need New Names*, 40 (Bulawayo 2013).
36. Ibid, 40.
37. Ibid., 41.
38. Suzanne Keen, "A Theory of Narrative Empathy," *Narrative*, 14.3. (2006): 209 (Keen 2006).
39. Juliana Makuchi Nfah-Abbenyi, *Gender in African Women's Writing*. Bloomington: Indiana University Press, 1997 (Nfah-Abbenyi 1997).
40. Bulawayo, *We Need New Names*, 42 (Bulawayo 2013).
41. In Chapter 4, I argue that female genital excision is a technology of power. It can also be seen as society's obsession with women's "thing" because it knows that women derive their strength for love of self and the power of resistance from there, as Cixous and Lorde have argued.
42. Bulawayo, *We Need New Names*, 42 (Bulawayo 2013).
43. Ibid.
44. Ibid., 43.
45. Sylvia Tamale, "African Feminism: How Should We Change?" *Development: Supplement: Women's Rights and Development; Association for Women's*, 49.1 (2006): 38–41. (Tamale 2006).
46. Joanna Zylinska, *The Ethics of Cultural Studies*. New York: Continuum, 2005, xii (Zylinska 2005).

47. Richard Rorty, *Contingency, Irony and Solidarity*. Cambridge: Cambridge University Press, 1989, 192 (Rorty 1989).
48. I acknowledge that some readers might be shocked by some stories. Such stories as these achieve effects other than empathy; indeed, they might achieve its exact opposite.
49. Paul Ricoeur, "Life in Quest of Narrative," in *On Paul Ricoeur: Narrative and Interpretation*, ed. David Wood. London: Routledge, 1991, 21 (Ricoeur 1991). [Emphasis in original.]
50. Ideologies such as racism, sexism or patriarchy package individuals as finished products.
51. For more on narrative understanding, see James Phelan and Peter J. Rabinowitz, eds, *Understanding Narrative*. Columbus, OH: Ohio State University Press, 1994 (Phelan and Rabinowitz 1994).
52. Paul Ricoeur, "Life in Quest of Narrative," 23 (Ricoeur 1991).
53. Ricoeur includes poetry and drama in his understanding of narrative. We do not need to hear every detail of the life of a character in order to come to a narrative understanding. Sometimes a particular incident suggests a more humane understanding of a given person.
54. We know, of course, that we are dealing with narrative works of fiction. It is true that there may be very negative characters in stories. They may not even be candidates for empathy given that they may have been responsible for their ugly fate.
55. Okparanta, *Happiness,* 35 (Okparanta 2013).
56. Ibid., 41.
57. Ibid., 40.
58. Ibid., 45–46.
59. Dave Beech, "Beauty, Ideology and Utopia." http://www.uwe.ac.uk/sca/research/vcrg/proj_beech.htm See also Dave Beech, ed., *Beauty: Whitechapel: Documents of Contemporary Art*. Cambridge, MA: The MIT Press, 2009 (Beech et al. 2009).
60. Bulawayo, *We Need New Names*, 67 (Bulawayo 2013).
61. Ibid., 67.
62. Martha Nussbaum, *Upheavals of Thought: The Intelligence of Emotions*. Cambridge: Cambridge University Press, 2001, 327 (Nussbaum 2001).
63. Okparanta, *Happiness*, 23 (Okparanta 2013).
64. Flora Nwapa, *Efuru*. Great Britain: Heinemann Publishers, 1966 (Nwapa 1966).
65. Marie Umeh, *Emerging Perspectives on Flora Nwapa: Critical and Theoretical Essays*. Trenton, New Jersey: Africa World Press, 1998 (Umeh 1998).
66. Okapranta, *Happiness*, 23 (Okparanta 2013).

67. Ibid., 25.
68. Ibid., 28.
69. Louis Althusser, *Lenin and Philosophy*. Trans. Ben Brewster. New York: Monthly Review Press, 1971, 170–178 (Althusser 1971).
70. Okparanta, *Happiness*, 32–33 (Okparanta 2013).
71. Ibid., 33.
72. Ibid., 34.
73. Hillary Rodham Clinton, "Women's Rights are Human Rights." http://gos.sbc.edu/c/clinton.html (Accessed May 15, 2013) (Clinton 2013). See also Hillary Clinton, Helping Women Isn't Just a 'Nice' Thing to Do." http://www.thedailybeast.com/witw/articles/2013/04/05/hillary-clinton-helping-women-isn-t-just-a-nice-thing-to-do.html (Accessed May 15, 2013) (Clinton 2013).
74. Elaine Scarry, *The Body in Pain: The Making and Unmaking of the World*. New York: Oxford University Press, 1985, 19 (Scarry 1985).
75. Bulawayo, *We Need New Names*, 89 (Bulawayo 2013).
76. Ibid., 90.
77. Ibid., 113.
78. Sabelo J. Ndlovu-Gatsheni, "Africa for Africans or Africa for 'Natives' Only? 'New Nationalism and Nativism in Zimbabwe and South Africa'," *Africa Spectrum*, 44.1 (2009): 61–78 (Ndlovu-Gatsheni 2009).
79. Bulawayo, *We Need New Names*, 120 (Bulawayo 2013).
80. Ibid., 121.
81. Ibid., 122.
82. Immanuel Kant, *Foundations of the Metaphysics of Morals*. Translated with an Introduction by Lewis White Beck. Upper Saddle River, NJ, 1997, 46. (Kant 1997). I will discuss Kant's idea more fully in Chapter 5.
83. Martha Nussbaum, C., "Patriotism and Cosmopolitanism," in *For Love of Country: Debating the Limits of Patriotism*, ed. Joshua Cohen. Boston: Beacon Press, 1996, 4. (Nussbaum 1996).
84. Pinkie Mekgwe, "Theorizing African Feminism(s): The 'Colonial' Question," *QUEST: An African Journal of Philosophy/Revue Africaine de Philosophie*, XX (2008): 21–22 (Mekgwe 2008).
85. Denis Ekpo, "Introduction: From Negritude to Post-Africanism," *Third Text*, 24.2 (2010): 177–187 (Ekpo 2010).
86. Gikandi, Ibid.
87. Chinua Achebe, *Morning Yet on Creation Day*. New York: Anchor Press/Doubleday, 1975, 71 (Achebe 1975).

88. Stephen Castle, "Mugabe's Presence Hijacks European-African Meeting," *New York Times*. 2007 (Castle 2007). http://www.nytimes.com/2007/12/09/world/africa/09summit.html?fta=y&_r=0.
89. Associated News, "Europe, Africa Seek New Relationship at Summit." 2007. (Associated News 2007) www.iht.com/articles/ap/2007/12/08/europe/EU-GEN-EU-Africa-Summit.php (January 30 2008).
90. BBC News, "UK Caused Cholera, Says Zimbabwe." 2008 (BBC News 2008). http://news.bbc.co.uk/2/hi/7780728.stm.

CHAPTER 4

The Body in Pain and the Politics of Culture

Nnedi Okorafor and Warsan Shire

In 2008, a number of Saudi Arabian doctors embarked upon a campaign to end the ancient ritual of female genital excision. Their action is surprising given the widely held opinion that Saudi Arabia is patriarchal, religiously conservative, and unconcerned about the rights of women. The more surprising aspect of the doctors' campaign was their justification, which they asserted was rooted in science: "Female circumcision is detrimental to women's sexual satisfaction." As a report in the *Guardian* details, "the study is part of an effort to build a collection of rigorous evidence about the long-term effects of FGM so that attitudes can be changed from within the countries where it is practiced."[1]

The truth of the "scientific discovery" of the Saudi doctors dovetails with the assumptions in a popular film that is credited with changing the attitude towards female genital excision in Kurdistan. The film, "FGM: the film that changed the law in Kurdistan – video"[2] produced in 2013, made a jarring comparison between female genital excision and neutering animals.[3] The comparison seems apt given that the ritual is particular to patriarchal cultures and religions that are characterized by rigid ideas about women's sexual expression. As Audre Lorde argues, pleasure in sex is liberating, and because a woman's discovery of the pleasures of her body liberates her emotionally and psychologically, she is considered wild and untamed. Women who discover the pleasure of their bodies are "empowered [and] dangerous. So we are taught to separate the erotic from most vital areas of our lives other than sex."[4] Hélène Cixous makes the same argument about women in relation to their bodies.[5] She urges them to reclaim their bodies by writing, speaking, and above all by discovering their erotic power, and that includes masturbation. Cixous makes an interesting comparison between the bodies of women under patriarchy and Africa under colonialism. Those two spaces, the woman's body and Africa, have been colonized, and made to hate themselves. Gloria Anzaldua reminds us that:

> according to Christianity and most other major religions, woman is carnal, animal, and closer to the undivine, she must be protected. Protected from herself. Woman is the stranger, the other. She is man's recognized nightmarish pieces, his Shadow-Beast. The sight of her sends him into a frenzy of anger and fear.[6]

If women's sexual pleasure is considered to be something wild, it is not surprising that some cultures have chosen to disable that condition at its source. Most parts of Africa, while no longer traditional, are still patriarchal, and sexuality is viewed as solely for procreation. The notion that women have the right to enjoy sex is exclusively associated with Western feminism, which is considered a form of decadence. In the first part of this chapter, I discuss the resistance to the idea that women have rights to their bodies. This resistance is often couched in the rhetoric of culture and heritage. In the second part, I discuss the works of two African women writers as an argument against the politics of culture in regard to women's sexuality.

The Politics of Female Circumcision

The idea of tampering with the female sexual organ is not peculiar to Africa; it has always been part of most patriarchal cultures. The practice of surgically altering the female sexual organ is an archaic ritual practiced in most parts of Africa. In our time, it has generated a politicized discourse. It is known by different names depending on one's cultural, social, or political persuasion: female circumcision, clitoridectomy, vaginal surgery, and female genital mutilation.[7] Some scholars insist on referring to it as female circumcision, and argue that the intention behind the ritual might be to do to women what is done to men in male circumcision.[8] For my discussions in this book, I will follow Chantal Zabus's and Elisabeth Bekers's example, and use the clinical term, female genital excision.[9] Regardless of the terminology one chooses, I am particularly interested in an analysis of the many ways through which society controls the relations between men and women. It is important that society understands the power relation implied in some rituals. This, I think, is what contemporary African women writers seek to expose in their narratives.

In *The History of Sexuality*, Michel Foucault explains that the body is the means through which society displays its power and control, and this is done through the control of pleasure, especially in sex: when it is exercised, how, and with whom. Strictly speaking therefore, to control sexual practice and relations is to control relations in society.[10] Patriarchal societies exercise their tightest control through series of norms of sexual behavior, especially for women. The idea of virginity applies only to girls. The same is not expected of boys because they are future men, and in matters of sex, "men have to be men." If men have to be men, then women have to be women, that is, compliant and submissive to the sexual expectations of men. Female genital excision, therefore, is a technology of power designed to make women compliant to men's power performance. Chantal Zabus's analysis of the Dogon myth of creation suggests that excision was introduced as a means of control. In that myth, Amma, the god of creation created the Earth and wanted to have intercourse with her. But the Earth's clitoris, in the shape of anthill, stood in the way. It blocked Amma's penetration in self-protection. Amma was furious and punished the Earth for her defiance; he excised Earth's erectile organ. In this way he subjected the Earth and her (female) descendants to his will.[11]

Judging from the testimonies of men in certain African communities, the cultural-political role of female genital excision appears to be close to the idea the creation myth suggests. The men justified female genital excision because it "impairs a woman's enjoyment [of sex]...[it reduces] sexual desire through making the act painful or removing pleasure...FGM is seen as a way of physically ensuring that a woman will be faithful to her partner."[12] It is not surprising then that in some African countries, female genital excision has firmly established itself in politics, and is exploited to win votes. For instance, in Sierra Leone:

> Patricia Kabbah, the late wife of President Ahmad Tejan Kabbah, had sponsored the circumcision of 1500 young girls in the presidential election, and other politicians had organised smaller initiation campaigns to gain popularity in virtually every district of the country.[13]

An African internet news agency, afrol.com, reported on the October 5, 2003 that three African imams were to be prosecuted in Norway for promoting female genital excision. There was a widespread practice of female genital excision among African immigrants in Norway and other European countries such as France, Britain, and the Netherlands. The news agency also quoted the Gambian president, A.J. Jammeh, as stating publicly that his "Government would not ban FGM, and that FGM is a part of the country's culture."[14] Jammeh's excuse echoes that put forward by Jomo Kenyatta in 1938. Kenyatta defended the practice as an integral part of African culture.[15] His countryman Ngugi wa Thiong'o also portrayed the practice in his novel, *The River Between* in the Kenyattan idiom.[16] Augustine H. Assah argues that in Thiong'o's:

> schematic portrayal of abolitionists as outsiders, zealous Christian converts, or western stooges, Ngugi has unwittingly influenced contemporary supporters of FGM keen to stigmatize opponents of the operation as western agents or at best as insensitive strangers/alienated Africans.[17]

Some of the African and African Diaspora intellectuals who support the right of African societies to practice their cultures the way they deem fit include Oyeronke Oyewumi, whose ideological stance on African feminism I have discussed in the introduction. Other important voices in the anti-Western, Afrocentric criticism of Western intervention in African ritual of circumcision are Joyce Russell-Robinson, L. Amede Obiora, and Nontassa Nako. I wish to establish their ideas as a prelude to the narratives and poetics of younger African women who now raise their voices against the practice. For these younger African women writers, the issue is no longer a West-versus-Africa discourse, but rather that of the explication of pain in their bodies. They want to reclaim the right to their bodies, and that includes right to pleasure; it is a matter of their rights as women. As human beings.

When Alice Walker published *Possessing the Secret of Joy*,[18] in which she sharply attacked the practice of female genital excision, she attracted much criticism from both within and outside Africa. Many accused her of exhibiting a missionary spirit. For Joyce Russell-Robinson it "echoes a missionary mentality in the worst sense of the term. The voices of the missionaries seem to be saying once more, 'Let's rescue those Africans.'"[19] She cautions that attacking certain rituals in Africa from the West could be counterproductive and that people should approach such rituals of initiation as female genital excision in Africa with a hermeneutic spirit in order to understand their cultural relevance to the people who practice them. Russell-Robinson neither condemns nor advocates the ritual of female genital excision; rather she argues that any change in that regard must come from within African communities. This is an interesting line of argument, and it has its own merits given the cultural arrogance that the West has exhibited toward Africa and the rest of the world. In the same breath though, she prefers that the West help Africans economically and otherwise:

> instead of harping on the ritual of female circumcision, let them save Africans from malnutrition, unhealthy environments and diseases. Let them save Africans from poverty and violence, themselves responsible for malnutrition, poor sanitation, lack of clean drinking water and infant mortality.[20]

This anachronism in Russell-Robinson's thinking underscores the intellectual and moral quandaries facing postcolonial Africa. How do you engage the West? What exactly can Africa take from the West; what should it reject? There is little doubt that the experience of slavery and colonialism has greatly influenced, alas, distorted the relationship between Africa and the West so that Africa is justifiably suspicious of any gestures from former slavers and colonizers. The condition has impacted African lives to the degree that African people's pains, such as those experienced in female genital excision, are often ignored within certain African cultures in pursuit of a specific cultural ideology.

Like Russell-Robinson, L. Amede Obiora cautions against overt outside intervention. She argues that "female circumcision is not simply a problem to be solved, it is also a complex culturally-embedded critical act which signifies continuity and meaning, and expresses social values."[21] She acknowledges that female genital excision has health consequences, and "where there is *well-founded* evidence that the practice causes harm, the custom should be challenged"[22] (emphasis in original). Oyeronke Oyewumi adopts a more forceful approach to the outsider interventions in African affairs. She interprets Alice Walker's intervention in the debates about female genital surgeries in Africa as a part of Western imperialistic involvement in Africa. In her view, Walker is acting as an "evangelist."[23] She therefore sets out to "interrogate Walker's representation of Africa in both *Possessing* and *Warrior Marks* (the book), examining the images of Africa presented and the strategies used to ground the picture [*sic*]."[24] Oyewumi argues that Walker should be read "within the context of Western imperialism in relation to Africa and the narcissism or naval-gazing of contemporary American life."[25] The issue for Oyewumi is not necessarily women's genital excision, though it is important; the issue is the power relations between Africa and the West. She argues that "if there were no female circumcision in some parts of Africa, Westerners would have invented it."[26] I cannot agree with this claim. I think that she was led to make such a bogus assertion because of her need to demonstrate the ubiquity of Western imperialism in the African life. This need is ideological to the degree that she ignores the likelihood that some Western critics of African female genital excision such as Alice Walker might just be interested in sparing African women the pain of the ritual itself.

Oyewumi seems not to be ready to challenge the practice of female genital excision. Indeed, she sees some agency in the fact that some African women willfully take part in it and even insist on their daughters taking part in the ritual. She argues:

> It is curious that in the larger debate on female circumcision in the United States media, instances of mothers who take the initiative to circumcise their daughters despite the objection of the fathers, are not interpreted as examples of female self-assertion and/or defiance of patriarchal authority. Instead, such women are often projected as having succumbed to community pressure, the community of course being defined as male-created.[27]

Oyewumi seems to have ignored how ideology succeeds in coopting individuals in its service by the process of what Louis Althusser has called interpellation or hailing,[28] and how, as Butler argues, subjects take an active part in their subjection if only to maintain their identity or to stay alive.[29] Part of her problem is that she is invested in an ideology, albeit a counter-ideology, based on race. Women who insist on having their daughters undergo the ritual of excision may only be trying to be good members of their society as keepers of the light of tradition. It is doubtful whether they are truly exercising their agency in so doing. Oyewumi's neglect of the insidious ways ideologies work does not negate her observation that Westerners often act as epistemic missionaries in Africa. Nor does it address the issue of female genital excision as an act that causes needless pain to the body of the circumcised, and, depending on the type, will to a greater or lesser degree negatively impact a woman's sexual life and possibly also her self-perception.

Obioma Nnaemeka's edited volume of essays, *Female Circumcision and the Politics of Knowledge: African Women in Imperialist Discourse* is devoted to the same issues Oyewumi examines. Most of the contributions are premised on the Western imperial gaze toward Africa. Nnaemeka's intervention captures the dilemma and the rewards of engaging the Western imperial othering of Africa:

> Female circumcision has been condemned as "torture" or "degrading treatment" that lacks any "respect for the dignity" of women and girls. And it should be. Unfortunately, some of the most egregious manifestations of "degrading treatment" and lack of "respect for dignity" lie in the modus operandi of many Westerners (feminists and others) who have intervened in this matter. The resistance of African women is not against the campaign to end the practice, but against their dehumanization and the lack of respect and dignity shown to them in the process... In my view, the ultimate violence done to African women is the exhibition of their body parts—in this instance, the vagina—in various stages of "unbecoming."[30]

Irrespective of one's ideological stance regarding the ritual of female genital excision, the most important question is: Why is it a cultural norm to damage the vulva in such a way that some women are forever traumatized by the experience? Could the ritual stop if men were to imagine the same thing done to them? This is one reason we must examine the narratives and poetics of the younger generation of African women writers, those who do not feel the need to confront the gaze of the Western world, but rather to address the unfairness that undergird how their world functions. I pointed out Sylvia Tamale's observation that "those that have never directly experienced gender discrimination" are more likely to downplay its effects on women.[31] She challenges the idea that African women are passive adherents to mostly patriarchal sexual mores. Her field research among the Banganda people of Uganda has revealed to her women's sincere, silent fight for equality also in sexual matters. Commenting on a particular cultural/sexual initiation institution among the Baganda called Ssenga, she writes:

> Explicit and daring topics regarding women's pleasurable sexuality, such as "female ejaculation" and "clitoral orgasm" have become part of *Ssenga's* repertoire of tutoring techniques. While the traditional message from *Ssenga* focussed on men's sexual pleasure, young *Baganda* women today are demanding that men also receive training in how to please their female partners. They have largely rejected the sexual ideology that privileges men

over women, one that locates female sexuality in a medicalised/reproductive realm. By insisting on pleasurable sex for themselves, these young women have refocussed culture and used the erotic as an empowering resource to claim justice.[32]

She thus directly refutes the arguments of those who suggest that African women who undergo female genital excision do so in support of their culture.

I Tell of the Body in Pain

One of the most renowned books condemning female genital excision in Africa is Waris Dirie's memoir, *Desert Flower*.[33] Dirie followed up her extraordinary memoir with a foundation dedicated to stopping the ritual that nearly cost her her life.[34] Other organizations and media outlets have joined women activists in protesting female genital excision.[35] Other African women writers actively engaged in ending the practice are Nawal El Saadawi,[36] Ayaan Hirsi Ali,[37] and Fauziya Kassindja.[38] I will base my discussions here on the fictional work of Nnedi Okorafor and the poems of Warsan Shire.

Nnedi Okorafor's magical realist novel *Who Fears Death*[39] chronicles the life of a young woman who was born with magical powers. She also learns that she was conceived in rape, and because of that she is socially stigmatized. She was circumcised at the age of 11. These two violent incidents in her life have filled her with anger. She wants to understand her people's culture and also to exact some measure of justice. The richly complex story encompasses many themes: female genital excision, genocide, human rights, globalization, the intermixing of peoples and cultures on the African continent, patriarchy, and solidarity among women, among others. The narrator threads the issue of female genital excision through the many instances of violence in her people's culture. The story begins with a richly symbolic event:

> It was evening and a thunderstorm was fast approaching. I was standing in the back doorway watching it come when, right before my eyes, a large eagle landed on a sparrow in my mother's garden. The eagle slammed the sparrow to the ground and flew off with it. Three brown bloody feathers fell from the sparrow's body. They landed between my mother's tomatoes. Thunder rumbled as I went and picked up one of the feathers. I rubbed the blood between my fingers. I don't know why I did that.[40]

The predator–prey relationship between an eagle and a sparrow foreshadows various encounters in the narrative. In this way, we are introduced to the story's major motifs: violence and pain. The narrator, Onyesonwu, considers herself tainted. But her contamination is understood as deriving from a culture that is hostile to the human rights of individuals. It is a culture in which violence is considered a means of survival. Ethnic groups enslave one another, and genocide is a norm. However, it is the violence done to individuals that attracts the narrator's lyric attention.

The narrative tells of how, during an outbreak of mass violence violence - the genocide of the Okeke by the Nuru – "all of the Okeke women, young, prime, and old, were raped. Repeatedly."[41] It is probable that Okorafor is recreating the genocide and mass rape that took place in Sudan. Genocidal rape as practiced in Sudan had the goal of introducing bloodlines of the victors into those of the vanquished. The women of the conquered tribe will carry the children of the conquerors to term and eventually groom the enemies within.[42] Speaking of herself, Onyesonwu links sex, an act that is inherently pleasurable, with violence, with pain: "But I didn't know about *this*—sex as violence, violence that produced children ... produced me, that happened to my mother."[43] Thus the motif that was announced at the beginning of the narrative—the pain that society visits on women's bodies—reasserts itself more fully. Onyesonwu can be understood as representative of the women of that society. She is "born of pain."[44]

Having established the experience of pain as a background, the narrator introduces the ritual that constitutes society's symbolic and actual violence on women: female genital excision. It is described as "a two thousand-year-old tradition held on the first day of rainy season. It involves the year's eleven-year old girls."[45] Onyesonwu is 11, has already developed breasts, and is now experiencing her periods. The meaning of the ritual has been lost in the thicket of oral tradition. Though the girls know that a piece of flesh would be cut from between their legs, they are unaware of "what that piece of flesh *did*." [46]

The italicized verb urges us to question what the women are missing. What does the excised piece *do* for women? The justification of the campaign by Saudi doctors to end female genital excision could help us understand what Okorafor is suggesting by the italicized verb. We are also reminded of Foucault's idea that the control of pleasure in society is intimately linked with power. The narrative raises the question: If that piece of flesh is useful to women, if it does something for them, why should society remove it? The question confirms our premise that destroying the clitoris has everything to do with society's goal of controlling women. In sex, the most intimate expression of oneself, women are denied power over their bodies; they become objects and means through which men achieve their ends. If women are reduced to sexual objects, then men become puppetmasters. The sexual relation that exists between "circumcised" women and their men therefore becomes symbolic of the gender relations in such a society. The narrator describes in detail what was done to her. She is among other girls who undergo the same ritual, and she describes how it was done to one of them. The woman circumciser "went for a small *perturbing* bit of dark rosy flesh near to top of Binta's *yeye*. When the scalpel sliced it, blood spurted. My stomach lurched."[47] It is curious that the narrator qualifies the clitoris as a perturbing piece of flesh. The dictionary definition of "perturb" suggests that that flesh is unsettling; it is a source of trouble. But we are left to ask: For whom does it cause trouble? Before the narrator provides an answer, she takes us through the girls' experience of pain. The description of the other girl's genital excision provides a close perspective to the actual organ that is cut. Yet the more persuasive aspect of the narrative comes when she talks about the pain of her own experience. "The pain was an explosion. I felt it in every part of my body and I almost blacked out. Then I was screaming."[48]

The description of this ritual of womanhood leaves no doubt that it was an initiation into a life of pain, a life of subjugation—in line with Dogon mythology. It describes the life of a person who has been objectified. Onyesonwu is therefore an embodiment of pain, both bodily and cultural. The former stems from the way she was conceived, and the pain in her own body, the throbbing wound, "the deep unprovoked pain [that] seemed to happen twice a day."[49] The latter form of pain comes from the fact that she is considered illegitimate. In narrating the painful ritual of female genital excision, Okorafor confronts us with questions of ethical relevance. Why does society cause such needless pain to women? Why does society make it painful for women to enjoy or control their bodies? We realize the ethical import of these questions when we, like the author, ignore the gaze of the West, that is, when we disregard the fact that Western feminists have adopted female genital excision in Africa as their cause. It is cruel to inflict unnecessary pain on people, to state the obvious. So, why would societies ingrain such cruel rituals in their cultures? In line with Adichie's injunction that we should all be feminists, we raise a fundamental question that hinges on fairness. Would men allow it if it was done to their bodies? Onyesonwu exhibits symptoms of trauma. She constantly questions her worth as a human being, and this suggests her awareness of herself as a disabled body. Pain, as Elaine Scarry argues, takes away our capacity for language. It robs us of our voice.[50] The Dogon creation myth could help us understand Onyesonwu's condition in regard to self-perception. According to the myth, the Earth and her female descendants are forever denied their selfhood by the violent act of excision. They are denied the capacity to resist violation. They are therefore made ready to be raped. They no longer have a wall of (emotional and psychological) defense. The pain that Onyesonwu's society has wreaked on her prevents her from achieving selfhood.

The narrator informs us that the Okeke people have forgotten the origin and reason for the practice of female genital excision. It is now simply an accepted part of Okeke culture. Over the course of history, female genital excision, like other cultural idioms, has acquired a symbolic power whose expression confers legitimacy on the people who undergo such rituals, regardless of the pain those rituals inflict. Yet Onyesonwu learns that the reason a girl's piece of flesh is cut off is to "align a woman's intelligence with her emotions."[51] In other words, its purpose is to curb women's emotions, to tame them. Thus she learns the real answer to the question of whom the women's clitoris perturbs. We understand the verb perturb as connoting women's desire to express themselves and to refuse to be controlled. There is, however, an added element of power in what is considered a harmless practice: "the scalpel that they use is treated by Aro. There's juju on it that makes it so that a woman feels pain whenever she is too aroused... until she's married."[52] Juju describes an object used as a fetish or amulet by peoples of West Africa. Juju is also the magical power attributed to such an object. In most African communities, only men are thought to possess the secret of juju. As a consequence, all men are feared. In this narrative, juju stands for the uncontested power of patriarchy, which intends to protect women from themselves. Of course, marriage will never bring back the function of the missing piece of flesh. In effect, the woman is expected to always align her intelligence with her emotions as conceived by the culture's patriarchs. Alignment here equals obedience. Elizabeth Anker has argued that the liberal notion of human rights is based exclusively on reason, which willfully suppresses the body.[53] It is revealing how the idea of women aligning their emotion with their intelligence echoes these liberal formulations of human rights. Patriarchy in Africa, portrayed in this narrative, raises reason above emotion. Indeed, intelligence (reason) must reign over women's bodies. This simply implies that women's bodies must be suppressed. The ideology of this ritual, as

Onyesonwu's narrative reveals, can be understood in light of what Audre Lorde and Hélène Cixous have characterized as women's erotic power. Society fears women's emotional expression, that is, their freedom and their pleasure, and the only way men can curb that power is to resort to the magical thinking involved in ideology. It is therefore no surprise that it was a man who came up with the idea of putting juju in the scalpel used in the genital excision. Indeed, after the ritual, the girls experience intense pain during sex. Those who have had sex with men before the ritual—kissing, touching, and intercourse—now know the sharp difference after having experienced the cutting.[54] Luyu, one of the girls, speaks of how she tried to do exactly what she had always done before the ritual:

> I have tried for three years. Then Gwan came one day and I let him kiss me. It was good but then it was bad. It...made me hurt! Who did this to me?... Soon we'll be eighteen, fully fledged adults! Why wait until marriage to enjoy what Ani gave me! Whatever the curse, I wanted to break it. I've been trying... Today it felt like I was going to die.[55]

It is interesting that Luyu identifies her vagina and its pleasures, as a gift from Ani. Ani is a Mother Earth figure in Igbo, the ancestral language of the author. To be sure, Onyesonwu is also an Igbo name, meaning "who fears death," hence the title of the novel. For Luyu, pleasure is a gift from Mother Earth. Yet the culture that promotes the suppression of women's pleasure invokes the same Ani. As Binta says, "it's Ani protecting us." Ani is protecting them "from enjoying boys."[56] There are obvious differences in the two instances in which Mother Earth is invoked. In the first instance, Binta sees herself as a member of the human community, as part of creation. There is an effort to locate her individuality as part of the larger whole. In her case, therefore, there is a healthy relationship between the individual and the community. Being part of a larger community should not, in her understanding, prevent one from being an individual with distinct wishes. Yet, in the second instance, her community or culture invokes Mother Earth in the abstract, as something that is omni-historical. She is used as an ideology that notoriously subsumes the individual within an imaginary whole. But the girls have seen through the ritual to the underlying belief system. Luyu, exasperated, says, "we're tricked into thinking our husbands are god."[57] They also recognize that women are not free of blame. The woman circumciser gave her consent to the whole ritual.[58] Onyesonwu speaks of how she discovered what the ritual had taken from her. She has read the great book of secrets, the book that had been hidden from women:

> I learned that my Eleventh Rite took more from me than true intimacy. There is no word in Okeke for the flesh cut from me. The medical term, derived from English, was clitoris. It created much of a woman's pleasure during intercourse. *Why in Ani's name is this removed?* I wondered, perplexed. Who could I ask? The healer? She was there the night I was circumcised! I thought about the rich and electrifying feeling that Mwita always conjured up in me with a kiss, just before the pain came. I wondered if I'd been ruined.[59]

The significance of Onyesonwu's discovery is that it is a testimony (albeit via the medium of art) from a woman of African ancestry about the effects of female genital excision on women's bodies. In Onyesonwu, the circumcised African woman's body accuses her culture, and asks the same question that the unnamed protagonist in Adichie's "Tomorrow is Too Far" has asked; it seeks to relate to the man's body as an equal.

Okorafor is concerned with the healing of the African community; this explains Onyesonwu's supernatural powers. With these powers, she can help others, but she cannot help herself in the area where she needs the most help. Her powers cannot help restore her Ani-given right to pleasure. For that, she needs the help of another person with supernatural powers, one who has also learned the secret of the people's cults. That is a young man named Mwita. With his intervention, Onyesonwu grows back her "tiny flesh," which eventually helps her to climax. It pleases her "that for once in [her] life obtaining something of importance was easy."[60] Does Mwita's help suggest Okorafor's belief that men are needed for the success of women's feminist causes? His help relates to Okorafor's conception of the flourishing community, to which I will return in the concluding part of this chapter. A flourishing community is one in which humans are not stuck in categories dictated by ideologies. Rather, it is one in which men and women relate to one another in freedom and on equal grounds.

Bodily Pain as a Trope for Existential Pain

Warsan Shire, born in Kenya of Somali parentage, now lives in England. She is the most vocal of contemporary African women writing against female genital excision. She states in an interview her motive for writing poems on the issue: "I write poems on FGM because I have been raised and loved by a community where many people I know have undergone this procedure. To work towards the eradication of this practice, their voices need to be heard."[61] Judging from her tone, she likely did not undergo the ritual of female genital excision. Her interpretation of her project as a poet can be read as a gesture of empathy. In a remarkable exercise of imagination, she suffers vicariously on behalf of other women who have been cut. In the remaining section of this chapter, I will examine four of her poems, three of which, "The Things We Lost in the Summer," "Tribe of Woods," and "Girls" are exclusively about female genital excision. I use the other poem, "Your Mother's First Kiss" as an introduction to her poetics of pain.

Like Nnedi Okorafor, Shire uses violence as an introductory motif for her poetics in the collection *Teaching My Mother How to Give Birth*. In the second poem, "Your Mother's First Kiss" the speaker uses images that suggest a violent origin. The first line of the poem shocks the reader with its positioning of the ritual of love alongside the violence of warfare.

> The first boy to kiss your mother later raped women
> when the war broke out. She remembers hearing this
> from your uncle, then going to your bedroom and laying
> down on the floor. You were at school.

Close attention to the wartime conditions that generated that act of violence provides a complex picture of Shire's poetics. The poem most likely refers to the Somalian war and the ensuing sociopolitical dysfunction in the country. This is the backdrop against which we can understand the series of violent acts that the women of that society experience. Men and women are victims of society's dysfunction, but men redirect their anger and frustration onto women's bodies. The second stanza amplifies the shock announced by the first:

> Your mother was sixteen when he first kissed her.
> She held her breath for so long that she blacked out.
> On waking she found her dress was wet and sticking
> to her stomach, half moons bitten into her thighs.

The experience of rape, we learn, is actually of the woman who received the kiss in the first scene. She shares her experience with another woman, who makes wine illegally, and claims that no man had ever touched her in that way before. The winemaker laughs sarcastically, and her laughter indicates the other woman's naïveté. She is only getting to know what has become a routine experience for many other women. It is possible that the reason the winemaker makes wine is to deal with the effects of trauma. It is also possible that she comes to the aid of all the other women who have been assaulted, and who did not want to carry their children to term. The fourth stanza rounds off the sorrowful tale:

> Last week, she saw him driving the number 18 bus,
> his cheek a swollen drumlin, a vine scar dragging itself
> across his mouth. You were with her, holding a bag
> of dates to your chest, heard her let out a deep moan
> when she saw how much you looked like him.

We have the picture of three persons marked by violence: the mother, the first man in her life, and her child. The last line of the poem suggests that the child was born from her encounter with that man. Atmosphere is a character in the poem, and the violent atmosphere of the speaker's conception sets the stage for the narrative of women's experience of pain in Somali society. The atmosphere is one of pain itself. The violence of the speaker's conception is similar to that of Onyesonwu in *Who Fears Death*.

"Things We Had Lost in the Summer" involves the pain of loss. Exactly what has been lost is kept from the reader, and this lends the poem its peculiar, ominous mood. There are insinuations of what might have been lost. Carefully chosen words reveal that the subjects are girls: "Amel's hardened nipples push through." The speaker is twelve years old and "swollen with the heat of waiting." Waiting for what? Menstruation? Initiation? Or some other thing that is peculiar to girls at that age in that culture? In the second stanza, we get a clear intimation of what might have happened, that is, what the speaker might have waited for.

> My mother uses her quiet voice on the phone:
> *Are they all okay? Are they healing well?*
> She doesn't want my father to overhear.

The "father" was excluded from what was going on between the mother and the speaker on the other end of the phone, who obviously has had something to say about healing. A wound? The wound could surely not have been a result of an accident. The mother must have been privy to what caused it. Mood plays an important role in our appreciation of "Things We Had Lost in the Summer" just as it did in "Your Mother's First Kiss." The poet creates a dizzying atmosphere of loss. The question, "are they healing well?" suggests a wound, a cut, pain, which in turn hints at something that has been excised. In the last stanza, the feeling of emptiness that comes from loss crystallizes.

> In the car, my mother stares at me through the
> rear view mirror, the leather sticks to the back of my
> thighs. I open my legs like a well-oiled door,
> daring her to look at me and give me
> what I had not lost: a name.

Even though the speaker claims that the only thing she has not lost was her name, we might wonder whether that too was not lost. Did she have a name in a culture that never considered her as an individual? Do women have names in such intensely patriarchal cultures? In the online version of the same poem a note indicates that the poem is about female genital excision. We have another helpful piece of information: "One of her earlier poems, The Things We Lost in the Summer was inspired by the experiences of people she knew who were to be cut when they were on the cusp of puberty [*sic*]".[62] That piece of information surely helps the reader to appreciate the poem all the more. Could the last line have been meant to be sarcastic? To be denied the right to pleasure in one's body is to be denied a name, an identity; it is to be denied human rights. It is not just the clitoris that is lost. So, what did those women lose? The mood insinuated by the poem prohibits us from answering this question because any answer will diminish the magnitude of the loss.

In "Tribe of Woods," a poem published online and not part of the collection, Shire explores the issue of female genital excision in a somewhat more obvious, though less detailed way. The poem has an explanatory note by the website's editor: "Female genital mutilation, the contradictions and sometimes cruelty of cultural traditions are tackled in this poem by this courageous and sensual 20-something Somalian poet."[63] The poem captures the perspective of a mother who, now informed by time and hindsight, appears to regret having submitted her daughter for genital excision:

> I held down my daughter last night
> spread her limbs across the forest

> laid her out to rest
> crushed berries across her mouth and
> gave her my knuckles to chew on.

The ritual takes place in a forest, a remote area where the women could be undisturbed by men for a more literal interpretation for the ritual of initiation. Nature contrasts with modernity and suggests a place where traditions are kept intact. It is a place where girls can be taught how to be women, and the mother is there playing an important role, albeit a violent one: she holds her daughter down, and the daughter's limbs are spread, obviously not of her own accord. The color of the crushed berries across the girl's mouth evokes the outcome of the application of force/violence in the process. But the daughter has to go through the ritual; she should never give up, and to help her persevere in that agonizing practice, her mother has to give her something to sink her teeth into: the mother's own knuckles. Knuckles are symbols of persistence and perseverance. In effect, the mother also suffers. Both mother and daughter experience intense pain merely to maintain a ritual that does not acknowledge them as individuals entitled to their own pleasures.

The second stanza paints the picture of the immediate outcome of the ritual on the girl's body. When the speaker gives her daughter to another ritual—that of marriage —she, the mother, learns that the daughter felt nothing when she had sex with her husband:

> I gave my daughter to a man
> an offering that made my stomach tight
> with want, he spread her limbs across the town
> I prayed she felt something,
> wriggled underneath him like
> the women across the border,
> I listened out to hear her moan
> but I heard nothing.

Realizing her mistake, the mother declares in the last line of the fourth stanza: "And I want different for my granddaughter." She now knows that her daughter, who will eventually produce a daughter of her own, will curse her in a foreign hospital "where her limp pregnant body /will be inspected by a bone lipped doctor /who'll ask "'what happened to this woman".'"

We assume that the woman whose own mother was complicit in her genital excision is now in another country where female genital excision is not practiced. The reference to the daughter's "limp pregnant body" alerts us to her zombie-like existence, resulting from the ritual. She felt no pleasure while her baby was being conceived and while the baby was growing inside her. The woman has been reduced to a breeding machine. If this sounds harsh in judgment then it might be even harsher in reality. Shire suggests that the only way to avoid the harshness of the act and of its narration is to let women be women, to let them experience the pains and pleasures that their bodies naturally experience, not those that culture imposes. This is the knowledge that the speaker has gained. While still expressing her regret, the mother requests her pregnant daughter to reveal to the foreign doctor who will attend to her the identity of the person who deprived her of her right to those experiences:

> tell him your mother took it
> a tribe of women the woodsmen
> a rusted blade the axe
> folklore and religion,
> but tell him your mother meant well
> and promise me
> that you'll teach my granddaughter
> that there is never any shame in want. [64]

The "rusted blade" in the third line is juxtaposed with "the axe" to suggest the effect of the ritual on the bodies of women. The blade is to the vulva what the axe is to a tree root. The next line, "folklore and religion" suggests the ideology that sustains that ritual. Folklore and religion notoriously ignore the feelings of individuals; they serve mostly the ruling classes or group, in this case, men.

The third poem, "Girls" was written as an expression of solidarity with Fahma Mohamed, a 17-year-old Bristol girl who began a campaign to educate people in England about the devastations of female genital excision.[65] The poet read out the poem as part of the campaign, at an event in (date, time):[66]

"Girls"
1

Sometimes it's tucked into itself, sewn up like the lips of a prisoner.
After the procedure, the girls learn how to walk again, mermaids with new legs, soft knees buckling under their new stainless, sinless bodies.

2
Daughter is synonymous with traitor, the father says. *If your mother survived it, you can survive it*, the father says. *Cut, cut, cut.*
3
On a reality TV show about beauty, one girl exposes another girls' [*sic*] secret. They huddle around her asking questions, touching her arm in liberal concern for her pleasure. *Can you even feel anything down there?* The camera zooms into a Georgia O'Keefe painting in the background.
4
But mother did you even truly survive it? The carving, the cutting, the warm blade against the inner thigh. Scalping. Deforestation. Leveling the ground. Silencing the devils tongue between your legs, maybe you did? I'm asking you sincerely mother, did you truly survive it?
5
Two girls lay in bed beside one another holding mirrors under the mouths of their skirts, comparing wounds.
I am one girl and you are the other.[67]

The change of perspectives in the three FGM poems is instructive. In "The Things We Lost in the Summer," the speaker, a twelve-year old girl, has obviously experienced the ritual. In "Tribe of Woods," the perspective shifts to a mother who has allowed it to be performed on her daughter. In "Girls," the perspective is that of the third-person point of view. "Girls" also dispenses with the more traditional format of the first two poems. It is a prose-poem that achieves its greatest impact in its voices. First we hear the voice of the father, the patriarch, who orders that the ritual take place. His belief that (his) daughter is synonymous with (a) traitor recalls the view held in most patriarchal societies that girls are of lesser value than boys. It is known that some families kill infant girls because they will only be a burden for the family.[68] However, in this instance, the patriarch's utterance is tinged with spite and the wish to control. "*If your mother survived it, you can survive it*, the father says. *Cut, cut, cut.*" We feel the sharpness of the cutting process in his words. The repetition of the word "cut" lends the act a patriarchal urgency. There is no room for doubt in the father's mind about the importance of the act. He obviously does not see his wife and daughters as individuals with rights that must be respected. He sees them in the ways that tradition—folklore and religion—stipulates.

But it is now the turn of a girl to question the wisdom of a patriarch. We assume it is the voice of one of the girls who had to learn how to walk again after the procedure. She chooses to direct her question to her mother. *"But mother did you even truly survive it?"* The question alludes to the physical and psychological devastations of the ritual. The girl knows that her mother has been disabled. The patriarchal tradition sees the woman's body only as a breeding machine that serves the needs of men; it does not consider other aspects of the woman's being: the inner world of the woman, her dignity. Through the girl's voice we too, through a process of empathy, wonder whether the patriarch knows what he is saying. How could he know whether the mother of his daughters survived the cut she had as a girl? In questioning the patriarch's knowledge, we also interrogate the assumptions of patriarchy, which is that the father knows everything, including the feelings of women.

The last stanza of "Girls" achieves the most impact, by giving an overview of the girls in bed comparing their wounds. They take us under their skirts, and what we could not have imagined all alone, they show us. The last line, "I am one girl and you are the other" is a sad comment on their existence. They see themselves as mere girls, that is, replaceable human beings whom society has denied rights and dignities. They have no names and are thought to have no feelings.

Narrative, Empathy, and Community

The question, "mother did you even truly survive it?" echoes disturbingly in the mind. I have argued that it is meant as an interrogation of the patriarch's epistemological assumptions, that is, his claim to understand his wife and daughter and to know what is best for them. Thus the daughter forms a bond with her mother, a bond from which the patriarch is excluded. How much would he know about his wife and daughters, he who has never listened to their stories? Perhaps they never told their stories because they did not have a voice. There is no way the patriarch could know that his wife did not survive the pain visited on her as a child because he operates under an ideology that notoriously ignores the feelings of individuals. He thus denies participation in the life of community to his wife and daughters and even to himself. The poet, in line with the virtues of narrative, gives a voice to the mother and others like her.[69] She narrates their stories. We, the community, also hear their stories on behalf of the ignorant father. We partake of the lives of these women; we suffer vicariously. But our vicarious suffering will have meaning only if we interrogate the system that enables such pains.

I suggested above that Nnedi Okorafor has the community in mind when her narrator tells how a man, Mwita, helped Onyesonwu regrow the piece of flesh responsible for pleasure. The presence of community in the narrative spheres of the African women writers under discussion is one of their outstanding traits. These writers are interested in human flourishing in African communities. Their ideal community is one that will not allow individuals to sacrifice their pleasure in the name of an abstract ideology. It could be argued that they seek to realize the ideals of *ubuntu*. Their conception of community is multicolored and political.[70] It is also rooted in empathy, in compassion for the other, and this is what their narratives seek to achieve.

Discussing Aristotle's concept of human flourishing, Alasdair MacIntyre examines the word *misericordia*, which is Aquinas's interpretation of Aristotelian sympathy, and states that it is precisely the virtue that communities require in order to thrive. "*Misericordia* has regard to urgent and extreme need without respect of persons. It is the kind and scale of the need that dictates what has to be done, not whose need it is."[71] For MacIntyre, virtue is necessary if human life is to flourish. We need a community in which those virtues thrive, one that encourages the common good, based not on prescribed rules but on the recognition of mutual empathy and dependence and on one another's freedom. MacIntyre argues:

> It is most often to others that we owe our survival, let alone our flourishing, as we encounter bodily illness and injury, inadequate nutrition, mental defect and disturbance, and human aggression and neglect. This dependence on particular others for protection and sustenance is most obvious in early childhood and old age.[72]

Between childhood and old age we go through many forms of dependence. The requisite virtue is that of acknowledged dependence on others, rather than the façade of exclusionary, misguided individualism. Stories bring us closer to our fellow humans by allowing us to encounter their vulnerabilities. For MacIntyre, the virtue of *misericordia* has political implications. "To treat someone else as someone for whom we have a regard" because of possible dependence on them, or theirs on us, "is to accord them political recognition."[73] This political recognition is especially welcome because it stems not from authority figures but from "everyday practical reasoning"; it is born in the "everyday activity of every adult capable of engaging in it."[74] Relating to others, having them within the reach of our imagination situates them within the axis of our feeling and consideration. They are no longer abstract entities; they are human beings who might depend on me and on whom I might depend.

The narratives of contemporary African women writers, as I have already argued, help us bridge the gap between others and us, and between genders. They make others real in our moral imaginations also by allowing us to put ourselves in their positions. The women in our lives are therefore no longer persons about whom society can make abstract laws, but rather persons whom men can relate to as fellow humans, as the moral beings that they are.

Notes

1. *The Guardian*, "Female genital mutilation denies sexual pleasure to millions of women." http://www.theguardian.com/science/blog/2008/nov/13/female-genital-mutilation-sexual-dysfunction (Accessed March 24, 2014) (*The Guardian* 2014).
2. Maggie O'Kane, Patrick Farrelly, Alex Rees, and Irene Baqué, "FGM: The Film that Changed the Law in Kurdistan – Video." www.theguardian.com/society/video/2013/oct/24/fgm-film-changed-the-law-kurdistan-video.
3. Maggie O'Kane and Patrick Farrelly, "FGM: 'It's like neutering animals' – The Film that is Changing Kurdistan." http://www.theguardian.com/society/2013/oct/24/female-genital-mutilation-film-changing-kurdistan-law (Accessed 10 December 2014) (O'Kane and Farrelly 2014).
4. Audre Lorde, *Sister Outsider: Essays and Speeches* Freedom, CA: The Crossing Press, 1984, 55 (Lorde 1984).
5. Hélène Cixous, "The Laugh of the Medusa," trans. Keith Cohen and Paula Cohen. *Signs* 1.4 (1976): 875–893. See especially pages 877–878 (Cixous 1976).
6. Gloria Anzaldua, *Borderlands/La Frontera: The New Mestiza*. San Francisco: Spinsters/aunt lute, 1999, 17 (Anzaldua 1999).
7. For more on the different forms of female genital excision, see Leonard Kouba and Judith Muasher, "Female Circumcision in Africa: An Overview," *African Studies Review*, 28 (1985): 95–110. (Kouba and Muasher 1985).
8. While it is true that male and female circumcision are compared in general discussions, apart from the fact that they both use some painful cutting, they are not the same procedure. What is done to women is very far from what is done to men. The motives of the cultures that practice female genital excision may not be evil in themselves, but that does not lessen to any degree the trauma of this procedure of physical mutilation. The effects on the female victims are not any different from what they would suffer if the practitioner's motives were in fact evil. I am grateful to Jim Fuhr for pointing this out to me.

9. Chantal Zabus, *Between Rites and Rights: Excision in Women's Experiential Texts and Human Contexts*. Stanford University Press, 2007 (Zabus 2007). Elisabeth Bekers, *Rising Anthills: African and African American Writing on Female Genital Excision*, 1960–2000. Madison: University of Wisconsin Press, 2010 (Bekers 2010). Zabus and Bekers capture the full range of the arguments about female circumcision in their important books. See especially Zabus (10–12).
10. Michel Foucault, *The History of Sexuality*, 1. Trans. R. Hurley. Penguin Books, 1978 (Foucault 1978).
11. See Zabus, *Between Rites and Rights*, 27 (Zabus 2007). See also Elisabeth Bekers's analysis of the same myth in Bekers, *Rising Anthills*, 3 (Bekers 2010).
12. IRIN: Humanitarian News and Analysis "In-depth: Razor's Edge—The Controversy of Female Genital Mutilation: KENYA: Justifying Tradition: Why Some Kenyan Men Favour FGM." http://www.irinnews.org/indepthmain.aspx?InDepthId=15&ReportId=62471&Country=Yes (Accessed September 4, 2014) (IRIN 2014).
13. IRIN: Humanitarian News and Analysis: "Razor's Edge—The Controversy of Female Genital Mutilation SIERRA LEONE: Female Circumcision Is a Vote Winner." http://www.irinnews.org/indepthmain.aspx?InDepthId=15&ReportId=62473&Country=Yes. For more on female circumcision, see Penelope Hetherington, "The Politics of Female Circumcision in the Central Province of Colonial Kenya, 1920–30," *The Journal of Imperial and Commonwealth History*, 26.1 (1998): 93–126 (Hetherington 1998). Lewis Hope, "Between Irua and Female Genital Mutilation: Feminist Human Rights Discourse and the Cultural Divide," *Harvard Human Rights Journal*, 8 (1995): 1–56 (Hope 1995).
14. http://www.afrol.com/Categories/Women/wom005_fgm_norway.htm. See also UNHCR, The UN Refugee Agency, "The Gambia: Report on Female Genital Mutilation (FGM) or Female Genital Cutting (GC)." www.refworld.org/docid/46d5787732.html.
15. Jomo Kenyatta, *Facing Mount Kenya*. London: Secker and Warburg, 1938, 133 (Kenyatta 1938).
16. Ngugi Wa Thiong'o, *The River Between*. London: Heinemann, 1965 (Wa Thiong'o 1965).
17. Augustine H. Assah and Tobe Levin, "Challenges of Our Times: Responses of African/Diasporan Intellectuals to FGM," *AFROEUROPA: Journal of Afro-European Studies*, 2.1 (2008) (Assah and Levin 2008). No page. http://journal.afroeuropa.eu/index.php/afroeuropa/article/viewFile/62/73. See also Haseena Lockhat, *Female Genital Mutilation: Treating the Tears*. Middlesex University Press, 2004 (Lockhat 2004).
18. Alice Walker, *Possessing the Secret of Joy*. New York: New Press, 1992 (Walker 1992).

19. Joyce Russell-Robinson, "African Female Circumcision and the Missionary Mentality," *A Journal of Opinion* 25. 1 Commentaries in African Studies: Essays About African Social Change and the Meaning of Our Professional Work, 25.1 (1997): 56 (Russell-Robinson 1997).
20. Ibid.
21. L. Amede Obiora, "The Little Foxes That Spoil the Vine: Revisiting the Feminist Critique of Female Circumcision," in *African Women and Feminism: Reflecting on the Politics of Sisterhood*, ed. Oyeronke Oyewumi. Trenton, NJ: Africa World Press, Inc., 2003, 199 (Obiora 2003).
22. Ibid., 211.
23. Oyeronke Oyewumi, "Alice in Motherland: Reading Alice Walker on Africa and Screening the Color 'Black,'" in *African Women and Feminism: Reflecting on the Politics of Sisterhood*, Oyeronke Oyewumi ed. (Trenton, NJ: Africa World Press, Inc. 2003), 161 (Oyewumi 2003a).
24. Ibid, 160.
25. Ibid.
26. Ibid.
27. Ibid, 170.
28. Louis Althusser, *Lenin and Philosophy*. Trans. Ben Brewster. New York: Monthly Review Press, 1971, 170–177 (Althusser 1971).
29. See Judith Butler, *The Psychic Life of Power: Theories in Subjection*. Stanford, CA: Stanford University Press, 1997 (Butler 1997).
30. Obioma Nnaemeka, "African Women, Colonial Discourses, and Imperialist Interventions: Female Circumcision as Impetus," in *Female Circumcision and the Politics of Knowledge: African Women in Imperialist Discourse*, ed. Obioma Nnaemeka. Westport, CT: Praeger, 2005, 274–276 (Nnaemeka 2005).
31. Sylvia Tamale, "African Feminism: How Should We Change?" *Supplement: Women's Rights and Development; Association for Women's Development* Houndmills United Kingdom, Palgrave Macmillan, 49.1 (2006): 38–41.
32. Tamale, "African Feminism," (61–62) (Tamale 2006).
33. Waris Dirie, *Desert Flower: The Extraordinary Life of a Desert Nomad*. London: Virago, 1998 (Dirie 1998).
34. http://www.desertflowerfoundation.org/en/.
35. See for instance *NPR*, http://www.pbs.org/speaktruthtopower/issue_female.html; *Huffington Post*, "Nearly 4,000 Treated For Female Genital Mutilation In London." http://www.huffingtonpost.com/2014/03/20/female-genital-mutilation_n_5000214.html and *The Guardian*, http://www.theguardian.com/end-fgm.
36. Nawal El Saadawi, *The Hidden Face of Eve*. New York: Zed Books, 2007 (Saadawi 2007).

37. Ayaan Hirsi Ali, *Infidel*. New York: Simon and Schuster, 2007 (Ali 2007).
38. Fauziya Kassindja, *Do They Hear You When You Cry*. New York: Delta, 1998 (Kassindja 1998).
39. Nnedi Okorafor, *Who Fears Death*. New York: Daw Books, Inc., 2010 (Okorafor 2010).
40. Ibid., 14.
41. Ibid., 8.
42. David Scheffer, "Sudan and the ICC: Rape as Genocide." http://www.nytimes.com/2008/12/03/opinion/03iht-edscheffer.1.18365231.html?_r=0. See also Jennifer Leaning, Susan Bartels, and Hani Mowafi, "Sexual Violence during War and Forced Migration," in *Women, Migration, and Conflict: Breaking a Deadly Cycle*, ed. Susan Forbes Martin and John Tirman. New York: Springer, 2009, 173–199 (Leaning et al. 2009).
43. Okorafor, *Who Fears*, 30 (Okorafor 2010).
44. Ibid., 31.
45. Ibid., 32.
46. Ibid., 33 (original italics).
47. Ibid., 39 (italics mine).
48. Ibid., 41.
49. Ibid., 50.
50. I have discussed Scarry in greater detail in Chapter 4.
51. Okorofor, *Who Fears*, 74 (Okorafor 2010).
52. Ibid.,76.
53. Elizabeth S. Anker, *Fictions of Dignity: Embodying Human Rights in World Literature*. Ithaca: Cornell University Press, 2012, 4 (Anker 2012).
54. Okorafor, *Who Fears*, 78. (Okorafor 2010).
55. Ibid., 78–79.
56. Ibid., 79.
57. Ibid., 80.
58. Ibid., 81.
59. Ibid., 90. [Original Italics].
60. Ibid., 130.
61. The Guardian, "Warsan Shire: Young Poet Laureate Wields Her Pen Against FGM." http://www.theguardian.com/society/2014/feb/17/warsan-shire-young-poet-laureate-michael-gove
62. http://www.theguardian.com/society/2014/feb/17/warsan-shire-young-poet-laureate-michael-gove
63. http://badilishapoetry.com/radio/WarsanShire/
64. Warsan Shire, "Tribe of Woods" http://badilishapoetry.com/radio/WarsanShire/

65. Fahma Mohamed, "Tell Schools to Teach Risks of Female Genital Mutilation Before the Summer." http://www.change.org/en-GB/petitions/educationgovuk-tell-schools-to-teach-risks-of-female-genital-mutilation-before-the-summer-endfgm
66. http://www.theguardian.com/society/video/2014/feb/14/girls-warsan-shire-fgm-video?INTCMP=
67. http://www.spreadtheword.org.uk/resources/view/warsan-shire-young-poet-laureate-for-london.
68. Palash Kumar, "India Has Killed 10 Million Girls in 20 Years." http://abcnews.go.com/Health/story?id=2728976.
69. See the introductory chapter for my discussion of Aristotle and Paul Ricoeur.
70. Aristotle understands human flourishing also in political terms. It is about people participating actively in the life of community.
71. Alasdair MacIntyre, *Dependent Rational Animals: Why Human Beings Need the Virtues*. Peru, IL: Open Court, 1999, 124 (MacIntyre 1999).
72. Ibid., 1.
73. Ibid., 141.
74. Ibid.

CHAPTER 5

Abstractions as Disablers of Women's Rights

Lola Shoneyin and Petina Gappah

During a question-and-answer session at the World Economic Forum in Davos, Switzerland, in 2010, President Jacob Zuma of South Africa defended his simultaneous marriage to four women by seeking recourse to his culture. Zuma answered: "That's my culture. It does not take anything from me, from my political beliefs including the belief in the equality of women... Some think that their culture is superior to others, that's a problem we have in the world."[1] In April, 2014, the Kenyan government legalized polygamy on the grounds that it was part of their culture and heritage.[2] My interest in Zuma's answer and the Kenyan polygamy law is entirely philosophical as I do not judge either of these. I am, however, more interested in whether culture could be used to justify one person's relation to another person. What happens to individuals when abstractions such as culture or nationalism insert themselves in people's relations?

Consider Zuma's other appeal to culture. During his rape trial in 2005, which made international headlines, he did not deny having any sexual contact with the woman who accused him of rape. Rather, he:

> told the court that in adhering to Zulu cultural norms, he had been obliged to have sexual intercourse with the complainant because she was sexually aroused. Had he walked away from the complainant when she was in this state, Zuma said, in Zulu culture his actions would have been tantamount to rape.[3]

What Zuma's two lines of defense and the Kenyan justification for legalizing polygamy have in common, apart from their generous exploitation of the argument of cultural relativism, is their use of abstraction to support actions that affect the lives of particular individuals. The thinking of the African feminist theorists I have discussed in the introduction has the same traits as Zuma's. For instance, in her discussion of Mariama Bâ's novel *So Long a Letter*, Chikwenye Okonjo Ogunyemi argues that Bâ depicted polygamy from the African perspective rather than from that of the West. In her reading, Bâ portrayed Ramatoulaye, the protagonist, as having accommodated herself to the fact that African men had the cultural right to have as many wives as they pleased. In the novel, Okonjo Ogunyemi argues, Ramatoulaye tells her friend:

> about the polygynous situation that has ruined her marriage because of her Western expectations of monogyny. Rather than collapsing, she remains undaunted, with little acrimony… Having accepted men with their libidinous disposition, she can create a stable life around her numerous children, male and female, along with their spouses. This is womanism in action; the demands of Fulani culture rather than those of sexual politics predominate.[4]

I have quoted Okonjo Ogunyemi in greater length in order to capture the ideological premise of her arguments. Her concern is to contrast African culture (polygamy) with that of the West (monogamy). It is interesting that Okonjo Ogunyemi reads Ramatoulaye's disappointment as resulting from her "Western expectations of monogyny." It seems to suggest that the idea of equality between men and women is essentially Western and that no African woman could (or should) aspire to that. To be sure, *So Long a Letter* is more complex than Okonjo Ogunyemi characterizes it. More than anything, it portrays Ramatoulaye's pain in the face of her husband's betrayal. Okonjo Ogunyemi's ideological need to defend African cultures seems to trump the necessity to explore the pain of an African woman who has been abandoned by her husband, and has to take care of their nine children all alone. Given the historical contexts of the time, one can understand why she would read *So Long a Letter* as supporting polygamy. But third-generation African women scholars and writers approach the issue from a different perspective. Even while not casting themselves as pro-Western, they seek to interrogate the premises of some of those African cultural practices; they question the abstraction in which the justifications of these cultures are couched.

In the introductory chapter, I discussed abstractions as manifestations of ideologies such as nationalism, heritage culture, tradition, religion, et cetera. I compared these abstractions with Emmanuel Levinas's notion of totality. For Levinas, Western philosophy, especially in the tradition of Descartes and Kant, subsumes the individual within the category of reason. He calls this category totality. He argues that for Western philosophy, in order to bring forth objective meaning the unicity of the present is sacrificed to a future thought to possess a definite goal; thought is what gives the individual meaning. "For the ultimate meaning alone counts; the last act alone changes beings into themselves. They are what they will appear to be in the already plastic forms of the epic."[5] It is therefore fair to claim that, in regard to the control of the individual, the category of reason is to Western cosmology what culture or tradition is to that of Africa. In this chapter, I argue that given the fact that people's lives are controlled by abstractions, especially in regard to marriage, women occupy the opposite pole of polar power relations; they have no voice. In the first part of this chapter, I examine polygamy as an institution that inherently disables women because its justification is in culture. In the second part, I examine the lives of women caught in the abstractions of nationalist politics and culture.

Lola Shoneyin: Polygamy as a Disabling Institution

In *The Secret Lives of Baba Segi's Wives*,[6] four women, Iya Segi, Iya Tope, Iya Femi, and Bolanle are married to one man, Ishola, known as Baba Segi. Ishola is confident in his virility and standing as a patriarch. The apparent barrenness of Bolanle, his beloved and educated fourth wife causes him much concern. His three other wives had, unbeknownst to him, solved the problems of childbearing in their own unique, crafty ways. But Bolanle insists that she and her husband do a test. In the course of a series of medical tests, he learns that he is, indeed, not as virile as he had claimed. Why did these women resort to secrecy in their lives with Baba Segi?

The narrative begins with a problem that, given traditional epistemologies, can only have been caused by women. "When Baba Segi awoke with a bellyache for the sixth day in a row, he knew it was time to do something drastic about his fourth wife's childlessness." Baba Segi makes it clear to Bolanle: "Your barrenness brings shame upon me."[7] In this overture, Shoneyin hints at the philosophical and, indeed, moral thread that will run through the narrative: the body in pain. Here we have two bodies.

One of them, Bolanle's, is supposed to be deficient, yet it is in the body of the other, Ishola, that pain is felt and taken seriously. Shoneyin does not intend to show Baba Segi's pain as a classic lesson in empathy; Baba Segi does not feel the pain of his wife's supposed barrenness because it disturbs his wife, but because it apparently makes people think that he is no longer a man. His concern is to prove his virility, and that blinds him to whatever pain his allegedly beloved wife might have felt.

Shoneyin seeks to achieve one particular goal with the structure of the narrative: the interrogation of patriarchy, and she does it by drawing attention to particular stories of individual women living in that system. That alone, listening to the women's stories, should recast the paradigms of relationships in society, and this is more important than seeking to crush an ideology, or to erect another in its place. Understanding the individual narratives of these women could aid us in our critical appreciation of the institution of polygamy.

For Terry Eagleton, feminism has been the paradigm of morality in our own times largely because it "insists in its own way on the interwovenness of the moral and political, power and the personal. It is in this tradition above all that the precious heritage of Aristotle and Marx has been deepened and renewed."[8] Eagleton reminds us of the difference between moralism and morality. Moralism is narrow and "believes that there is a set of questions known as moral questions which are quite distinct from social or political ones." Morality on the other hand, means "exploring the texture and quality of human behaviour as richly and sensitively as you can." This implies that one cannot talk about morality or about existence in general "by abstracting men and women from their social surroundings."[9] In order to examine the texture of the lives of her female characters fully, Shoneyin employs the riches of the first-person point of view, and allows each woman to tell her own story. She, in a way, gives each woman a voice: Iya Femi lost her parents as a child. Her uncle sold her into "house slavery" with the justification that a "girl cannot inherit her father's house." A woman is denied her father's property because, as her uncle says, "she will marry and make her husband's home her own."[10] Iya Femi spends more than 20 years in the household into which her uncle sold her. She meets Taju, Baba Segi's driver and begs him to help her find a husband. Taju tells her that only Baba Segi has enough money to marry several wives. Iya Femi pleads: "Then make him marry me. Convince him and put me in your debt forever. I have no relatives so there is no one for him to pay homage to."[11]

Iya Femi's story reveals a lot of things about the condition of certain women, one of which is that their only escape from the misery of their life is marriage to a man. In examining her life, we are allowed to interrogate the cultural patterns that denied her access to her own father's estate. The source of her economic dependence lies in her inability to inherit her father's property. Would she have needed to beg a man to marry her if she had had the means to sustain herself economically? We understand her seeking to be wedded to a married man as an effort to stay alive in a culture that has limited space for her. Hers is therefore a life-and-death struggle; she is fighting to stay alive within the narrow structure her culture has for her. She has limited choices; indeed, her choices have already been made for her by her culture. This is one of the instances in which abstractions disable women. In defining her needs and desires, Iya Femi's culture literally freezes her in an ontological category because of her gender. In line with Levinas's critique of Western philosophy, the unicity of Iya Femi's presence is sacrificed to maintain the culture's presumed goal.

Iya Tope's conditions are not much different from those of Iya Femi. Iya Tope's father was a hired farmer in the service of Baba Segi. That year, drought destroyed the crops. Iya Tope's parents presented her to Baba Segi as compensation for "the failed crops." Her father praised her in the presence of Baba Segi as being "strong as three donkeys" just as if she were on the auction block. He thus underlined Iya Tope's utilitarian value. Influenced by the way her father narrated her, Iya Tope, now telling her story, describes herself as being like the tubers of cassava in the basket.[12] Certain that he has secured a valuable commodity, Baba Segi describes Iya Tope in the same mercantile language. For example, when he begins to worry about her failure to conceive, he tells her, "if your father has sold me a rotten fruit, it will be returned to him."[13] Without alternatives and hemmed in by the identity conferred on her by her father, acting on behalf of her culture, Iya Tope seems to be reconciled to her fate, recognizing that Baba Segi, the master, is her only saviour.[14] She thus falls under the protection of one man or another without her consent. Is she therefore a true African woman to whom her culture is more important than her own rights and dignities? Based on just the stories of these two women, it is perhaps no longer a secret why Shoneyin shows the pain and humiliation of women in societies where culture determines people's relation to one another.

Tracing the development of the idea of human rights, Lynn Hunt argues that eighteenth-century European novels provoked a "torrent of emotions"[15] in their readers because of the way they shed light on the pains of their protagonists. In Jean-Jacques Rousseau's *Julie or the New Héloïse*, Julie sacrificed enough for love that people empathized with her. Hunt suggests that such novels like Rousseau's and Richardson's *Pamela* (1740) and *Clarissa* (1747–48) contributed to the thoughts captured in the proclamation of "the rights of man,"[16] the cornerstone of the ideas of the French revolution. The writers put people's identification with the pain of others in easily graspable narrative formats. The French Declaration of the Rights of Man and of the Citizen in 1789, Hunt argues, presaged the Universal Declaration of Human Rights, article 1 of which states that "All human beings are born free and equal in dignity and rights. They are endowed with reason and conscience and should act towards one another in a spirit of brotherhood."[17]

Could we compare what African women writers do for the African world with what the European writers of the eighteenth century did in regard to the pains of their fellow citizens? Literature does not prescribe how people should live. Strictly speaking, literature exposes the "texture and quality" of characters as figurative of the way we live. Martha Nussbaum sees the relationship between philosophy and literature, and draws attention to the important connection between form and content; she points out that in narratives, "a view of life is told."[18] We respond to this view of life and its characters as if they existed in (our) reality. In this regard it is justifiable to argue that Shoneyin exposes the objectification of women and thereby insinuates associations with the absence of these women's rights. The fact that Baba Segi refers to his wife as a thing reveals the quality of their intersubjective relationship. Of course, he has the impetus to do so because he knows how dependent she is on him. Her dependence on him was necessitated by the socio-cultural structure that froze her in a category. Assessing their relationship to one another, we get the impression they are not two free adults; they are master and indentured slave.

Iya Segi is the first of Baba Segi's four wives and over time has acquired a prominent role in the family. She is nearest in rank to the paterfamilias and therefore is a symbol of authority. The other women take orders from her. But none of this makes her condition as a person, whose existence is already overdetermined, any more tolerable. She too, came from a poor background. She worked hard and "aggressively" like a man. She was able to make a considerable amount of money, enough at least to buy a place in Baba Segi's home.

As Cavarero and Butler have shown, the ultimate question central to recognition of the other is: "Who are you?" This question is the basis for stories. In having these women tell their stories, Shoneyin assumes the relation between text and reader, that is, between the reader and the women whose stories are an answer to the question implicit in our reading. We listen to them and in so doing establish a condition for relation. Their stories calls us to meet them face-to-face, that is, engage them ethically. Shoneyin allows us to feel the different traumas that women experience because of their bodies. The women's individual narratives highlight their poor backgrounds, suggesting that their only hope of escape from their insignificance and the curse of their poverty and gender is their having a husband, any husband. And they are grateful to have found a husband, even if it means sharing him. They are grateful to be alive. Their lives or what could have been perceived as their subjectivities are subsumed within the abstract, ubiquitous presence of the man.

Hegel's dialectic of master and bondsman reveals that it is in the nature of the master to desire. The slave, on the contrary, does not desire; he is there to fulfill the desires of the master since the slave has no claim for recognition.[19] In a patriarchal society in which the relationship between man and woman can be represented in Hegelian terms, the woman is considered to have no desires.[20] A woman who desires rejects the subservient, traditional role meant for her. In *The Secret Lives of Baba Segi's Wives*, women, from the perspective of tradition, have no desires. They affirm the master, and satisfy his desires; the master does not affirm them. To affirm them would imply acknowledging that they, too, have rights and therefore are no longer at the service of the master; affirming them would make them his equal, and therefore negate his condition of being.

We have a better understanding of the women's self-perception in relation to their husband at the moment Bolanle, the fourth wife arrives. The other three grumble among themselves about her. Bolanle will make their already scarce commodity, their common master, even scarcer. Iya Femi complains: "Is it that our food wasn't tasty enough? Why would Baba Segi marry another wife? Has he condemned our breasts because they are losing their fists?"[21] It is revelatory about Iya Femi's self-perception that her frustrations are focused on her services to her master; she is concerned with his pleasure: the food she prepares for him and her breasts that she presents to him. Only after mentioning the master's desires does she remember herself as an individual that deserves attention, and even more so only in relation to another woman: "I will not be cast aside because she is a graduate... I do not want her in this house."[22] Shoneyin's presentation of the women's concerns reveals some of the inner workings of polygamy. From the perspectives of these women, we learn what it feels like for different women to compete for the favor of one man. The condition that results from that arrangement incapacitates women. Iya Tope takes her inferior position in life as given. Her

> only worry was that Bolanle's arrival would disrupt the sex rotation. Baba Segi normally went from wife to wife, starting each week with Iya Segi. By Thursday, he'd start the cycle again, leaving him with the freedom to choose whom to spend Sunday night with.[23]

In his relation to his wives, Baba Segi is the one who exercises some form of freedom. The women have no access to him the way he has to them. Shoneyin seems to be suggesting that African polygamy turns women into objects in their relation to their common husband. Theirs is not a relation founded on reciprocity and mutual respect. In the spirit of the early proponents of human rights in the eighteenth century, Shoneyin raises fundamental ethical questions: what is my relationship to this other human being of a different gender? Do I consider her as a means to an end or as an end? How would I want to be treated if I were in her position?

As a result of the conditions into which they are forced, the women turn against one another; they especially taunt and mock Bolanle. They scheme against her, hoping that she will be chased out of the house, especially when it becomes clear that she is *barren*.[24] Knowing that Baba Segi is a man whose world is controlled by traditional narratives and idioms, the women plant a *juju*—a totem thought to possess evil magical powers—in his room, and accuse Bolanle of having done that because she wants to get rid of Baba Segi in order to cover her barrenness.[25] The dramatic turning point in the narrative is when the truth of Baba Segi's infertility becomes known. The problem that was introduced in the first scene of the narrative is, after all, not the fault of the women in Baba Segi's life; rather it is with the patriarch himself. But even after Baba Segi has been shown not to be who he presented himself to be, his power over the family is undiminished. On the contrary, his power increases dramatically. He threatens his wives with a nuclear option in the exercise of authority in order to bring them under his total control; he wants to send them back to where they came from, knowing full well that they have nowhere to go. He spells out the conditions under which they can stay:

> You can stay if you promise to be the wives *I* want you to be. He promptly banned them from leaving the house without his permission. Iya Segi was instructed to close down all her shops and relinquish every kobo she had saved to him. Iya Femi was forbidden to wear makeup and there would be no more church.[26]

Again Shoneyin exposes the peculiar social and economic conditions women are subjected to. They are the conditions that make polygamy possible in the first place. The conditions portrayed raise the question: would these women marry Baba Segi if they had more options in life? Might it be that Shoneyin is not against polygamy per se? She is against the circumstances that lead to four women vying for one man. Her primary concern is that the women's unhappy life is made possible by culture and tradition. It is precisely their culture and tradition that prevent Baba Segi from seeing them as having rights and dignity.

Raising Questions, Raising Awareness

Baba Segi's first three wives accept the conditions he lays out for them after his sterility is made known; this effectively reduces them to the status of house slaves. They have no claim to dignity and human rights because such are simply inconceivable in their world. The fact that they accept the conditions spelt out for them by the patriarch, who has been revealed to be impotent and empty, suggests that women's bodies are controlled by an abstract construct, nullity. For Bolanle, living under the new restrictions imposed by Baba Segi is unacceptable; she divorces him. In this regard, she stands in sharp contrast to the other three. She turns her back on the past, understood as tradition, and as symbolizing abstractions that have defined her body. She thus embraces the future, understood as open, and that in which the individual makes choices that might contrast with traditional expectations, choices based on her awareness of her rights and dignities.

Given that Bolanle is a well-educated young woman, one might wonder why she chose to become the fourth wife of a polygamist in the first place. One answer is that she chose a life of polygamy with full knowledge of what she was getting herself into; she thus asserted her individuality specifically because she exercised the full extent of her freedom to choose, even if that choice is a retreat from what could be seen as the modern lifestyle of monogamy. Bolanle does not dismiss polygamy out of hand as a Westerner might. She thinks for herself. In refusing to judge a lifestyle or an aspect of tradition from a distance, she asks not to be judged, but rather to be understood. She wants people to listen to her story, which is unique to her. She was raped at 15, she had an abortion, and she has lived with a deep pain ever since then. Her mother wanted her to live a modern lifestyle by being the only wife of a young, rich man. Her mother, however, went about it by ignoring that important aspect of Bolanle's life: choice. Bolanle chose an older man, hoping that his maturity would suit her own circumstances. "Baba Segi wouldn't be like younger men who demanded explanations for the faraway look in my eyes. Baba Segi was content when I said nothing."[27] In her thinking, marrying a man who accepted her, one who did not ask too many questions about her "quietness," would definitely help her on her way toward healing. Ultimately she rejects her mother's dictatorial impositions. It might appear to some that she is, indeed, running away from her life so that marrying a polygamist becomes a way to avoid confronting her trauma. We may not agree with her decisions, but we need to understand their context. On a more profound, aesthetic level, it is only logical that Bolanle is a disruptive tool in the hands of the author; she interrogates the culture from within, and in so doing, raises questions that direct our attention to the humanity of the women in polygamous marriages. It is at this point in the narrative that we feel the triumph of Bolanle's journey. In a way she becomes a means with which Shoneyin lays bare the structure of the traditional marriage arrangement, especially how it denies women their rights and dignities.

Bolanle is aware of herself as a desiring being. It is ultimately fulfilling that Bolanle's actions are deliberate; she asserts her freedom to determine the course of her own life:

> I chose this family to regain my life, to heal in anonymity. And when you choose a family, you stay with them. You stay with your husband even when friends call him a polygamist ogre. You stay with him when your mother says he's an overfed orangutan.[28]

It is instructive for our understanding of Shoneyin's ethical goal that, even though Bolanle finds herself surrounded by forces and norms that impinge on her life as a woman, she harbors no anger. Rather she focuses on affirming herself with the means available to her. In her choices she demonstrates her moral maturity. She touches on several important issues, the most obvious of which is the woman's self-perception as a human that can and should steer the course of her body. Her body is not an object at the disposal of society. That body feels pain just like the bodies of men do.

NATIONALISM AND HUMAN RIGHTS

In the concluding section of Chapter 3, I discussed the phenomenon of Mugabe syndrome, which is the rejection of introspection and self-criticism and the attendant delusion of moral excellence. Mugabe is a master at fending off opposition and criticism of his (mis)rule by a clever recourse to anti-imperialist rhetoric. Each time people point out his mistakes he incites pan-African nationalist feelings by lambasting the West for colonialism and imperialism. Even though his observations are correct, they are merely part of his insidious technique to hold on to power. Using nationalism as a metanarrative of power, he has built a one-party state under an ideological cloak of anti-imperialism. It is within the contexts of Zimbabwe's deployment of nationalist or totalitarian rhetoric that we can appreciate Petina Gappah's *An Elegy for Easterly*,[29] a collection of thirteen stories. My discussions will focus on three stories, "An Elegy for Easterly," "At the Sound of the Last Post," and "The Maid from Lalapanzi." A central concern that will guide my discussion is the relation between the nation, conceived in a totalitarian paradigm, and the individual. How do abstractions disable people in general and women in particular, and how do people respond to their abuses?

"An Elegy for Easterly" is a story about a slum, Easterly Farm and about Martha Mupengo, who is mentally disabled and pregnant. The unborn child's father is Josephat, husband of Ellen, who cannot conceive. Accidentally, Josephat's wife, as she is popularly known, discovers Martha having contractions and delivers her baby. Martha dies in the process and Ellen takes the child back home, to the shock of her husband for whom the event is an epiphany; it causes him to remember the night he raped Martha Mupengo. To Josephat, as to the nation, Martha Mupengo is an object; she has no rights.[30] She is therefore figurative of the greater tragedy of the informal settlement, and of Zimbabwe as a nation. The illegal settlement and its many shanties sprang up as a direct consequence of the president's ruinous government; specifically, it was due to the government's earlier attempt to sweep the streets of poor people because of the visit of the Queen of England. Those who were displaced in that cleansing effort found a new home in Easterly Farm. They were dispensable. The country had become a nation of informal traders.

Gappah uses the four countries that border Zimbabwe to reveal the country's chaos:

> to the north, Zambia, formerly one-Zambia-one-nation-one-robot-one-petrol-station... to the east, Mozambique... to the west, Botswana... and to the south... South Africa... They had become a nation of traders... at the end of the day, smelling of heat and dust, they packed up their wares and they returned to Easterly Farm, to be greeted again by Martha Mupengo.[31]

Easterly Farm is a microcosm of the country. Before Mugabe took power, these countries, with the possible exception of South Africa, were worse off than Zimbabwe. Now, the opposite is true. Yet Zimbabweans are fed with official lies designed to make them believe their country is still flourishing. Like the rest of the citizens, the residents of Easterly Farm have, however, learned to decode the government's lies. For them, truth is the exact opposite of the government's official proclamation. "If the government said inflation would go down, it was sure to rise. If they said there was a bumper harvest, starvation would follow."[32] In a particularly revealing scene, *Ba*Toby, an elderly man, explains to a group of children some of the symbols on the coins of the old currency, coins which had been in use as recently as in 2000. The five-cent coin had a rabbit, the 10-cent, a baobab tree, while the dollar coin showed the Zimbabwean ruins. He repeats a popular joke to the children:

> Before the President was elected, the Zimbabwe ruins were a prehistoric monument in Masvingo province. Now, the historic Zimbabwe ruins extend to the whole country. The children looked at him blankly, before running off to play, leaving him to laugh with his whole body shaking.[33]

*Ba*Toby symbolically blends lessons in history with a humorous reproach of the government. His laughter exposes the dysfunction undermining the new, independent country. The ruins of Masvingo represent the internal decay which the nationalist smokescreen seeks to cover. Human rights are one of the aspects of the country that are symbolized by the Masvingo ruins. Though Mugabe is not named in the story, we assume that "the president" refers to him. It is true that the entire country has become a site of ruins since Mugabe took over the reins of government, as it has become a site for many illegal settlements. But the people laugh about it. How might we interpret their laughter? Might it be gallows humor? Perhaps they deploy laughter as a deconstructive means. Even in their helplessness, they are aware of their subjectivity and agency. In this regard therefore, their laughter suggests their awareness of better alternatives.

In "Nietzsche's Last Laugh: Ecce Homo as Satire," Nicholas D. More discusses Nietzsche's clever uses of humor and satire as rhetorical devices for his philosophical truths. According to More's reading of *Ecce Homo*, "satire became the philosopher's stone that turned the dark details of Nietzsche's life and philosophy into the comic, and made them bearable, even enjoyable. Humor distanced Nietzsche from his own life just enough to face and embrace it."[34] But it is not only the difficulties of his personal life that Nietzsche confronts with humor and satire; he brings humor to bear on philosophy and life in general. In Chapter 8, Section 1 of *Thus Spoke Zarathustra*, "Reading and Writing," Zarathustra exhorts his listeners to write with blood, but never to take themselves or their wisdom too seriously. Doing so easily leads to a dangerous gravity. God and the Devil are all products of grave spirits or constructs of ideology that can be defied by a simple act: laughter. The people of Easterly laugh in the Nietzschean deconstructive sense; they slay the spirit of gravity, that is, the spirit of abstraction.

Gappah's narratives are not only realistic; they are also, in some instances, a near mimetic presentation of Zimbabwe's political and social realities, if only designed to mock them. Gappah satirizes Zimbabwean society, especially its understanding of heroism; she laughs at the system and those who proclaim its excellence with a typical anti-imperialist, abstract mindset. Ironically, whereas the president spins his propaganda, average Zimbabweans know what is at stake; they feel the pains of political dysfunction. They laugh.

The story, "At the Sound of the last Post" is told from the perspective of a sharp-witted widow, Esther, who, though she has tears in her eyes does not fail to record, in mocking tones, the social and political dysfunction playing itself out before her. The story is of the burial of Esther's husband, an unnamed hero and freedom fighter. The party and state officials are present: the president, the chief justice, the police commissioner, and the governor of the central bank. The widow sits beside the president; she observes him and notes the obvious: he is an old man: "Unexpected pity wells up inside me. Half-remembered lines of poetry come unbidden to my mind: he grows old, he grows old; he shall wear the bottoms of his trousers rolled."[35] The lines from T.S. Eliot's "The Love

Song of J. Alfred Prufrock," which put her in an innocent childlike state of mind, reveal more than the fact that old men no longer wear their trousers the way they did in their youth; they suggest that the ruler's senses have deserted him. He sees the world in simplistic terms, the way children do.

Yet the old man fights against the perception that he has outlived his usefulness in office. Esther imagines him counting his years or months and days in the position. When it is time to put her husband's coffin in the ground, she prepares to walk down to the grave. "The president moves also, and I watch him, an old man still but one who is Commander of the Armed Forces, Defier of Imperialism, and, as he was just moments ago, Orator of the Funeral of Dead Heroes."[36] The widow's tone suddenly becomes cynical and mordant, making reference to the now redundant anti-imperialist rhetoric that has become part of the president's political repertoire. Gappah achieves her goal of exposing the tension in society as soon as the widow's tone turns from pity to derision. We hear immense pain in the widow's tone. She embodies the grief and disappointment we feel at the ruins of the postcolonial country. From the widow's perspective, we behold an old man who has literally and figuratively moved towards the grave, but who, in his spirit of gravity, stubbornly clings on to life at the expense of the nation. Being aware of the absurdity of the incident, we laugh with the widow.

The widow relates the president's funeral speech in a sarcastic tone that exposes the president's grand narrative as a farce. "We must move forward today and strive ahead in togetherness, in harmony, in unity and in solidarity to consolidate the gains of our liberation struggles."[37] The president's catchwords, "togetherness"; "harmony," "unity," and "solidarity" are built around the symbolic relevance of the people's common experience, which is supposed to contrast with everything the colonial master stands for. Secondly, it is his effort to create a common identity for the people. But the people laugh at his efforts because they know that common identity is an illusion. Harmony is an ideological construct which notoriously ignores the body of the individual. In parodying the president's speech, the widow counters the president's abstractness with lightness. "There was a nugget of newness in the use of trillion and not million as a measure of the impossibility of re-colonisation," she says, and goes on to make a subtle comparison between the president's impossible trillion and the unimaginable rate of inflation, that is, between rhetoric and reality: "It is three months since inflation reached three million three hundred and twenty-five per cent per annum, making billionaires of everyone, even maids and gardeners."[38]

In the earlier parts of this book, I discussed the idea that those in a position of power anywhere tend to privilege reason over feelings, the abstract over the body, culture over the individual. This resonates with Elizabeth Anker's critique of the liberal formulation of human rights. In Nnedi Okorafor's *Who Fears Death*, we learn that female genital mutilation is designed to "align a woman's intelligence with her emotions."[39] Abstractions are some of the easiest ways to avoid personal responsibility because they ignore the demands of the other's body. Oppressive institutions rely on the abstractions of ideologies as effective means of control of the body. By his adept uses of nationalist tropes that have obvious symbolic control over the masses, the president successfully maintains his hold on power to the detriment of the citizens. Gappah's goal is to make us laugh, and we do so as soon as we see through the folly of the president's ideas. Even the microphone felt irritated, and "gave a piercing protest at the *trillion trillion*."[40]

Satire "seeks to criticize and correct the behavior of human beings and their institutions by means of humor, wit, and ridicule."[41] According to Jean Weisgerber, "the satirist is a paper tiger: he assaults his victim by proxy, that is, through the medium of language and more especially of literary language." For Weisgerber, the rhetorical feature of satire is "closely related to the satirist's social motive, which consists in disclosing what is 'right' by deriding what is 'wrong.' Satire ultimately aims at enlightening and correcting."[42] Weisgerber further argues that "not only does satire require a social background even when it exposes individual follies or vices, but its aim is to convince as many readers as possible that society, as matters stand, is inferior to what it should be."[43]

One of the ironies in the understanding of heroism in post-independence Zimbabwe lies in the identity of heroes. Who are they? It is emblematic that Esther constantly refers to the hero being buried as "my husband"; she never calls him by name. He remains anonymous even to her; he is therefore a man who can easily be replaced by another man. He is not sufficiently present in her life to mean something to her. He is not even the person she had thought he was, hence her declaration: "I thought I loved him; but that was in another country." Both of them had lived in exile while his compatriots fought the racist, minority government of Ian Smith, and while in exile she "helped him to write furious letters of righteous indignation condemning the white-settler regime and the situation in his country."[44] There in exile, they engaged in highbrow revolutionary discussions associated with Frantz Fanon, Steve Biko, Marx, and Engels. These are obviously heroes of every revolutionary struggle, but Esther's husband, a revolutionary hero, is everything but a true opponent of the oppressor, and he had not been forthright with her; he had made her believe she was a wife who shared in his dreams, an equal, not a subordinate. Esther, however, finds out that he had been married before, and had children whom he gave names that bore the characteristics of revolutionary struggle: "Rwauya, meaning "death has come," and the second Muchagura to mean "you shall repent," and the last Muchakundwa, "you shall be defeated." They are messages for the white oppressors, warning signs to the white man."[45] Given the fierce nationalism in these names, there is little doubt that the dead husband was a true nationalist who did indeed love his people. But we know that the love was nominal just as his dedication to his country was. His heroism was a product of ideology.

Gappah suggests that the hero stands for the ideology of nationalism and, just as Martha Mupengo was a subject of abuse in society, so does the hero's first wife become a victim of abstraction. We learn that the first wife was summarily divorced so that the hero could marry Esther. The issue is not that he divorced his wife; it is how he divorced her. He merely gave her a *gupuro* (a local symbol of divorce) which she would take to her family. Indeed, "he picked out a pot with a red and yellow flower on it and gave it to her as a sign that he had divorced her. She died three years after that."[46] The widow is dispensable, just as the residents of Easterly Farm are.

The divorce incident raises questions about women's rights; it suggests that women are easily disposable. Women are substitutable for one another. Like Shoneyin, Gappah reveals the socio-cultural conditions that shape gender relations. If a man could easily dispense with his wife as if she were a rented car, then there are more questions not only about the man's moral compass, but also the culture that made it possible in the first place. The fact that the divorced woman died three years later speaks to the precariousness of the lives of women in society. Women flourish only in marriages because they depend on men. Given that the hero is presented without a name, it is possible that Gappah sees in him a symbol of the excesses of *chimurenga*;[47] and given the idea of conceiving identity in essentialist paradigms, it is only fitting that the hero's widow mocks the hero as soon as she has narrated his divorce from his wife. "Like the worthless dogs that are his countrymen, my husband believed that his penis was wasted if he was faithful to just one woman."[48] Now that we know about the dead hero, Esther's bluster seems to be in order. Her anger is directed at the beneficiaries of patriarchal privileges. She laughs at their empty performances and reminds us that the casket which has been lowered into the grave is indeed bereft of her husband's body.[49] The most portentous symbol of the emptiness of the postcolonial nation in this respect is the idea of people rallying to bury an empty coffin.

Esther is a means through which Gappah interrogates history, and with her (Esther's) help, we discover that the new, post-Independence nation is a sham. Esther also reminds us of the obligation everyone owes to a world that has been held hostage by its rulers and a socio-cultural system that makes tyranny (political and patriarchal) possible.

When Right Means Life

Shoneyin has demonstrated how the three women, who originally shared Baba Segi, have ganged up against Bolanle for fear that she would deprive them of their own share of their husband, and eventually lay bare their common secret. Subsequently, the relationship among the women becomes one of hatred rather than of solidarity. It is, indeed, revealing that the women turn against Bolanle, who came into the marriage arrangement of her own free will. She is also the one who, acting as a catalyst, threatens to expose the sordidness of their common condition as co-wives. As a catalyst, her role becomes highly symbolic. On the one hand, it exposes the weaknesses of traditional African gender relations. On the other, and this is perhaps pertinent to the women's self-perception and solidarity, Bolanle shows the limitation of women's love of self and of freedom within traditional patriarchal contexts. They are unable to appreciate themselves because of the strictures imposed on them by society. They perceive themselves as having no rights because they have to fight for bare survival. But Shoneyin seems to suggest that the absence of self-appreciation ultimately leads to death. Segi, the first child of the marriage, and the daughter of the matriarch, Iya Segi, accidentally bonds with Bolanle after an incident in the market place. Segi and Bolanle walk together to Bolanle's room, where a plate of food, part of the ongoing birthday festivities, awaits Bolanle. The food is poisoned. Now relishing the comfort that comes with the new friendship with Bolanle, Segi asks Bolanle whether she could taste the food. Bolanle does not deny her request.

Segi's death is richly symbolic, especially given the atmosphere of mutual hatred in which the women live. That hatred leads to the death of one of their own, and it is a signifier of their own death. It is also significative that the poison attacks those body parts that women take pride in: their hair and their breasts. Segi's "breasts were flattened against her chest. What used to be firm, supple skin sagged like beaten leather. All her hair was gone; her scalp shone like a marble."[50] It is also ironic that she confides her secrets and feelings in Bolanle precisely at the time her death looms. She spends the night in Bolanle's room, apparently relishing Bolanle's singular, positive mindset, which flows from her decision to set herself on the path of healing. Their friendship hints at a more positive outlook for women. By bonding with Bolanle, Segi rejects the negative world of her own mother, and welcomes the positive, life-affirming spirit that Bolanle embodies. In Shoneyin's poetics, Bolanle's self-esteem is posited as a life force. Implicitly, to be aware of one's rights is synonymous with being aware of one's life. Shoneyin is concerned with the bodies that are served by that culture or tradition. She imagines individuals enjoying their freedom, making decisions, and being morally responsible for the consequences of those decisions; she imagines them being humans.

In November 2013, Shoneyin organized the Ake Arts and Book Festival (or Ake Festival) with the theme "The Shadow of Memory"[51] in Abeokuta. It attracted many national and international writers and producers of culture. The idea is part of her project of engaging her culture from within. The most significant paradigm-shifting moment of the festival was the adaptation of her already mentioned novel, with emphasis on the gay sexual orientation of one of Baba Segi's wives. Reporting on the event, Christie Watson remarks that:

> the panel discussion about sex and sexuality, which focused on representations of homosexuality in African literatures, was standing room only. It felt radical. At times the discussions felt almost dangerous: the treatment of gay people in Nigeria remains appalling. But Ake gave me hope for the future. The public talking has begun.[52]

In exposing the inner workings of polygamy and introducing the discourse of gay sexual orientation into the minds of her fellow countrymen and women, Shoneyin opens new ways of exploring the African experience beyond the conventional postcolonial discourse that presumes a monolithic African identity and culture. This expansion of the notion of African culture is, in my judgment, part of Shoneyin's project of enhancing human flourishing in her community. She urges us to engage people as individuals who make up the cultures identified as African. Empathy is an important step in that direction.

Gappah also employs the riches of empathy to highlight the abuse of people's human rights in Zimbabwe. The narrative of women ex-soldiers that Yvonne Vera fruitfully explored in *The Stone Virgins*[53] is taken to a new level by Gappah, in "The Maid from Lalapanzi." Gappah engages the myth of the glories of the liberation struggle, which, sadly, have morphed into a state of government dysfunction. *Sisi*Blandina had fought in Zimbabwe's war of liberation. As a girl, her job was to serve in the kitchen and, at night, in the beds of guerillas.

Like most Zimbabweans who have witnessed the struggles of liberation, *Sisi*Blandina still nurses a triumphant frame of mind. When Munya, one of the toddlers she is looking after, complains to her that his sister, Chenai, has jumped over him with her fingers crossed in order to stop him from growing, *Sisi*Blandina corrects him, telling him that the idea of crossing one's fingers while jumping over someone was the invention of white people. "Why must you always believe what those white children tell you? Did their parents not lose the war?"[54] What is important in *Sisi*Blandina's response is not the sense of the children's superstition or lack thereof; it is the tenor of her argument. Whites have lost the war; consequently they have lost every argument, and all moral claims to reality. This does not escape the attention of Chenai, the narrator: "We won the war, we had conquered the conquerors. Our parents said it all the time. The television said it, the radio too. We had won the war."[55] She thus replicates the nationalist ideology of the freedom fighters who are now in power. Yet her story raises questions not only about the nature of *chimurenga*, but also about whether the war was actually won. Did women, for whom *Sisi*Blandina occupies a figurative role, win? Did the people win the war? What about their individual rights and dignities, which have been subjected to the putative glories of the post-Independence world? As a maid, *Sisi*Blandina had already lost out in the new dispensation. Chenai makes a critical observation about how maids are treated in her parents' family. "They came and went, dismissed for various flaws as my mother searched for the perfect housemaid, leaving behind the uniform dress and matching hat that they all wore which seemed to stretch and shrink to fit each one."[56]

Gappah allows Chenai to be a judge of her own mother when she paints her as a tyrant in her own way, lacking empathy for those not in her class. Like other maids, *Sisi*Blandina is seen as having no individuality; she has to fit into the model designed for her by her rich host family, for whom she has sacrificed herself. She is pliant, already humbled by the harsh experience of the war, which, ironically has given her pride of identity, but this will be her undoing. It is revealing, as Chenai tells us, that *Sisi*Blandina now suffers at the hands of women. The maids have no individuality; they are presented in the abstract and are therefore thought not to possess dignity.

The family in which *Sisi*Blandina serves as a maid is figurative of a country that, blindsided by the abstraction of nationalism, has little or no concern for the pains of its members, the less privileged women. While serving the guerillas, *Sisi*Blandina took a revolutionary name, like other boys and girls:

> I wanted to call myself Freedom, but there were already seven with that name, and even one called Freedom-now, and four other people called Liberty. Then one of the commanders told us that we were fighting for autonomy and for self-rule and for self-determination, and so that became my name.[57]

The listing of synonyms for independence exposes the absurdity of Zimbabwe's national autonomy and the condition of individual Zimbabweans. But this is also what prevents her and her people from thinking about their rights. It not only makes the idea redundant; it makes us wonder whether the freedom fighters ever understood what they fought for. After many years, and when it begins to seem as if *Sisi*Blandina will never experience the true love of a man or a family, she falls in love with *Mukoma*George. She is pregnant, and hopes that *Mukoma*George will marry her. But he denies responsibility for the pregnancy, accusing her of sleeping around with men. That was, after all, what she had done during the war, he alleges. In rejecting *Sisi*Blandina, *Mukoma*George exhibits the moral attitude of the pure/impure binary, which undergirds the patriarchal sexual imagination. He fails to go beyond the fact that *Sisi*Blandina was no longer a virgin when he met her. Not being a virgin, for the patriarchal imagination, has moral implications; the woman is impure and undesirable.

*Sisi*Blandina is trapped by her past; despite her *chimurenga* name, she has not been liberated. She has been used by the guerillas in the forest of

Mozambique, and she has been used by *Mukoma*George. She begs Chenai's mother to take her back, but is refused because of her (*Sisi*Blandina's) pregnancy. Rejected by everyone, she drowns herself in the Mukuvisi River. *Sisi*Blandina shares the same fate as that of the first wife of Esther's husband. They are the victims not only of political dysfunction, but also of gender relations, in which women are at a disadvantage.

Notes

1. BBC News, "Davos 2010: South Africa's Zuma Defends Polygamy." http://news.bbc.co.uk/2/hi/8485730.stm (Accessed June 8, 2011).
2. It would amount to cultural arrogance for outsiders to dismiss the law, even if it was pushed and enacted by the male-dominated parliament. It is, however, a different issue if we consider the law from women's perspective. How does the law impact the relationship between two persons, man and woman, who consider themselves as equal in rights and dignity? This, in my judgment, is the more urgent question, one that goes to the core of the moral foundations of the gender relations in that society. See Faith Karimi and Lillian Leposo, "New Kenya Law Legalizes Polygamy; Women's Group Applauds It" (2015). http://www.cnn.com/2014/05/01/world/africa/kenya-polygamy-law/.
3. Nolwazi Mkhwanazi, "Miniskirts and Kangas: The Use of Culture in Constituting Postcolonial Sexuality." http://www.darkmatter101.org/site/2008/05/02/miniskirts-and-kangas-the-use-of-culture-in-constituting-postcolonial-sexuality/ (Accessed May 15, 2013). See also "Timeline of the Jacob Zuma Rape Trial." http://mg.co.za/article/2006-03-21-timeline-of-the-jacob-zuma-rape-trial.
4. Chikwenye Okonjo Ogunyemi, "Womanism: The Dynamics of the Contemporary Black Female Novel in English," in *The Womanist Reader*, ed. Layli Phillips. New York: Routledge, 2006, 31 (Ogunyemi 2006).
5. Emmanuel Levinas, *Totality and Infinity*. Trans. Alphonso Lingis. Pittsburgh: Duquesne University Press, 1969, 22 (Levinas 1969).
6. Lola Shoneyin, *The Secret Lives of Baba Segi's Wives*. New York: William Morrow. 2010, 1 (Shoneyin 2010).
7. Ibid., 1.
8. Terry Eagleton, *After Theory*. New York: Basic Books, 2003, 144 (Eagleton 2003).
9. Ibid.
10. Shoneyin, *Secret Lives*, 135 (Shoneyin 2010).
11. Ibid., 144.

12. Ibid., 91.
13. Ibid., 93.
14. Ibid., 94.
15. Lynn Hunt, *Inventing Human Rights: A History*. New York: W.W. Norton & Company, 2008, 34 (Hunt 2008).
16. Ibid., 39.
17. United Nations, "The Universal Declaration of Human Rights." www.un.org/en/documents/udhr/.
18. Martha Nussbaum, *Love's Knowledge: Essays on Philosophy and Literature*. New York: Oxford University Press, 1990, 5 (Nussbaum 1990).
19. Wilhelm Gottfried Hegel, *Philosophy of Mind: Being Part Three of the Encyclopedia of the Philosophical Sciences* (1830). Ed.William Wallace. Oxford: Clarendon Press, 1971, 170–175 (Wallace 1971).
20. The Dogon myth of creation reveals as much. See Chapter 4 for my discussion of the Dogon myth of creation.
21. Shoneyin, *Secret Lives*, 54 (Shoneyin 2010).
22. Ibid., 55.
23. Ibid., 53–54.
24. Ibid., 59.
25. Ibid., 67.
26. Ibid., 278 (Emphasis in original).
27. Ibid., 16–17.
28. Ibid., 19.
29. Petina Gappah, *An Elegy for Easterly*. London: Faber and Faber, 2009 (Gappah 2009).
30. I am grateful to a reviewer for pointing this out to me.
31. Ibid., 34–37.
32. Ibid., 43.
33. Ibid., 33–34.
34. Nicholas D. More, "Nietzsche's Last Laugh: Ecce Homo as Satire," *Philosophy and Literature*, 35.1 (2011): 2 (More 2011).
35. Gappah, *An Elegy*, 3 (Gappah 2009).
36. Ibid., 5.
37. Ibid., 6.
38. Ibid., 7.
39. Nnedi Okorafor, *Who Fears Death*. New York: Daw Books, 2010, 74 (Okorafor 2010).
40. Ibid., 7.
41. Edwin J. Barton and Glenda A. Hudson, *Contemporary Guide to Literary Terms: With Strategies for Writing Essays About Literature* (2nd edition). Boston: Houghton Mifflin Company, 2004 (Barton and Hudson 2004).

42. J. Weisgerber, "Satire and Irony as Means of Communication," *Comparative Literature Studies*, 10.2 (1973): 159 (Weisgerber 1973).
43. Ibid., 160.
44. Gappah, *An Elegy*, 9 (Gappah 2009).
45. Ibid., 11.
46. Ibid., 11.
47. Shona name for the war of independence.
48. Gappah, *An Elegy*, 11–12 (Gappah 2009).
49. Ibid., 11–12.
50. Shoneyin, *Secret Lives*, 229 (Shoneyin 2010).
51. Ake Festival. www.akefestival.org (Accessed November 8, 2013).
52. Christie Watson, "Ake Festival, Nigeria—Where Kids Want to Fly in Colour," 2013 (Watson 2013). www.bookbrunch.co.uk/article_free.asp?pid=ake_festival_nigeria_where_kids_want_to_fly_in_colour.
53. Yvonne Vera, *The Stone Virgins*. New York: Farrar, Straus and Giroux, 2004 (Vera 2004).
54. Gappah, *An Elegy*, 154 (Gappah 2009).
55. Ibid., 154.
56. Ibid., 158.
57. Ibid., 161.

CHAPTER 6

The Enslaved Body as a Symbol of Universal Human Rights Abuse

Chika Unigwe

As I have shown in the preceding chapters, contemporary African women writers highlight women's rights by addressing the relationship between men and women, and the pain that arises from that. In drawing attention to the pain experienced by individual African women, they make a micro argument for empathy as a portent tool for human rights. In this chapter, I discuss Chika Unigwe's novel *On Black Sisters' Street* as segue to the macro argument about human rights. In the introductory chapter, I raised the question of whether human rights are universal and a Western invention. Unigwe suggests an answer by urging a broader thinking about human rights in Africa. She does that by situating her narrative in Africa and Europe. She establishes her belief in the universality of human rights by making a United Nations agency an instrument that enhances people's rights in Africa.

In *On Black Sisters' Street*, women are sex slaves, and I read the narration as a metaphor for the relationship between men and women in societies that operate under a rigid, oppressive patriarchal order. In treating slavery as a metaphor, Unigwe has precedence in Buchi Emecheta's *The Slave Girl*. Slavery is, without doubt, the worst expression of failure in intersubjective relationships. The relationship is not that of person to person, but rather that of person to object. The enslaver does not consider the enslaved as a person with rights and dignity; the enslaved is a thing. Like Emecheta, Unigwe understands her project as a writer as enhancing the global understanding of women's rights and dignity. She wrote a doctoral dissertation on the efforts of Igbo women writers before her to draw attention to the inequalities and unfairness faced by women in their society. She herself regretted that she came from a background in which women were considered as second-class citizens. But these women did not succumb to the inferior positions their tradition had subjected them to. They told stories and, according to Unigwe, "their stories first sensitized [her] to the gender-inequality around [her], as a young girl growing up in Enugu and gave [her] the first stirrings of rebellion."[1] Unigwe has discussed the works of Flora Nwapa, who is to African women's fiction what Chinua Achebe is to African fiction in general. She has also discussed Zulu Sofola, who occupies in the world of drama the same position that Flora Nwapa has in fiction. In *On Black Sisters' Street*, Unigwe fleshes out the arguments she had established in her doctoral dissertation. The novel is about the outright objectification of women. It documents the plights of female African bodies fleeing pain and annihilation: Sisi, Ama, Efe, and Joyce are young women from Nigeria and Sudan. They work as sex slaves in Belgium. As Jack Donnelly argues:

> Human rights are not just abstract values such as liberty, equality, and security. They are rights [and they need] particular social practices to realize those values. A human right thus should not be confused with the values or aspirations underlying it or with enjoyment of the object of the right.[2]

To think about human rights is to think about how abstract values affect my relation to others, that is, how values are translated into social practices; it is to provide answers to the question: What are other people to me? It makes no difference whether this other is my relative or a stranger.

SLAVERY AS A METAPHOR OF ABUSE OF HUMAN RIGHTS

In *On Black Sisters' Street*,[3] four African women work as prostitutes in Brussels. One of them, who falls in love with a white man, attempts to escape the control of their pimp and is killed by the mafia. Her death brings the remaining three closer, and the fear they have for their lives moves them to tell one another their stories and to give a closer consideration to those lives. Can humans own other humans the way we own pets or other animals? This question goes to the heart of article 3 of the Universal Declaration of Human Rights (UDHR): "Everyone has the right to life, liberty and security of person."[4] The naturalist school of human rights, to which the UDHR owes its philosophy, as Marie-Bénédicte Dembour argues, would answer in the negative to the above question.[5] Humans cannot own other humans. That would be slavery, and slavery is a crime against humanity. Yet, the fundamental assumption of patriarchy raises the question of whether women's bodies really belong to them. Patriarchy assumes that women's bodies belong to society, that is, men.

On Black Sisters' Street derives its depth largely from its subliminal association with transatlantic slavery, which is one of the grossest instances of the abuse of people's rights in history. Dele owns a business, "Dele and Sons Ltd: Import-Export Specialists"[6] that offers women "a passage to Europe."[7] His company purports to help girls escape the misery of Nigeria, which he calls a nonsensical country. Most of the girls are well aware of the type of jobs they will be doing in Europe. Nevertheless, given the economic stress they and their families face in Nigeria, they grudgingly agree to take part in the business. In exchange for making the necessary connections and for sending them to Europe, Dele charges them €30,000 each. They have to pay only when they arrive in Europe.[8] They instantly become slaves—if only indentured slaves. Dele's use of the phrase "passage to Europe" is one of Unigwe's deliberate acts of association with transatlantic slavery, the Middle Passage. In so doing she provides us with answers to the question that these displaced bodies in pain ask about human rights in Africa. We are alerted to the fact that these women are not being accorded the dignities they deserve as human beings, who, according to the UDHR, "are born free and equal in dignity and rights"; rather, they are being accorded a passage just like their kin had been three centuries before.[9]

Dele is a synecdoche for the patriarchs of his society; his relation to women is that of master to his servants. Women exist in his life to serve his material needs, which includes functioning as sex slaves. If we understand Dele as a synecdoche, we must also read his relationship to women as figurative of the male–female relationship in Africa. While seeking to convince Sisi that she is a good product, Dele praises her body parts in obviously mercantile language. "See your backside, kai! Who talk say na dat Jennifer Lopez get the finest yansh."[10] Dele obviously fails to see Sisi as a person with dignity; he sees her as an object, something whose utilitarian value easily stands out. We observe a parallel between Dele and Baba Segi in regard to their attitudes towards women. There is nothing to suggest that Sisi sees herself as possessing rights and dignity; in this respect they are like Baba Segi's first three wives. Furthermore, unlike the African slaves of the past,

Sisi is complicit in her objectification, and this presents a unique moral quandary. How can one empathize with a person who willfully accepts her own suffering? Yet it is important to understand the backstory of her self-destruction. The severe economic conditions of her country have robbed her of the courage to lay claim to rights. What occupies her mind at the moment she agrees to Dele's terms is how to escape the economic misery of her country; yet in agreeing to his conditions, she runs into a more difficult situation. She becomes someone's property. Based on our discussion of polygamy in the preceding chapter, we establish a parallel between the conditions that drive women into polygamous marriage and those that force them to become sex slaves. In regard to women's dignity, polygamy is not better than sex slavery. Both accord women no equal relation to men.

Nigerian sex trafficking in Europe is a highly organized business just like transatlantic slavery. In Belgium Sisi is received by Madam, the European representative of Dele's company; Madam promptly seizes Sisi's passport and tells her to declare herself an asylum seeker, a gesture meant to underscore her lack of status.[11] Madam's role in the enslavement of other women is troubling. But, as Althusser argues, no ideology functions without the cooperation of its victims. Ideology co-opts individuals and makes them subject.[12] The seizure of Sisi's passport is eloquent enough to let Sisi know that she has lost any claim to rights. But when her application is rejected, Madam shows no surprise. She tells Sisi that the rejection papers issued to her by the Ministry of Foreign Affairs mean nothing, and goes on to enunciate the symbolic relevance of the seizure of the passport: "All you need to know is that you're persona non grata in this country. You do not exist. Not here...Now you belong to me."[13] In Madam therefore, patriarchal ideology disrupts the relationship between women so that they, too, see one another as objects. Her utterance brings to full circle in Europe the dehumanization that was begun in Africa. Again, this appears to be a subtle recreation of the experience of transatlantic slavery. In Europe, during that era, African slaves, some of whom had been betrayed by their village or townspeople, became part of the estates of their many European slave owners, just as Sisi has become part of Dele's company. Unigwe dramatizes the crime of modern sex trafficking in Africa in hopes of rousing people to indignation, and thereby establishing the universal application of the principles of human rights. If we condemn transatlantic slavery—as we should—then we should also condemn Dele's enslavement of his fellow Africans today.

On Black Sisters' Street plays with the theme of slavery and racism not only by allusion to transatlantic slavery, but also directly through the story of Joyce, who is otherwise known as Alek. She is a Sudanese refugee who was raped into unconsciousness by members of the Janjaweed militia, who called her a "stupid African slave."[14] In Joyce's story we are reminded of an often neglected aspect of slavery in African history, which is that from the Arabian Peninsula. The Janjaweed militias obviously did not see themselves as Africans. By the time Alek has regained consciousness, the militia has left; she is cared for by the members of a UN refugee organization. It is important to remark here that the UN has organized refugee camps in keeping with its commitment to the concept of human rights. At this point, the UN acts not only as an immediate foil to the Janjaweed militia in Alek's world; it also acts as a symbol of Unigwe's belief in universal solidarity, one that defies ethnic or racial boundaries, and aims at the humanity of each individual person. The Janjaweed inflict pain while the UN agency provides care. The UN therefore functions on figurative and literal levels. On the figurative level, it stands for the inviolability of human dignity, an idea that was inscribed in its human rights charter. On the literal level, it actually takes care of Alek.

Unigwe does not suggest that the abuse of human rights is only an interracial crime; it is also intra-racial. It manifests itself not only in violent forms like that of the Janjaweed militia; it shows itself also in more subtle ways, such as in regarding members of other groups within one's own race or ethnicity as unmarriageable and therefore of less value as persons. At the refugee camp, Alek meets Polycarp, a Nigerian soldier on a peacekeeping mission in Sudan. He falls in love with her and takes her back to Nigeria where they live as partners with intentions of starting a family. But this is not to be. Polycarp's mother rejects Alek, claiming that she is a stranger; she insists that Polycarp, her first son, should marry an Igbo girl, not a foreigner, who is thought to be inferior and by implication, as possessing no dignity. Alek is shocked and disappointed by this experience of prejudice, which she had thought she had escaped. Did the UN not restore her belief in the universal brotherhood and sisterhood of all people? The actions and beliefs of Polycarp's mother are, in regard to Alek's dignity, equally heinous. We have thus far different levels of disregard for the rights of individuals: slavery, rape, and ethnicism. Unfortunately, the ethnicism exhibited by Polycarp's mother pales when Polycarp leads Alek to Dele, knowing that Dele will help her make the "passage to Europe." And, like the African slaves centuries before, Alek receives a new name, one thought out by Polycarp and Dele: Joyce. Unigwe displays some touch of irony in the selection of name for this "chattel." Joyce is supposed to announce or bring *joy* to Alek. But she obviously does not see it that way. She feels that she has been objectified:

> Dele pointed at her, slapped his thighs and burst into fresh gales of laughter, holding his head in his hands, as if the force of the laughter would snap it off.... Anger rose in Alek's throat and threatened to make her shout but she pushed it down. She had no energy left for anger. The soldiers that raped her that night in Daru had taken her strength, and Polycarp's betrayal had left her unwilling to seek it back.[15]

It is perhaps no accident that the Janjaweed, Polycarp, and Dele all have targeted Alek (Joyce) as a woman. With them, the oppression of women crosses geographical boundaries and becomes no longer just cultural, but transnational.[16]

Dreams as an Expression of Human Rights

In her macro argument for universal human rights, Unigwe allows us to look at the socio-economic realities that enhance the objectification of humans, and how patriarchy condemns women's bodies to the status of mere objects that are meant to serve society, that is, men. Unigwe exposes some of the remote causes of the dysfunctional system that ultimately encourages the dehumanization of women. Some of them have to do in part with the history of colonialism, which caused the loss of fundamental human solidarity in Africa. Colonialism, which forced different ethnicities (nations) into one state, indirectly sowed the seed of mutual distrust among these peoples. Of course, as Fanon states, there is also a failure on the part of the colonized to adopt ethnicity-transcendent moral visions that would allow people to see individuals, even from other ethnicities, as having rights and dignities. For Fanon, the nationalist consciousness in postcolonial states morphed into various forms of "race feeling."[17] In Fanon's thinking, and in line with Unigwe's narrative, post-independence African states have yet to become exemplary spaces where individuals, regardless of ethnicities, can achieve their dreams of true freedom and human rights. In such African states as Nigeria, many people have abandoned the honest search for true freedom and solidarity; they fight for survival, even if it means enslaving one another

Ethnic thinking and patriarchy are ideological; both of them diminish the humanity of the other. Unigwe draws on the pitfalls of ethnic thinking to demonstrate the effects of abstraction on people in general and women in particular. Her ultimate goal is to expose the contexts in which dehumanization and human rights abuses take place. Sisi has dreams, and she eventually dies without realizing them. Dreams are the expressions of that intangible thing she has in common with the rest of humanity, her wish to relate to the men and women of her society in more meaningful ways. These dreams could also be seen as the expression of her human rights, which are universal. Her dreams also link her with other characters in the novel. We get to know this especially because through the shock of her death, the others—Joyce, Efe, and Ama—reveal their own dreams to one another. They realize that they share a common destiny that demands their solidarity with each other, if only to keep their dreams alive. Their dreams are also Unigwe's way of demonstrating the universality of human rights. When we encounter Sisi (born Chisom) at Efe's birthday party, she seems to be at an emotional crossroads, having by now experienced the indignity of her new profession. Yet, having come from a dysfunctional society, one that, in Fanon's thinking, has failed to expand its nationalist aspirations to embrace universal moral paradigms, Sisi knows she has no better alternatives. In Nigeria she would have ended up in a worse situation than where she is now. Before embarking on her passage to Belgium, she lived in squalor in Lagos, having shared an apartment with her parents in Ogba:

> Chisom dreamed of leaving Lagos. This place has no future. She tried to imagine another year in the flat her father rented in Ogba. She tried not to breathe too deeply because doing so would be inhaling the stench of mildewed dreams. (15–18)

Like most postcolonial fathers who believed in the promises of modernity that independence would usher in, her father's dream of a university education was tied to his belief in his daughter's destined future: "Yet, two years after leaving university, Chisom was still mainly unemployed."[18] Jobs are not offered on the basis of merit, but of ethnic or tribal connections.[19] Things get worse when her father loses his job of 24 years because, as he observed, "I am not from Lagos State."[20]

If we understand Sisi's dreams as expressions of human rights, then the society that keeps those dreams from being realized also actively obstructs her human rights. But it is also noteworthy that some dreams are dreamed without regard for the human person as an end, but only as a means to an end. When Chisom (Sisi) was born:

> a gap-toothed soothsaying neighbor... raised the new baby up to the skies, looked deep into her future and declared to the waiting parents, "This girl here has a bright future ahead of her ooo. You are very lucky parents oooo".[21]

The soothsayer saw in the child's future her utilitarian value to her parents, a promise of good luck for them. Their luck was not based on the life of the child in the here and now, or on the child as an end in herself, but on the future of the child, on what the child will achieve. To be sure, every parent wishes the best for their children, but in this instance it is clear that the hopes and joys of Sisi's parents are rooted in her future only on the basis of the expectation that she will take care of them. The fulfillment of the soothsayer's prophecy comes in the nature of Sisi's utility, in the glitzy lights of brothels.[22] Unigwe has taken seriously Terry Eagleton's idea about feminism examining the texture of human existence, and in Sisi's story she proves that one cannot judge humans in the abstract. Feminism is not about abstract formulations or ideological stances towards people; it is about taking individual lives seriously.

The ideologies of patriarchy and capitalism also turn the former victims into victimizers. A Nigerian sex worker has yet to pay off her "indenture," after which she can purchase her own girls. She plans to buy African girls from Brussels because it is more convenient to get girls who are already in the country.[23]

It is ironic and unsettling that Efe, a former sex slave, plans to buy other women in order to set up her own business. She appears to have learned nothing from her own experience of pain. We understand that through her own history of objectification, she has lost esteem for herself and those who look like her. One would think that a victim of violence would be in a better position to understand others who go through what they have experienced. We know, however, that that is not always the case. A lot has to do with the system in which the victims find themselves. They internalize the oppression that has subjected them to pain and humiliation. It is therefore not surprising that Efe has failed to exhibit empathy toward others in a situation like hers. Efe has been hailed by the ideology that has kept her a slave; she is willing to serve the machinery of oppression because through that she gains power and becomes a subject. The problem is therefore not just the dysfunctional state in which the people live, but also the people's willingness to make profit from that state even if it means violating others. In this way, Unigwe highlights the importance of attention to personal moral responsibility, that is, people's duty to break the cycle that turns the oppressed into oppressors. This cycle could be broken if people raise questions about the degree to which they may be complicit in the inhumanity of their system.

WOMEN IN SEARCH OF LOST DIGNITY

In Chapter 4, I discussed Elaine Scarry's idea of physical pain as destroying language, how it reduces us to the prelinguistic stage of human development, the stage in which tears are forms of communication.[24] Scarry's reading of physical pain as destroying language equally applies to Unigwe's narrative in the sense that the characters' silence and tears challenge people to respond. In *On Black Sisters' Street*, the pain of the characters we have thus far encountered seeks to make not only political but also moral demands. From the moment Sisi has her first client, the moment she has sexual intercourse with a stranger for money against her will, she realizes she has lost what is most valuable to her: her dignity. She is clueless as to what to do with the first client: "She [sits] still, her second glass of beer untouched, her heart heavy with a sadness that was close to a rage." She tells herself: "*This is not me. I am not here. I am at home, sleeping in my bed. This is not me. This is not me. This is somebody else. Another body.*"[25] When her first client forces himself on her, "she baptize[s] herself into it with tears...feeling intense pain wherever he touche[s], like he [i]s searing her with a razor blade."[26] Sisi's pains are not transient, and they are especially relevant because they are her efforts to salvage her dignity; they are her cry for help, and they appeal to people's empathic faculties. In her desperate search for dignity, she seeks to connect with other people. It is in light of Scarry's understanding of pain as having political consequences that we can interpret Unigwe's feminist sensibility as a political statement. It is political to the degree that it raises fundamental questions about the organization of society. I employ the understanding of politics as used by Hannah Arendt in *The Human Condition*, which suggests that it is a fundamental organization in human community.[27]

In Chapter 5, I argued that contemporary African women writers are interested in human flourishing in African communities. Their notion of community is, as Martha Nussbaum put it, a "community of human beings."[28] The same can be said of Unigwe's vision. These communities are to be understood as diverse rather than homogenous, multicolored rather than monochromatic, empathic rather than inconsiderate of the pain of others. It is a community in which the ideals of the UDHR are realized. Sisi's story alone stands as a homage to such a community ideal, in the sense that it tells of her yearning for a world in which people treat one another with dignity. While standing in line to register as an asylum seeker, she wonders what story each person standing in line has to tell, what fate brought them there. She wishes she could ask a man next to her what his story is: "What's your story? You want to hear mine? Would you like to trade stories? Mine for yours?"[29] Her question "what's your story?" is another way of framing the Cavarero/Butler question, "who are you?" We get a glimpse of Sisi's inner life as one who is aware that she has a story, that her story is a means to connect to others. Her story is her only possession; it is also what she has in common with the rest of humanity. It occupies the same position in her life as does her dream: both are intangible possessions, her rights. The larger, more embracing morality that Eagleton talked about urges us to see and respond to the life conditions of this individual who tells a story that mirrors some aspects of our lives.

As Margaret Atwood argues, one of the reasons we tell our stories and listen to those of others is to invite people to partake of our lives, and for us to partake of theirs. For her, stories have anthropological and ethical relevance.[30] Granted, there could be many other reasons we might be interested in other people's stories, one of which could be to compare ourselves with those people. But in most cases, we are moved by other people's pain. Literature does not prescribe how people should live. Rather it exposes the "texture and quality" of characters as figurative of the way we live. Literature is a conscious reaching out to the world in a text. Literary texts are worlds packaged in accessible forms; they speak to us through figures that we, by generous acts of suspension of disbelief, take to be real. Stories are already mediated since what we experience in the text is a reflected experience of the other (the narrator) and the author. As I have pointed out in the introduction, Martha Nussbaum draws attention to the important connection between form and content, and points out that in narratives, "a view of life is told."[31] We respond to this view of life and its characters as if they existed in (our) reality.[32] Seizing on what Lawrence Buell has called "the turn to ethics" in literary discourse, Amanda Anderson explores the importance of character as a "more elaborate, individualized way of life," that evokes "settled dispositions, habits, and temperament."[33] She explains that any discussion of character:

> should include a recognition of the historical conditions out of which beliefs and values emerge, as well as the possibility for the ongoing recognition of the many forces (psychological, social, and political) that can thwart, undermine, or delay the achievement of such virtues and goods.[34]

Anderson's discussion of character is consistent with what Terry Eagleton identified as feminism's contribution to literary and cultural theories. Eagleton argues that feminism explores "the texture and quality of human behavior as richly and sensitively as [it] can."[35] Anderson's and Eagleton's ideas agree with what Boyce Davies's statement about the standard for critiquing African women's writings. Anderson's thinking also points to the understanding of characters in a novel as a way to explore people's dignities and their human rights. It is in light of the power of literature to bring the pains and joys of our fellow humans to our attention that I understand not only Unigwe's writing but also other African women's writings, which center heavily on Africa without reference to the West as an imperial agent. I have argued elsewhere, citing Richard Priebe's essay, that violence in African literature is not portrayed merely for pornographic ends. Rather, contemporary African writers call attention to the African body in pain. I echoed Priebe's argument that "we need a rhetoric of motives, and perhaps a grammar of motives," for their representations.[36] Unigwe's motive is ethical given her attention to people's pain.

It is the handwriting of pain on Sisi's body that attracts Luc, a white man, to her. Luc responds to Sisi's call for empathy, to her humanity. He even falls in love with her. Luc recognizes Sisi's dignity and rights as a human being. He is ready to help her. At this point, when she finally makes the decision to escape the control of Dele's company, Sisi meets her death at the hands of Segun, who is the brothel's handyman as well as being an important member of the company.[37] It is ironic that it is a white man who recognizes Sisi's humanity at the same time that her fellow African sees her as an object. There is, of course, nothing essentialist in this gesture. That irony suggests that love and human dignity are universal, and their recognition is not bound to color or ethnic origin; it is also Unigwe's way of suggesting that human rights are universal.

Sisi's death, the ultimate marker of her humanity, brings her former colleagues to reflect on their own humanity and their dignity. Her death becomes cathartic as well as catalytic, especially with regard to stories and recognition of our humanity and that of others.[38] The narrator takes us through the backstories of the other women: Ama and Efe. Shortly after Ama turned eight, her stepfather began to molest her sexually. During the night of her eighth birthday he stole into her room and "fumbled under her nightdress."[39] As time went on, he began to have sex with her.[40] Since then, Ama's dream had been to flee her environment and to escape to London.[41] Perhaps more painful than the actual sex abuse was the fact that her mother did not believe Ama when she eventually told her of her experience. We understand that Ama's mother suppressed the knowledge or belief that her husband was abusing her daughter. She depended on her husband for sustenance. Thus while we are left with the impression that women fail to show solidarity with their fellow victims of patriarchal violence, the undercurrent narrative describes how an oppressive system turns them against one another: mothers against daughters. The idea of a mother turning against her daughter and of lack of solidarity among women recalls the situations in Chinelo Okparanta's stories, "Fairness" and "Wahala." The patriarchal system that exploits women sets them against one another in the manner of divide and conquer.

At the age of 16, Efe begins trading her body for cash with Titus, 45 years old. When Efe's mother dies, Efe's father starts drinking, and the responsibility of holding the family together falls back on the 16-year old, who has to quit school. Titus promises Efe money in return for sex. After this initial painful experience, sex with Titus becomes a routine, and she eventually becomes pregnant. Titus abandons her; she has to do menial work in order to support her child and her siblings. As a teenager with a child, Efe sees herself as damaged goods.[42] As these women are linked by their dreams, so are they bound by their resolve to reclaim their dignity in a world whose structure has none for them.

As is already evident, what all these women have in common is the fact that their world sees them as means to its ends rather than as ends in themselves. Simon Baron-Cohen has argued that evil is no more than "empathy erosion." It is the situation in which people begin to treat other people as objects. Those people who treat others as objects have "Zero Degrees of Empathy," and this is for Baron-Cohen the force behind what has always been identified as evil.[43] People inflict pain on other people because they are unable to imagine themselves in the position of those on whom pain is inflicted. Stories help us bridge the gap between us and others; they enhance empathy and connection between peoples. These stories allow us to understand feminism as taking an interest in the dignity of individual women, rather than adopting an ideology that seeks to deliver a group. As Efe, Ama, and Joyce tell their stories to one another, they realize the degree to which they have been humiliated, and they ask questions of moral and existential significance. Most importantly, they offer one another recognition just by listening to one another's accounts. To listen to a person's stories is to recognize the person; it is to complete the storyteller's circle of subjectivization. Having listened to each other's life histories and therefore having affirmed one another's humanity, they realize how offensive it was that Madam showed no feelings of loss at the death of Sisi. She merely shrugs it off and promptly demanded that they go about their business as usual. But Joyce can no longer take it. She shouts:

> We're human beings! Why should we take it? Sisi is dead and all Madam can think of is business. Doesn't Sisi deserve respect from her? What are we doing? Why should she treat us any how and we just take it like dogs?[44]

Joyce's bluster is a cry for help. It is also an acknowledgement of her own dignity, and an attempt to reclaim her human rights. Yet she and her fellows are well aware that they are trapped in a world marked with vicious profiteering. While acknowledging the truth of Joyce's words, Ama tries to let her understand that there is little they can do. Madam works with the police. Yet Joyce does not want to accept the situation. She harbors the belief that the police would come to the slaves' rescue if only they could summon the courage to report Madam. The only support for that belief is her instinctive trust in the inviolability of her rights as a human being and in her trust that humanity has the means to conquer evil. She makes her own personal declaration of human rights: "Madam treats us like animals. Why are we doing this? ... Madam has no right to our bodies, and neither does Dele."[45] Her words sound as if she were reading from the official UN document, especially article 4, which states that "no one shall be held in slavery or servitude; slavery and the slave trade shall be prohibited in all their forms."[46] Joyce's words sum up the moral core of the narrative world of *On Black Sisters' Street*. In spite of everything she has experienced, she still clings to the universal truth that all persons are created equal, that they are endowed with rights, and that no one should be subjected to inhuman or degrading treatment or punishment.

Historical Consciousness and Human Rights

In *A Room of One's Own*, Virginia Woolf argues for the relevance of literary tradition to the individual talent. She, of course, gives this modernist idea, shared also by T.S. Eliot, a characteristic feminist bent:

> For we think back through our mothers if we are women. It is useless to go to the great men for help, however much one may go to them for pleasure... The weight, the pace, the stride of a man's mind are too unlike her own for her to lift anything substantial from him successfully... Perhaps the first thing she would find, setting pen to paper, was that there was no common sentence ready for her use.[47]

As well as the relevance of tradition, Woolf suggests solidarity among women. To understand the need for resistance and struggle for human rights, one only needs to look back to how people like oneself had been treated. The awareness of how women have been treated in history would invariably nourish the consciousness of solidarity among them. No one can articulate the pains and joys of being a woman more than women. The only person an adolescent female can turn to for confirmation of the changes taking place in her body is her mother or elder sisters. Men have no experience of such, and when they narrate about the world, they do so from the wealth of their own experiences. Woolf argues that male writers construct sentences "out of their own needs for their own uses," and their uses have largely flourished at the expense of women.[48] It is therefore the task of women to rediscover their images and themselves from the spoils of history.

In the introductory part of this chapter, I mentioned Unigwe's doctoral dissertation about her literary foremothers. I interpret her project in light of Virginia Woolf's injunction that women think through their mothers. In that dissertation Unigwe examined Igbo women's writing as "counter-discourses to oral traditions," the latter of which she identifies as a trove of patriarchal epistemology that hinder women's rights. She also examines how women's writing challenges "the dominant (written) male tradition" and their characterizations of women. These women writers, Unigwe argues, "transgress the boundary set for them by an earlier male-dominated tradition." Equally important is the fact that "female authors have been creating their own traditions."[49]

Unigwe's discussion of Flora Nwapa as a writer is emblematic of her understanding of her foremothers as champions of women's rights.

Nwapa, for Unigwe, "commits herself to first righting the fallacy about women in her society. *Efuru* is also principally important because it signifies women as the text. Efuru is its protagonist. The text is both her and of her."[50] Unigwe observes how Nwapa creates two women characters as contrasts in order to enhance her argument about the representation of women in society. Efuru's mother is largely absent; all we know about her comes from what other characters, mainly men, say about her. So they define her, shape her identity: "The impression we get of Efuru's mother is that she is a female contained within the patriarchal order. She is beautiful and in life has never annoyed her husband. Her absence can be read as a lack of substance."[51] It is therefore no surprise that Nwapa creates Efuru as an opposite of her mother. Where her mother was seen only as an absence, she is a presence. Efuru's presence therefore more than makes up for her mother's absence. For Unigwe, "it is obvious that Nwapa's reason for writing this book is to create a character like Efuru, a character who challenges the truth of Igbo women as submissive (as pronounced in folktales and encouraged in proverbs)."[52]

The critical observations Unigwe makes about Flora Nwapa apply to most other pioneer women writers: they seek to establish women as a presence rather than an absence; where women have been presented as submissive and voiceless in oral narratives, or works by men, they are presented as assertive and as having agency in women's narratives. In *On Black Sisters' Street*, Unigwe extends Nwapa's task of making women present. This she does by exposing the system that conspires to make them an absence. Making women present, or bringing those characters to our axis of empathy is understood as her effort to highlight their human rights. Furthermore, making women present means drawing attention to the supremacy of the body in regards to rights.

Conclusion: The Rights of One Are the Rights of All

Having identified and honored her foremothers, and having established the tradition of Igbo women writers, Unigwe carefully positions herself among these women, and highlights the unique challenge facing her generation of writers: "If knowledge is power, then Igbo women of my generation are empowering themselves to carry on the fight begun by the pioneers."[53]

Unigwe is not interested in presenting images of strong women, or necessarily in challenging the stereotypical images of women. That work has already been done by her foremothers. She is more interested in drawing attention to the bodies of women as a theater of universal human rights abuses. What she has done in *On Black Sisters' Street* can best be understood with the help of what Toni Morrison has identified as one of the most important challenges of our times. Morrison is a master in the art of storytelling as a means of preserving memory and survival. In November 2006, she inaugurated a six-week, multidisciplinary exhibition in Paris titled "Etranger Chez Soi." As the presiding spirit of the exhibition, she chose Theodore Gericault's painting *The Raft of the Medusa* (1819) as the focal point of the exhibition. *The Raft of the Medusa* is a depiction of the tragedy of the French ship *Medusa* off the coast of Senegal. In June of 1816, the *Medusa* set sail to the Senegalese port of Saint-Louis. The ship sailed too close to the African shoreline and hit a sandbar. After the wealthy and the well connected had been saved, the rest, numbering more than 100, were forced onto a makeshift raft. It sailed for more than two weeks in stormy seas. There were cases of brutal murders, insanity, and cannibalism on board, and only about 15 passengers survived.

In Morrison's reading, the survivors depicted in the painting have a story to tell; they present an effective metaphor for the millions who, in our times, are set adrift, wandering "like nomads between despair and hope, breath and death." The bodies of present-day migrants, mostly on ships to Europe and Australia, or crossing the boundary to the US, tell stories, and their stories have a common theme: they demand that we witness people as bodies fleeing pain and extinction and that we accord them respect and dignity. Morrison draws special attention to "the body as the real and final home" of reality; to lose it is to lose everything, and for one to control another body is to control everything that comes with the body.[54] What Morrison says about the bodies of the present-day migrants applies to the bodies of the four women around whom the narrative of *On Black Sisters' Street* revolves. It is also the story of African women fleeing patriarchal oppression. Their flight can be seen as a symbol of a universal call for the inviolability of every individual body's dignity. They represent *every body* fleeing oppression, and seeking a place where that dignity can be assured. We recall what Richard Rorty said about the world deriving moral progress from descriptions of individual lives rather than from philosophical or religious treatises. We empathize with people whose stories we know, and we even love to do so.

To write about the wrongs of society is to take steps towards righting them by drawing people's attention to them. Unigwe has undertaken nothing less in *On Black Sisters' Street*. Slavery in Africa is not a thing of the past; it is very much alive just as it is in many other societies, including those in the West. Chattel slavery, to be sure, may be a thing of the past, but people are still being exploited and held against their will in bondage. In many ways the oppressive patriarchal structures in many African societies hold women in servitude, or in conditions close to that.

Notes

1. Chika Unigwe, *In the Shadow of Ala. Igbo Women Writing as an Act of Righting*. Ph.D. Thesis. Leiden University, 2004, 140 (Unigwe 2004).
2. Jack Donnelly, *Universal Human Rights in Theory and Practice*. Ithaca: Cornell University Press, 2003, 11 (Donnelly 2003).
3. Chika Unigwe, *On Black Sisters' Street*. London: Vintage, 2009 (Unigwe 2009).
4. United Nations, "The Universal Declaration of Human Rights." www.un.org/en/documents/udhr/ (Accessed October 5, 2011) (United Nations 2015a).
5. Marie-Bénédicte Dembour, "What Are Human Rights? Four Schools of Thought," *Human Rights Quarterly*, 32.1 (2010): 2–4.
6. Unigwe, *Black Sisters*, 78 (Unigwe 2009).
7. Ibid., 247.
8. Ibid., 32–35.
9. United Nations, 1948.
10. Unigwe, *Black Sisters*, 42 (Unigwe 2009).
11. Ibid., 120.
12. Louis Althusser, *Lenin and Philosophy*. Trans. Ben Brewster. New York: Monthly Review Press, 1971, 170–177 (Althusser 1971).
13. Unigwe, *Black Sisters*, 182 (Unigwe 2009).
14. Ibid., 190.
15. Ibid., 231.
16. To be sure, I do not mean to conflate "internationalism" with "universalism." I think, however, that the idea that the concern for the dignity of the body cuts across boundaries of ethnicity and race is precisely what the "universal" in the UDHR means.
17. Frantz Fanon, *The Wretched of the Earth*. Trans. Constance Farrington. London: Penguin Books, 1967, 127 (Fanon 1967).
18. Unigwe, *Black Sisters*, 21 (Unigwe 2009).
19. Ibid., 23.
20. Ibid., 33.
21. Ibid., 245–246.

22. Ibid., 245.
23. Ibid., 278.
24. Elaine Scarry, *The Body in Pain: The Making and Unmaking of the World.* New York: Oxford University Press, 1985, 19 (Scarry 1985).
25. Ibid., 212 (emphasis in original).
26. Ibid., 213.
27. Hannah Arendt, *The Human Condition.* Chicago: University of Chicago Press, 1998 (Arendt 1998).
28. Martha Nussbaum, "Patriotism and Cosmopolitanism," in *For Love of Country: Debating the Limits of Patriotism*, ed. Joshua Cohen. Boston: Beacon Press, 1996, 4 (Nussbaum 1996).
29. Unigwe, *Black Sisters*, 173 (Unigwe 2009).
30. Margaret Atwood, "Why We Tell Stories." 2010. *Big Think.* www.bigthink.com/ideas/24259 (Accessed June 3, 2012) (Atwood 2010).
31. Martha Nussbaum, *Love's Knowledge: Essays on Philosophy and Literature.* New York: Oxford University Press, 1990, 5 (Nussbaum 1990).
32. See also Wolfgang Iser, *The Act of Reading: A Theory of Aesthetic Response.* Baltimore: The Johns Hopkins Press, 1978 (Iser 1978).
33. Amanda Anderson, *The Way We Argue Now: A Study in the Culture of Theory.* Princeton University Press, 2006, 118 (Anderson 2006).
34. Ibid., 122.
35. Terry Eagleton, *After Theory.* New York: Basic Books, 2003, 143 (Eagleton 2003).
36. Richard Priebe, "Literature, Community, and Violence: Reading African Literature in the West, Post-9/11," Research in African Literatures, 36.2 (2005): 48 (Priebe 2005).
37. Unigwe, *Black Sisters*, 293 (Unigwe 2009).
38. Ibid., 180.
39. Ibid., 132.
40. Ibid., 47.
41. Ibid., 134.
42. Ibid., 75.
43. Simon Baron-Cohen, *Zero Degrees of Empathy: A New Theory of Human Cruelty.* New York: Allen Lane, 2011, 4–9.
44. Ibid., 289.
45. Ibid., 290.
46. United Nations, "The Universal Declaration of Human Rights." www.un.org/en/documents/udhr/.
47. Virginia Woolf, *A Room of One's Own.* New York: A Harvest Book, 1989 (original 1929), 76 (Woolf 1989).
48. Ibid., 77.
49. Unigwe, *In the Shadow of Ala*, 2 (Unigwe 2004).

50. Ibid., 11.
51. Ibid., 17.
52. Ibid., 26.
53. Ibid., 140.
54. Alan Riding, "Rap and Film at the Louvre? What's Up With That?" *The New York Times,* 2006. www.nytimes.com/2006/11/21/books/21morr.html (Accessed 5 October 2011) (Riding 2006).

CHAPTER 7

Human Rights as Liberatory Social Thought

Sefi Atta

This chapter is premised on the idea that writing is a social activity and that to think of the human rights of individuals is to think of these rights in society at large. The practice of human rights liberates not only the individual, but also society.

The history of African literature cannot be fully conceptualized without reference to sociopolitical and cultural liberation.[1] Harry Garuba, writing about Nigerian poetry, suggests that the Achebe-Soyinka generation were "Modernist-Nationalists." He argues that nationalist tropes characterized the writings of the age, and "since such tropes often require a looking back in time, sometimes to pre-historic times, to recall the original unity and coherence of self and society, a recuperative urge is certainly present in their poetry."[2] By recuperative urge, Garuba means the need of the age to recover aspects of the past as a means of justifying the present. Therefore, nation, culture, and people were very much present in the thinking of this age, and the ideals surrounding these were presented largely in contrast to those of the West. What Garuba says about Achebe and Soyinka, of course applies to Ngugi wa Thiong'o, Sembene Ousman, and other African writers of their generation.

The third-generation writers are still engaged with the task of liberation, but this time around they are more interested in liberating people from themselves, from their delusions of grandeur and from the everyday violence they use against one another. These writers are engaged in an ethical reconstruction as a social project. Sefi Atta articulates this project best; and she does so by showing the role of moral consciousness as a sociopolitical tool. Based on readings of her two novels, *Everything Good Will Come*[3] and *Swallow*,[4] this chapter seeks to show the nexus between the abuse of the human rights of individuals and of those of society. Atta's macro argument is directed at society as a place where human rights thrive. I do not imply that the other writers I have discussed thus far are not interested in their societies. Quite the contrary; they are. In Atta's writing, however, the connection between the private and public spheres in regard to human rights are more forcefully established. In the introduction, I referred to Marie-Bénédicte Dembour's discussion of four schools of thought on human rights. Atta's writing suggests that human rights in Africa must be made to exist not only when Africans talk about them, but also when they make them part of their social thought. For Atta, to think of women's rights is not only to liberate oneself from the morally constricting ideologies of patriarchy and tradition, but also to imagine communities in which humans realize their lives in the ways they deem best for themselves.

Human Rights as Social Thought

Human rights, as we know them today, are self-evident. They are born of political grievances and people's demands for freedom and dignity. But because of the inherent desire of every person to be free, and given the expression of this desire over the ages, the framers of human rights formulated them as a goal to be pursued and as self-evident. Lynn Hunt traces the history of human rights by examining Thomas Jefferson's famous sentence: "We hold these truths to be self-evident, that all men are created equal, that they are endowed by their Creator with certain unalienable Rights, that among these are Life, Liberty and the pursuit of Happiness."[5] Jefferson helped the French draw up their own declaration of the basic tenets of human rights. The French Declaration of the Rights of Man and of the Citizen's ample references to "'every man,' 'all men,' 'all citizens,' 'each citizens,' 'society,' and 'every society,' dwarfed the single reference to the French people."[6] Thanks to these references, the declaration gave the first hints of the universality of the core idea of human rights. Hunt argues that the "declaration of the Rights of Man and Citizen incarnated the promise of universal human rights" Ibid., 17. as laid down in the 1948 UDHR.

Implicit in both the American and the French declaration of human rights or rights of man is the understanding of the human person as endowed with free will and reason, which are the dominant philosophical ideas in eighteenth-century Europe, ideas which formed the basis of the Enlightenment. Hunt points out the obvious contradiction between these declarations of human rights and their implementation in practice. Those who claimed that rights were universal were not inclusive in their treatment of their fellow humans.[7] Yet, the fact that they were not inclusive does not vitiate the self-evident nature of their notion of rights. Hunt suggests that it is precisely the idea of self-evidence that renders rights their universality. The reverse also holds. As she argues, in order for autonomy, an essential aspect of human rights, to be possible:

> two related but distinct qualities were involved: the ability to reason and the independence to decide for oneself. Both had to be present if an individual was to be morally autonomous. Children and the insane lacked the necessary capacity to reason, but they might someday gain or regain that capacity.[8]

Thus, even though the Declaration of the Rights of Man excluded certain groups, the thinking also granted the possibility of these groups "growing up" or achieving the essential condition for the practice of rights. The declaration envisaged human rights as a part of being human, though they had to be attained through a rigorous process. Freedom and rights are interior feelings associated with the capacity to reason, and can be learned and nurtured. As I have sought to explain, citing Mugo, the African conception of human rights differs from the Western notions in the sense that the individual is already embedded within a given community. You do not need reason in order to possess rights and dignity. You have rights because you are part of a community. But an important strain in the evolution of human rights in the West stands out, and when examined closely, can enhance our appreciation of human rights in general. It is the role of empathy. As Hunt argues, human rights become self-evident in the cultural practices that recognize that "others feel and think as we do, that our inner feelings are alike in some fundamental fashion." Hunt argues further that "autonomy and empathy did not materialize out of thin air in the eighteenth century; they had deep roots" in the maturation of European culture over time.[9] Part of that maturation is what she calls "imagined empathy," by which she means "the sense that empathy requires a leap of faith, of imagining that someone else is like you."[10]

Atta's writing, like those of her contemporaries, also functions on the basis of the same assumption of imagined empathy. Atta therefore believes in the self-evidence of human rights in the sense that humans are born into an *ubuntu* community. This is a community in which empathy plays an important role in human interaction. Within this understanding, empathy is the basis for every form of successful social activism, which in itself begins in the family. She describes the insufferable patriarchal conditions in which African women live, and she does so in hopes of provoking people's imagined empathy across the wider society. The idea of treating others as we would like to be treated starts in the family. For Atta, family is society writ small, and the degree to which people accord one another respect and dignity in that small unit equals the degree to which they do so in society. A man who never considers his wife as an equal partner, worthy of respect and dignity, can hardly consider others in society in the same way. Because of the ideology of patriarchy that prevents him from imagining the pain society inflicts on women, he is more prone to see others as means to his ends.

Violence and the Curse of Silence

Everything Good Will Come has attracted much discursive attention at international conferences and in some scholarly publications. Ayo Kehinde and Joy Ebong Mbipom see the novel as dealing with the "smallest unit of the society," the family as a microcosm of the nation.[11] Jonas Akung argues that Atta has given the African woman a voice. She "must speak out because silence is no longer golden; it has become a destructive metaphor."[12]

Everything Good Will Come is about three women, Sheri, Enitan, and Arinola, Enitan's mother. These women struggle not only to raise their voices, but also to save their lives in a world closely guarded by patriarchal norms. Arinola's world disintegrates when she loses a son whom she had hoped would assure her a permanent place in her husband's heart and home. Her husband, Sunny Taiwo, eager to have a male heir, has a concubine who eventually fulfils his wish for him. The loss of her child and Sunny Taiwo's infidelities drive Arinola insane. She eventually dies broken-hearted. Another traumatic incident that exposes the poverty of intersubjective relationships in society is the rape of Sheri by a group of boys. She never recovers from the resultant trauma. She learns to cope in her unfriendly world by being like the rest of the population. *Swallow*, on the other hand, is about Tolani and Rose, two young women who fall prey to the capitalist and patriarchal excesses of Lagos. Rose is not only sexually assaulted; she is also used as a drug mule. Mr Lamidi Salako is the manager of Federal Community Bank, and he sexually assaults Tolani. She files a complaint, and she is dismissed. While Rose dies pushing drugs for her male boss, Tolani goes back to her ancestral home, Makoku, in what could be seen as an effort to draw inspiration from her place of birth. In these stories, Atta shows the interrelatedness of the private and social spheres.

What binds all the women in these stories in a common fate is the near absence of intersubjectivity in their relationship to the menfolk of their society. Arinola's personhood is reduced to her function as the producer of an heir for her husband. She is therefore a means. On the basic human level, Sheri's rape reveals the degree of the boys' relation to her.[13] They are driven by male-oriented, patriarchal thinking that sees women as a means to the satisfaction of men's carnal desires. When women are subjected to the position that patriarchal ideology has foreseen for them, they are literally violated by the totality and totalitarian dictates of that ideology. Levinas argues that ideology obliterate the face. This ideology only manifests itself in a concrete format in the very instance of violence such as rape. If totality subsumes the unicity of the present within the conception of an end, the face acts as a foil; it resists containment. He states:

> The face is present in its refusal to be contained. In this sense it cannot be comprehended, that is, encompassed. It is neither seen nor touched—for in visual or tactile sensation the identity of the I envelops the alterity of the object, which becomes precisely a content.[14]

We can also understand the violence of ideology with the help of Fanon's examination of the effects of racism on the black body. Perhaps the most insidious aspect of control of a people is the control of knowledge about them (epistemic violence), which emerges from theory, constituted over the years through anecdotes and rituals that are passed from generation to generation so that with time they assume an air of essence. As Fanon argues, when a white child points at a black man and tells his mother, "mother, look, a Nigger," the child merely makes present all the negative ideas his culture has woven around the black man.[15] What is said of the black man in the West can be said of women in patriarchal societies; they are constituted by anecdotes and mythologies that shape their identities so that it becomes very difficult to see them as individuals with distinct feelings, dreams, and aspirations. Their faces are obliterated by the mere fact of their being seen through the spectrum of patriarchal ideology.

Sheri is seen not as an individual in her own right, but as something that belongs to an amorphous group already categorized (and totalized) by patriarchal thinking. The thinking of the boys who raped her had already removed her from their range of empathy. The rape, vicious as it is in itself, assumes a symbolic relevance to the degree that it is a microcosm of society's violence on women. It is in this regard that Sheri is synecdochic of women of that society, and she is so in the sense that she is a part of a group whose members the system rarely recognizes as individuals with unique pains and pleasures.

Augustine H. Assah calls rape of women "a horrendous aspect of patriarchy and dominator ideology."[16] Commenting on the devastating effect of rape in society, he argues:

> Since the determining principle in the perpetration of rape is force, and women have been socialized by the patriarchal order to accept subservient and non-assertive roles in society, it stands to reason that most rape victims are girls and women.... Rape becomes then a form of phallocratic violence, that is violence prompted by the use of force and the dictates of male hegemony.[17]

A particular detail stands out in the narration of the incident of rape as observed by Enitan. She describes what she sees in a seemingly harmless way: the portly boy on top of her friend Sheri. His hands are clamped over Sheri's mouth. "It was a silent moment; a peaceful moment. A funny moment, too. I didn't know why, except my mouth stretched into the semblance of a laugh before my hands came up, then tears filled my eyes."[18] Why does Enitan feel like laughing? We have a classical instance of trauma and helplessness in Enitan's reaction. One would have expected her to call the police, but she knows she cannot do that. Her society has no provision for this, and this is part of her trauma. In her helplessness, she turns to blame Sheri:

> If she hadn't smoked hemp it would never have happened. If she hadn't stayed as long as she did at the party, it would certainly not have happened. Bad girls got raped. We all knew. Loose girls, forward girls, raw, advanced girls. Laughing with boys, following them around, thinking she was one of them.[19]

Perhaps the major reason the boys raped Sheri was precisely because she refused to conform to the docile image society has of women. At this juncture, Enitan could be seen as an extended arm of her society, which also sees raped women as having brought their condition upon themselves. Sheri therefore experiences double violence. She is violated physically by the boys. She is also violated morally when Enitan blames her for bringing rape upon herself. Ironically, in condemning Sheri, Enitan condemns herself as a woman. Atta seems to suggest that society has succeeded in distorting not only women's relation to one another, but also to their individual selves, especially in regard to rights. They blame themselves when they are assaulted.

Sheri's crimes are self-confidence and her sense of freedom. She therefore has to be cut down to size. Thus the symbolic and actual function of rape is to put women in their place. Rape is implicitly seen as a corrective means through which women who "go astray" are brought back to order. We recall the exorcism scene in NoViolet Bulawayo's *We Need New Names*. Women who dare to go beyond the parameters society has defined for them are forced back, especially by that special patriarchal tool: the phallus. They are reminded of the defined space in which they are meant to be.

Atta obviously draws attention to the violation of women. But she also sees such violation as figurative of that of the Nigerian people by the military, which could be seen as the crystallization of patriarchal privileges. In a discussion with two other female Nigerian writers, she acknowledged:

> I was in my early thirties when I wrote *Everything Good Will Come*. I was frustrated about what I was seeing in the Nigerian community in America and what I had witnessed growing up in Lagos. I just needed to vent. As you know, the novel is about a girl/woman at odds with patriarchy and reads like angry rants in parts.[20]

She declared in an interview that "fighting for human rights is a sacrifice rather than a luxury."[21] I read Atta's anger as a cry for justice. Her narrative asks why these young men raped Sheri; it also interrogates the society whose system allows for such violence. She wants to liberate Nigerians from themselves, and she does it by highlighting the pains of individuals. These pains are caused neither by colonialism nor by the military, but by friends and relatives of the victims, enabled by their systems.

Though Sheri is figurative of women in society, she is also an individual in her own right, especially when she chooses to respond to her experience in a manner that betrays the dignity of her gender. She take recourse in her body, not as a way of pleasing herself, but as a pornographic item. She would go on to "become part of the sugar daddy circuit in Lagos, hanging around senators, and going on shopping sprees abroad."[22] She eventually becomes a full-time concubine of one of the rich sugar daddies, Brigadier Hassan, a man "who collected ponies and women as young as his daughters." Her life circles around the monotonous duty of cooking for him, and then the rest of the time she spends preparing for his coming: "her hair, her nails, dabbing perfumes and cooking meals."[23] As an indicator of the general moral decadence in her society, Sheri, a victim of rape, chooses to be a passive facilitator of her oppressive patriarchal system; she believes that it's easier to walk around a rock, to get to your goal, than to break it down.[24] Indeed, hers is the philosophy of generations of women of that society, particularly in regard to their men; it is also the philosophy of men. For these women, the gender relation in their society is set by tradition, and it should not be disrupted regardless of the pain it inflicts on them. In Sheri, Atta demonstrates the mutual relationship between private and public spheres in regard to human rights abuses. Sheri is a kept woman, one who has elected to live with the fact of her subjection, very much like her society has.

Monogamy is often seen as the form of marriage that, despite its weaknesses, goes a long way to assure women some grounds for equality with men in their marriages. Sheri, however, becomes suspicious of this very system, believing it is a Western import;[25] here she is the exact opposite of her former self, who had easily mingled with boys as evidence of her belief in her equality with them. The total change in attitude towards herself and those who look like her should therefore not come as a surprise to us. As Althusser and Butler have demonstrated, often victims of oppression help to perpetuate the system that oppresses them. This is largely due to the consequences of the trauma they suffer. They are frightened into self-spite. Their attitude, in turn, empowers their oppressors all the more. Nigerian society has no mechanism in place to address abuses such as rape. It therefore lets Sheri down. Sheri, in turn, believes that the appropriate attitude for her to take is to turn her back on society and approach life without much consideration for it. She, too, lets society down. There is therefore a pernicious dialectic between the society that disables the individual and that individual. The society disables itself indirectly through the actions or indifference of the individual. Atta has established a hermeneutical circle as far as the relationship between an abused individual and an abused society is concerned: As it goes with the individual, so it goes with society. It is not accidental that Sheri runs into the arms of a military man.

As the Family Goes, So Does the Nation

It is troubling that Sunny Taiwo does not seem to have noticed the direct correlation between his allegiance to patriarchal tradition and his wife's pains. He sees his wife as a person whose meaning is exhausted in her role as the bearer of male heirs. The circumstances of the birth of Arinola's son expose the barren moral conditions against which her mental breakdown can best be understood. After giving birth to Enitan, Arinola attempts to no avail to convince her husband that they should not bear another child because of the danger of sickle cell. Her effort is destined to fail because she is going up against an intractable tradition. And so she succumbs; she gives birth to a son with sickle cell.

One might not blame Sunny Taiwo for not being a hero in the face of a strong tradition. His moral failure, the wretchedness of his intersubjective attitude to Arinola is, however, revealed when he blames her for not sending their son to the hospital even though he knows that there is no cure; he secretly marries another woman, who gives birth to a healthy son.[26] Perhaps the seeming intractability of the patriarchal tradition succeeds in producing insincere humans. Thus, Sunny Taiwo, an otherwise loving, educated man, who even gives Enitan the feminist impulse of self-esteem as a woman, is shown to be a hypocrite and one who disables Arinola.

The philosopher Martin Buber suggests conditions under which human rights can flourish. He differentiates between experience and relation. One experiences the world of things, but stands in relation to the world of humans. When we relate to people, we cease to see them through the lens of utility; rather we begin to understand that they make our existence whole. Relation is not a one-way attitude; it is reciprocity, and reciprocity recognizes the dignity of the other.[27] Experience, for Buber, is "remoteness from you," but relation reduces that remoteness.[28] If the remoteness between me and you is nullified, there is then the possibility of encounter, which is the basis of actual life.[29] In this encounter, the individual, "I," could meet the other, *You*, as "my You." The phrase "my You" seeks to present the other, who is otherwise an indifferent "You," as very close to the subjectivity of "I" to the degree that there is no longer an estranging distance. We exchange positions, so to speak. When I confront the other as my You, our world is basically guided by the I–You operational model. When this is the case, according to Buber, the other:

> is no thing among things nor does he consist of things. He is no longer He or She, limited by other Hes and Shes, a dot in the world grid of space and time, nor a condition that can be experienced and described, a loose bundle of named qualities. Neighborless and seamless, he is You and fills the firmament.[30]

The phrase "he is You" puts us in the mindset of perspective switching. We put ourselves in the position of the other to the degree that we feel what he feels. This can be achieved if, as Buber argues, "nothing conceptual intervenes between I and you, no prior knowledge and no imagination; and memory itself is changed as it plunges from particularity into wholeness."[31] When Buber prohibits the conceptual from intervening between two persons he, like Gabriel Marcel, suggests that no ideology or prejudice should hinder one person from encountering the other as a being in whose position they can easily imagine themselves. This corresponds to what Emmanuel Levinas calls the command of the face of the other.

Martin Buber's differentiation of experience and relation helps us to understand what has happened between the characters, the men and the women whom Atta writes about. The men's relation to women is controlled by what Buber has identified as experiencing, which we do to the world of things. When we experience people, we do not see them as possessing rights and dignity, and this is because we see them as means to our ends. The men fail to relate to the women the way humans are supposed to relate to the world of humans. Atta exposes how men see women through the lens of utility in the society she describes. That society is dysfunctional because men experience women rather than relate to them. In that way the men's existence is fragmented, unfulfilled, and morally deficient, just as women are disabled by the abstractions of ideologies. The same can be said of society in general.

With the violence surrounding the lives of these women, Atta suggests that it is impossible to talk about human rights where people fail to encounter one another; when they see one another as means to their individual ends. The ends to which people (in this case men) put others (women) are often hidden in society's norms, values, heritage, and other concepts that merely embody a particular ideology of the dominant class or gender. As I argued in Chapter 4, with reference to Jacob Zuma, it is easier for a man to have a concubine, or even marry several wives, if he can find an excuse in his tradition or heritage that allows for that. That tradition already gives him an upper hand in any ethical confrontation with his wife. Unfortunately, that heritage completely ignores the subjective world of woman, her feelings of pain or her right to pleasure. The tradition literally puts a wedge between the I and the Thou of the world of men and women. As Nfah-Abbenyi suggests, we can recover the dignity and rights of these women by paying attention to their subjectivities.

In what could be seen as an allegory, Atta suggests a connection between the family and the nation. The nation is the family writ large. For her, the failure of intersubjectivity on micro levels such as that of the family (for example, a man ignoring the discomfort of his wife and children) parallels, or even directly leads to, that on macro levels such as that of the nation (for example, dictators tramping on the dignity of citizens). Over the course of the story, Enitan matures morally and politically, and deriving this from the riches of her experience, she makes the connection between individual actions and the fate of the society/country very clear. The military government has become extremely repressive, and Sunny Taiwo is now a victim of violence. He dares to challenge the authoritarian army regime, and is consequently incarcerated. Enitan, now a lawyer, is faced with challenging the military government the way she challenged her father on behalf of her mother. Before this, though, Atta allows us a glimpse of Enitan's mind; how she sees the connection between the country and the family. This becomes evident in a scene of intense encounter between her and her husband, Niyi. They talk about her father's being in detention. Niyi is eager to blame the Northerners for the mess in the country, but Enitan thinks that the problem cannot simply be explained using the North versus South dichotomy: "We have all played a part in this mess, not caring enough about other people, how they live. It comes back to you. Right back. Look at us in this house, paying Pierre pittance."[32] Enitan puts her finger on the core of the problem in her country; the problem of how people relate to one another, how they care or do not care about one another. The issue is that they live in a society that lacks empathy. Her observation does not sit well with her husband, who does not see any parallel between his bossiness and that of the military dictator. He believes that the situation is just how things are meant to be. He responds: "That's life, o-girl, unless you want Pierre to come and sleep in our bed tonight."[33] When Niyi makes that comment Enitan feels a strong aversion for him. But she quickly controls her feelings, knowing that he, too, is a child of his time. He is like the rest of the country. "There was a feeling that if people were at a disadvantage, it was because they somehow deserved it. They were poor, illiterate, they were radical, subversive, and they were not us."[34]

In Enitan's thinking, disregard for the pain (abuse of the rights) of one's immediate relative almost always leads to a disregard for the common good of society. If a man gets used to his pregnant wife cooking for him while he amuses himself with his colleagues in his sitting room, soon he also gets used to seeing hundreds of beggars, who are mad men and women whom society has obviously forced to their miserable fate by its lack of care. In Enitan's musings, we understand that dictators do not jump fully formed into existence as adults, nor are they creations of the gods; they are groomed by a society that fails to nurture a caring ambience in families where individuals, men, women, and children are given their due respect and dignity. In families where men beat or fail to respect their wives, children cannot suddenly become adults who are sensitive to other people's pains. For Enitan, children bear the brunt of society's misperception of human rights.

> Teachers beat, neighbors beat. By the time a child turned ten, the adults they know would have beaten out any cockiness that could develop into wit; any dreaminess that could give birth to creation; any bossiness that could lead to leadership. Only the strong would survive; the rest would spend their lives searching for initiative.[35]

Atta addresses the reader as part of society, drawing attention to the vicious circle of violence between the private and public spheres. If people can understand the root cause of society's decadence as the failure of intersubjectivity on a micro level, then it is possible to heal society, not by engaging in mega social projects, but by readjusting individual moral compasses towards intersubjectivity. That could break the vicious circle of violence and oppression in the social order.

How to Liberate an Oppressed Society

Swallow grafts well into the sociopolitical context of *Everything Good Will Come*, and furthers its exposition of Nigeria. To demonstrate the importance of a healthy self-appreciation, Atta presents us with a character that exhibits no lack in that regard. Arike utters a surprising wish: "I want to be a widow."[36] The wish is stunning not only because of the age of the person who utters it—merely a girl—but also because of its wide-ranging implications. Why would a girl want to be a widow?

After her unsuccessful efforts to make her living in the ever difficult and corrupt city, Lagos, Tolani flees to her ancestral village, Makoku, where she reconnects with her roots by learning the history of not only her birth, but also that of the long line of strong women in her ancestry. We are taken through the backstories of Tolani's lineage. Her mother, Arike, herself a woman with a strong character, had grown under the tutelage of another strong-willed woman, Iya Alaro, who lost her husband without bearing a child. Growing up, Arike admired Iya Alaro's sense of freedom and responsibility, believing that Iya Alaro achieved all that because she lost her husband. This is the genesis of her childish desire to be a widow.

Atta hints at the visible and invisible obstacles in the way of women's rights and dignities. The obstacles are not marriage or children; rather they are the expectations, norms, or mores that society has woven around the institution of marriage. Without a husband and children, Iya Alaro has no expectations/obstacles in the way of her self-fulfilment. She has time to herself, and can engage in trades that women with family obligations could not. When therefore Arike, having been influenced by Iya Alaro, utters her wish, it is not because she desires to get rid of men. Rather it is a demonstration of her longing for freedom and responsibility. These are traits of an individual who has a high self-regard. Even as a child, Arike signals her desire for agency, and in so doing placed far-reaching demands on society: the demand that she not be seen as a tool for others. She wants to relate to them on equal grounds. This is, perhaps, the most radical feminist thrust of the narrative, one that has profound implications for the liberation of society from the ideologies of tradition. It is also an important sociopolitical aspect of the novel, especially as we get to know more about the life of Iya Alaro, the woman Arike has imitated. One could also see in Arike's wish some audacious feminist suggestion: if men stand in the way of women being who they desire to be, then it is only justified that a woman would wish to someday be rid of her husband, or possibly not to have one. Thus it is better to live alone than to be in an abusive relationship.

Like most Nigerian women, Atta is skeptical about being labeled a radical feminist.[37] It is, however, to her credit that her ideas go to the roots of problems that violate women. It is safer to say that she writes with a strong sense of history; this is specifically the justification for Tolani's going back to her ancestral home. After being assaulted by her boss in Lagos, she has nothing to fall back on but the significant people in her life: her mother, her grandmother. She goes to find out her history, and learns that it is a potent means to fight not only patriarchal but also political oppression.

When I say that Atta writes with a sense of history, I also imply that she is aware of what she is doing with the characters she locates in Yoruba cosmology. The idea of women's agency is not foreign to the Yoruba world, and this is what Tolani has to learn. She has to know that she carries in her the blood of two generations of powerful women. We do not get Iya Alaro's story directly; we get it filtered through Arike's telling. Iya Alaro obviously was ahead of her time, and because of her self-confidence, people thought she had supernatural powers. In Arike's words:

> Women were not allowed to form secret societies as men did, but my aunt did as she pleased. People were afraid of her. They said she was a reincarnation of a witch who had long ago terrorized our town. The witch had no husband or children to speak of and was driven away to the forest. They claimed she'd brought bad luck, caused illness, and destroyed crops.[38]

When the new Oba (ruler) begins to terrorize Makoku, Iya Alaro gathers the women of the village and, using her power of oratory, reminds them of how the women of Abeokuta caused commotion for their Alake (ruler) and his chiefs. They too could cause troubles for their tyrannous Oba. Indeed the women listen to her, and they form a resistance group that is joined by farmers, fishermen, hunters, and Shango devotees. They carry tree branches and march to the palace, chanting. There they *"informed the new Oba that the town would no longer tolerate the practice of forcing women into marriage."*[39] They challenge the unequal power relation between the people and the Oba, and by implication that between women and men.

When Arike sits Tolani down to tell her stories of her past, we feel how Atta layers her narrative almost as a systematized social and political lecture. She seems to be telling the present-day Nigerian women (and men) that they have no reason to succumb to the tyranny of the political class. All they need in order to fight the gender and political oppression of their times is right there inside them, in their veins. Atta couples feminist concerns with those of a society under political oppression. Indeed, Atta uses fiction to enhance feminist and political arguments. Larry Diamond argues that:

fiction is more than a passive reflection of society and history. It is also an active influence, reinforcing or refashioning values, beliefs, ideas, perceptions and aspirations. The teller of a story can become a powerful force in shaping the way a people think about their social and political order, and the nature, desirability and direction of change.[40]

I understand politics in its most fundamental usage as the art of organizing people or people taking an active part in the affairs of state. In Iya Alaro, Atta allows us to think of great black women in history who have fought oppression in their different ways. One thinks of Sojourner Truth, who believed that women had the ability to turn their world around if only they could believe in themselves. Like Sojourner Truth, Iya Alaro believes that rights are not gifts that could be handed out like candies. Rights are what they are because they are inalienable parts of every human being, and people should stand up to take what belongs to them. She used her co-op as a means of protecting women and children against the excesses of the men of Makoku, who, led by their ruler, were busy raising taxes and squandering them:

> passing edicts and banning women and children from festivals, threatening even the smallest baby with a barren womb if her mother dared to break a taboo; and while people thought the royal court had all the power in our town, elders and men in that order, it was the women of my aunt's co-op who were busy policing quietly and silently.[41]

In order to underline the relationship between human rights in private and public spheres, Atta has this story contrast with the modern instances of abuse of power in the city. Tolani, Iya Alaro's great-niece, is the link between the present and the past. She too, has stories to tell about male abuse of power. In Makoku, she learns that oppression and abuse of power are not modern phenomena; they exist where humans exist. Every abuse of power, however, needs to be challenged. Arike's stories about herself and Iya Alaro teach Tolani that women have not always been helpless. Quite to the contrary; women have agency, and they can put it to use if they believe in themselves. Arike concludes her story thus: "You see, we had our own ways of keeping our rulers in check, and they were quite effective, long before the oyinbos came along."[42] As if making a reference to Tolani's office experience, Arike makes an incisive observation about power abuse and how it oppresses the victim. "Someone in power does something wrong to you and everyone treats you as if you are at fault. You yourself begin to feel you're at fault. And for what? No reason. No reason at all"[43] In the manner of eighteenth- and nineteenth-century European writers, who ingrained the idea of human rights in the consciousness of their contemporaries, Atta uses her character to create awareness of the dignities of each individual human being, and the need to organize and fight oppression.

Fighting oppression is one thing, improving oneself in the sense of earning one's living is another. Arike's strength is in her ability to aim for higher goals and to be creative. She was interested in overcoming her self-doubt. "I was consumed with creating innovative designs and trying untested methods of cloth dyeing."[44] In relating her story, Arike seeks to pass her tenacity on to her daughter. Freedom is won not merely by an act of "No" to oppression, but also by an act of "Yes" to oneself, yes to reality. The ultimate question for Tolani, as for all the women, is how to resist their erasure and assert themselves as humans with rights and dignity. Atta suggests that the first step for them in this regard is to develop love of self. Audre Lorde understands feminism as people letting free their erotic force:

> The erotic is a measure between the beginning of our sense of self and the chaos of our strongest feelings. It is an internal sense of satisfaction to which, once we have experienced it, we know we can aspire. For having experienced the fullness of this depth of feeling and recognizing its power, in honor and self-respect we can require no less of ourselves.[45]

When the group of boys rape Sheri (*Everything Good*), they not only inflict severe bodily pain on her; they also take her self-esteem. Sunny Taiwo achieves the same with Arinola, as does Mr Lamidi Salako with Rose and Tolani. Women react to their oppression in different ways. However, the most potent weapon against an oppressive system, in Audre Lorde's understanding, is to discover the "kernel within myself."[46] Arike seems to be alluding to the same idea, not only in her stories to her daughter, but also in pointedly telling Tolani never to tolerate insult from any person: "If you sleep in dirt, you will eventually begin to smell like it."[47] What Arike tells her daughter applies without qualification to all Nigerians, who have accommodated themselves to indignities imposed on them by their rulers, and to all women in patriarchal cultures. Atta engages in a profound political and moral education of Nigerians. She carefully props up Tolani and Enitan as agents of feminist and sociopolitical transformations both on micro and macro levels. Though Tolani gives indications that she will take her mother's words seriously, it is, however, in Enitan that we see a woman who is ready to discover her erotic force. She is prepared to confront her husband even if it means separating from him. Enitan's understanding of self-respect, or love of self, to be sure, is not equal to divorce, yet she knows that if distancing herself from a husband who does not treat her with respect is all it takes for her to appreciate her life, then divorce should not be taboo.

Enitan never bases her happiness on what others think. Rather she is ethically informed and, armed with her fearless intelligence, she believes that whoever has a voice must use it "to bring about change."[48] She believes that the ability to make a change in society begins with the ability to affect a change in oneself and in the family. What Sheri and Arinola lack will be made up for in Enitan's resolve to stand up for herself and those who look like her. She fought to get her father to transfer the house in which her mother lives to her mother's name, and she did that with the goal of empowering her mother. In her own marriage, she maintains the same proactive stance in defence of her dignity; she insists that Niyi should change some of his patriarchal attitudes, and begin to see her as a partner in marriage.[49] Niyi does not budge. But then Enitan has to move on. "Niyi was so tall," she ruminates. "I'd always thought he deserved more space. The shrinkage I experienced was never worth it...He was fighting as though we were vying for the same cylinder of air: the more I breathed, the less there was for him."[50] It is the consciousness of the dignity of her body that grants her the courage to tell him that he is hurting her, and that she is not a mule of the earth;[51] her body has the right to experience pleasure and avoid pains. At this juncture, she points to the possibilities open to oppressed people if only they could learn to appreciate their worth as human beings.

Tolani's journey to her ancestral home not only exposes her to the strength of the women in her lineage; it also reveals to her the nature of the patriarchal order which has justified her oppression. In reconnecting with her mother, Tolani confirms the truth of what she has always suspected: that the man she had always known as her father was not her biological father because he was impotent, and that her mother did not perceive herself as a victim.[52]

Solidarity as an Exercise in Empathy

The discovery of the sterility of the paterfamilias has a symbolic relevance as far as patriarchy is concerned. Patriarchy is a construct; it is not rooted in something indubitably given. Tolani could still have existed without her father. Indeed, Tolani's world has been possible largely because of her mother's *efforts*. In Tolani's family, men are not only biologically sterile; they are also economically so. Without Arike, the Ajao family would not have been. She takes the initiative to conceive when she discovered that her husband was impotent. Arike is the breadwinner of the family, and this is because she has always perceived herself as a strong, independent-minded individual who did not need the permission of a man to be that way. She learnt to dye cloth from Iya Alaro.[53] Atta suggests that given the peculiar position that women occupy in traditional patriarchal settings, they are uniquely placed to remind the rest of society of what it means to be human, which supports the saying that women's rights are human rights.[54] The attention these women call to their pain has the potential to humanize us, and it does so by inducing "imagined empathy" in us. Being well educated, and possessing a good knowledge of her society, Enitan is able to establish a parallel between the excesses of patriarchy and the abuse of power by the military; what both of them have in common is the sheer abuse of power and the tendency of the person in power to see others as means to their ends. Enitan does not succumb to these forces. Rather she gains a new inspiration to fight oppression by entering into solidarity with the other victims of these two forces. She reveals her moral trajectory in her musings about her country, but more specifically those about the city in which she was born, and in which she lives. For her, the city is a space that necessarily calls for universal solidarity because it reduces all to a common condition by exposing their vulnerability and negating any mythology of autochthony. In the city, nothing is fixed; everything is in a flux, including identity. This is so because of encounters with strangers with whom one must negotiate. Enitan tells: "My father was from a town in the middle belt of Nigeria; my mother, from the West. They lived in Lagos. I was born here, raised here."[55] She understands herself as com-posited. She is aware that she can neither be described as pure, nor can she afford to adopt a tribal attitude in Lagos. Her allegiance is therefore tilted toward a composite, what is merged. She is, by nature, disposed to mediate between opposites, to go beyond the one-dimensionality of the world of either/or. This is the source of her understanding of her country, which is also made up of different regions, tribes, and ethnicities. The nature of the country therefore requires nothing less than negotiations and solidarity with the downtrodden. In this regard, the city is synecdochic of the nation just as the ethical assumptions of the private sphere are for the public, especially in regard to gender relations.

Notes

1. For more on the history of African literature see O.R. Dathorne, *African Literature in the Twentieth Century*. Minnesota: University of Minnesota Press, 1976 (Dathorne 1976); Charles Larson, *The Novel in the Third World*. Washington, DC: Inscape, 1976 (Larson 1976).
2. Harry Garuba, "'The Unbearable Lightness of Being': Re-Figuring Trends in Recent Nigerian Poetry," *English in Africa*. New Nigerian Writing, 32.1 (2005): 58 (Garuba 2005).
3. Sefi Atta, *Everything Good Will Come*. Boston: Interlink Books, 2004 (Atta 2004).
4. Sefi Atta, *Swallow*. Boston: Interlink Books, 2011 (Atta 2011).
5. Cited in Lynn Hunt, *Inventing Human Rights: A History*. New York: W.W. Norton & Company, 2008, 15 (Hunt 2008).
6. Hunt, Ibid., 16.
7. Ibid., 18.
8. Ibid., 28.
9. Ibid., 29.
10. Ibid., 32.
11. Ayo Kehinde and Joy Ebong Mbipom, "Discovery, Assertion and Self-Realisation in Recent Nigerian Migrant Feminist Fiction: The Example of Sefi Atta's *Everything Good Will Come*," *African Nebula*, 3 (2011): 67 (Kehinde and Mbipom 2011).
12. Jonas E. Akung, "Feminist Dimensions in Sefi Atta's *Everything Good Will Come*," *Studies in Literature and Language* 4.1 (2012): 114–122 Accessed October 10, 2012.(Akung 2012).
13. Atta, *Everything Good*, 62 (Atta 2004).
14. Emmanuel Levinas, *Totality and Infinity. Alphonso Lingis, trans.* (Pittsburgh: Duquesne University Press, 1969), 194 (Levinas 1969).
15. Frantz Fanon, *Black Skin, White Mask*. New York: Grove Press. 1967, 109–111.
16. Augustine H. Assah and Tobe Levin, "Images of Rape in African Fiction: Between the Assumed Fatality of Violence and the Cry for Justice," *Annales Aequatoria*, 28 (2007): 333 (Assah and Levin 2007).
17. Ibid., 336.
18. Ibid., 62.

19. Atta, *Everything Good*, 65 (Atta 2004).
20. Unoma Azuah, "Of Phases and Faces: Unoma Azuah Engages Sefi Atta and Chika Unigwe," *Research in African Literature. Nigeria's Third-Generation Novel: Preliminary Theoretical Engagement*, 39.2 (2008): 112 (Azuah 2008).
21. Ike Anya, "Sefi Atta: Something Good Comes to Nigerian Literature." http://www.africanwriter.com/sefi-atta-something-good-comes-to-nigerian-literature/ (Accessed March 06, 2015).
22. Atta, *Everything Good*, 76 (Atta 2004).
23. Ibid., 157.
24. Ibid., 251–252.
25. Ibid., 246.
26. Ibid., 180.
27. Martin Buber, *I and Thou*. New York: Simon and Schuster, 1970, 58 (Buber 1970).
28. Ibid., 60.
29. Ibid., 62.
30. Ibid., 59.
31. Ibid., 62.
32. Ibid., 228.
33. Ibid., 228–229.
34. Ibid., 321.
35. Ibid., 131.
36. Atta, *Swallow*, 47 (Atta 2011).
37. Azuah, Ibid., 112 (Azuah 2008).
38. Atta, *Swallow*, 46 (Atta 2011).
39. Ibid., 95 (original italics).
40. Larry Diamond, "Fiction as Political Thought," African Affairs, 88.352 (1989): 435 (Diamond 1989).
41. Atta, *Swallow*, 47 (Atta 2011).
42. Ibid., 96.
43. Ibid., 96.
44. Ibid., 149.
45. Audre Lorde, *Sister Outsider: Essays and Speeches*. Freedom, CA: The Crossing Press, 1984, 54 (Lorde 1984).
46. Ibid., 54.
47. Ibid., 162.
48. Atta, *Everything Good*, 259 (Atta 2004).
49. Ibid., 326.
50. Ibid., 330–331.
51. Ibid., 256.
52. Atta, *Swallow*, 290–295 (Atta 2011).

53. Ibid., 45.
54. See also J. Oloka-Onyango and Sylvia Tamale, "'The Personal Is Political,'" or Why Women's Rights Are Indeed Human Rights: An African Perspective on International Feminism. *Human Rights Quarterly*, 17.4 (1995): 691–731 (Oloka-Onyango and Tamale 1995).
55. Atta, *Everything Good*, 299 (Atta 2004).

CHAPTER 8

The Obligation to Bear Testimony to Human Rights Abuses

Patricia Jabbeh Wesley

The poet Patricia Jabbeh Wesley acknowledged in an interview that her primary goal in poetry was to immortalize the suffering of her people. What exactly does she mean by that? What are the implications of remembering human rights abuses, of keeping sorrows alive, especially in narratives? This chapter examines these questions in light of Primo Levi's envisaged moral obligation to bear testimony to the victims of the Jewish Holocaust, as well as Giorgio Agamben's thoughts on the latter. As in the other works discussed thus far, ethics is central to Jabbeh Wesley's poetics. The difference between Jabbeh Wesley's and those other works, as I mentioned in the preface, is Jabbeh Wesley's macro concern with human rights abuses, her record of the history of her people's pain. The poet has a calling: the moral responsibility to bear testimony to the dead, the dispossessed, and the abused. I will discuss Jabbeh Wesley's poems as both a tribute to the victims of the Liberian civil wars and as an appeal to the living to change their lives.

Jabbeh Wesley is one of the most prolific African poets of the twenty-first century. With four collections of poetry spanning over 15 years, and having won prestigious awards and garnered rave reviews, she is also one of the most renowned of African women poets. While she is known to many students of African literature, it is a shame that she has not yet

© The Author(s) 2016
C. Eze, *Ethics and Human Rights in Anglophone African Women's Literature*, Comparative Feminist Studies,
DOI 10.1007/978-3-319-40922-1_8

attracted as much scholarly attention as she deserves, especially given the depth of her poetics and the thematic relevance of her works. To my knowledge, the only scholarly article on her works is that of Carol Blessing.[1] Jabbeh Wesley occupies a metonymic position in writings about Africa, a continent that has experienced brutal historic traumas, but one that has an abundant will to heal, to live, and to flourish. What is said of Jabbeh Wesley applies in some respects to her native country, Liberia, whose former head of state, Charles Taylor, was convicted of war crimes in 2012 by a special court in The Hague.

Liberia was born of the efforts of an American colonization society, founded in 1816, to resettle freed black slaves. The resettlement took place on a strip of coastal land in Mesurado. The colony was initially called Christopolis but was later rechristened Monrovia, after the American president, James Monroe.[2] The colony expanded to become what would later be known as Liberia, a place of freedom. For John-Peter Pham, social divisions "have characterized the complex tapestry of Liberian society from the very beginning."[3] Yekutiel Gershoni states that Liberia's ruling elites, comprising exclusively the descendants of free slaves, "chose to adopt attitudes and tactics...which were borrowed from the colonial administrators of white powers" towards the "indigenous Africans."[4] The Americo-Liberians, as they were called, were largely "perceived by the Africans as foreign rulers in every sense."[5] George Klay Kieh Jr. rightly argues that while the ethno-cultural antagonisms between and among the various ethnic groups were not what led to the eventual political and social collapse of the country, they certainly did not create political cohesion.[6] When Jabbeh Wesley was asked about her references to the conflict between the Americo-Liberians and the indigenous population as "a metaphor for Liberia," she did not minimize this conflict. She acknowledged that the descendants of freed American slaves "actually did some enslaving of indigenous people—who were my ancestors— similar to what they had suffered in the American South."[7]

Though Jabbeh Wesley has addressed the conflict between the Americo-Liberians and the indigenous populations, it is not her intention to revive old identity-based encounters or conflicts; the major goal in her poetry is to bring to discourse the Liberian people's human condition. She understands that literature involves the experiences of people. "It doesn't exist in isolation of the experiences of a specific group of people."[8] More specifically, "poetry is an outlet for my grief and a way to immortalize some of the suffering that we've endured, my family, my people, Liberia."[9]

To immortalize people's suffering in narratives is to bear testimony to their struggles, to give voice to the voiceless. Her specific intention is to bring about healing by demonstrating that the pain of one is the pain of all. Yet we have to ask if narratives can actually bring about healing. One way to approach this question is from the perspective of Primo Levi, who, having survived Auschwitz, began to give voice to the imperative not to keep silent, to speak. So, why do we tell stories of human tragedies?

Stories and the Ethics of Testimony

In the introduction, I referred to James Dawes's concern about the paradox involved in speaking for others: it is "both a way of rescuing and usurping the other's voice."[10] The paradox can be approached more fruitfully by imagining the alternative: not speaking for the voiceless. Speech is an imperfect act, while silence is perfect in its negativity. Speech is imperfect in the sense that there will always be the unsaid, the unexpressed that demands more speech to bring it to life. Speech initiates a discourse. Empathy, when expressed in a form that does not seek to patronize people, bridges the gap between silence and speaking for the voiceless. Storytelling is by its very nature an imperfect act. It does not claim to capture the totality of the subjects. To the contrary, it situates its subjects at the center of discourse.

In Chapter 3, I discussed Paul Ricoeur's understanding of the function of poetry, one that goes to the core of the relation of narrative and ethics. Poetry enables the imagination to piece together, in ways acceptable to human flourishing, bits of human conduct, the elements of our happiness and misfortune. In line with Ricoeur, Richard Kearney states that "what is peculiar to the ethical quality of narrative understanding, especially in literary works, is that it gives priority to the perception of particular people and situations over abstract rules."[11] The situations described in the narrative force us to engage the individual not in abstract or universalistic terms, but in our own terms or in terms that our pain or humiliation has dictated, and this requires prudence. I also discussed Martha Nussbaum's understanding of empathy. To be sure, people do not always empathize with others who are in pain. Empathy can be blocked, for example, by the kinds of conditioning that Germans were subjected to during the Nazi regime. However, it is also true that to be human is to reach out in gestures of empathy to others. People can even derive pleasure in feeling the pain of others, as Susan L. Feagin argues. For her, pleasure from tragedy is a meta-response, and it is gratifying to know that there is "a unity of feeling among members of humanity, that we are not alone, and that these feelings are at the heart of morality itself."[12]

In Aristotle's understanding, the writer who imitates people's actions in tragedy bears witness to humanity's experience of pain. In provoking pity and fear in us when we witness the pain of others in narratives, the writer indirectly seeks to put a stop to the source of that pain. This, in my understanding, is where Aristotle, Levi, and Jabbeh Wesley's understandings of narrative merge. When Jabbeh Wesley states that she writes as a way to keep her people's suffering alive or that writing provides a way for her to grieve, she touches at the heart of Aristotle's idea of tragedy as illuminating ethics by initiating some form of purification in people. She crafts her poems as testimonies in pursuit of life in its fullness. Testimony is also at the core of Levi's poems and memoirs of survival in the German concentration camps.

The Jewish Holocaust is, no doubt, the most fully documented horror of the twentieth century, excepting, of course, the two world wars themselves. Geoffrey Hartman argues that "no other man-made catastrophe has been so voluminously recorded and publicized as the Shoah."[13] Accounts of Holocaust survival are also veritable templates for survival of all large-scale ethnic or racial traumas. Simon Wiesenthal, Eli Wiesel, Viktor Frankl, and Levi provide some of the best examples of testimonies about the evils of the Holocaust and the healing power and moral obligations of such testimonies. In the concluding chapter of his memoir, *The Drowned and the Saved*, Levi offers a rationale for speaking about his experience in the concentration camp:

> We see it as a duty and, at the same time, as a risk: the risk of appearing anachronistic, of not being listened to. We must be listened to: above and beyond our personal experiences, we have collectively witnessed a fundamental, unexpected event, fundamental precisely because unexpected, not foreseen by anyone. It took place in the teeth of all forecasts; it happened in Europe.[14]

Levi's assertion that "we must be listened to" underscores his belief in the fundamental insight of Aristotle's understanding of tragedy. Levi believes that the survivors of the Shoah have stories that are capable of provoking "pity and fear," stories that ultimately lead to a more ethically conscious life. There is, therefore, a moral urgency to inform the living of what happened to the dead. He issues an urgent warning: "It happened, therefore it can happen again: this is the core of what we have to say."[15] The moral obligation of all survivors of horror is to prevent it from happening again, and this, of course, presupposes that all have been moved to pity and fear by the narrative of what happened. In *Survival in Auschwitz*, Levi makes his most robust ethical case for revealing the horrors of the camps. He notes that the book was written to satisfy certain needs, primarily that of "an interior liberation."[16] He confronts his audience with an ethical responsibility. He does this in a short, epigraphic poem, "If This Is a Man," in which the speaker addresses the reader directly, thus situating him in the center of Levi's moral imagination:

> You who live safe
> In your warm houses,
> You who find on returning in the evening,
> Hot food and friendly faces

Now that readers feel directly addressed, Levi reveals, in the second stanza, the core moral issues to be faced when he paints the pictures of inmates of the camps: a man who "works in the mud" and who "fights for a scrap of bread"; a "woman without hair... her eyes empty." The concrete details of the man and woman who have been humiliated by their fellow humans should trouble every person who lives safely in their warm house. Levi however urges these readers further to:

> Meditate that this came about:
> I commend these words to you,
> Carve them in your hearts
> At home, in the streets,
> Going to bed, rising;
> Repeat them to your children.[17]

As Nicholas Patruno argues, this epigraphic poem, written in January 1946, is a "loosely paraphrased interpretation of one of the most often invoked Hebrew prayers, the Shema."[18] The imperative not to forget is a well-known component of Jewish history and culture. Remembrance is the holy grail of survival. Conversely, to forget is to subject oneself to extinction. For Patruno, the title of the poem is intended to raise a "rhetorical question of conscience whose impact is so powerful that any reply would be superfluous."[19] Jonathan Druker contends that the ethical import of Levi's memoir is highlighted by the poem, which "commands the 'safe' reader, surrounded by 'friendly faces,' to reflect on whether the dehumanized victim, unable to assert his or her own subjectivity, is yet a human being for whom the reader is responsible."[20] Druker, alluding to Emmanuel Levinas, further points out that "the human face is the focal point of the poem's gaze as the 'friendly faces' (*visi amici*) of the first stanza give way to the dehumanized victim's blank stare 'her eyes empty'; (*vuoti gli occhi*)."[21]

By inviting the reader to look closely at the faces of the camp inmates, Levi asks the reader indirectly: Would you keep silent if you knew this was happening in your own time and place? Do you still feel comfortable among your friendly faces? Do you not recognize the humanity of that other human who has been forced to waste away? Would you still keep silent? Levi knows the destructive force of silence, for, as he notes, the silence of the majority of the German population, their failure to let the secrets about the concentration camps be known, is a moral failure. This failure, Levi argues in *The Drowned and the Saved*: "represents one of the major collective crimes of the German people and the most obvious demonstration of the cowardice to which Hitlerian terror had reduced them."[22]

To keep silent when one should have spoken out is to refuse to acknowledge the humanity of others, of those in pain. Perhaps the many genocides that took place after the horrors of Auschwitz bear him out. The 1994 genocide in Rwanda, and those in Bosnia and Herzegovina between 1992 and 1995, and the horrors of the Liberian civil wars come readily to mind.

Jabbeh Wesley's Poetics of Attention

My discussion of Jabbeh Wesley's poetics is based on the poems that, in my view, best demonstrate what I have already identified as the ethical thrust of her writing, the remembrance of human rights abuses. Jabbeh Wesley writes in the tradition of Aristotle's understanding of tragedy discussed above. In her faithful rendition of the observed world, she imitates people's action in pleasurable language with the ultimate goal of affecting the reader. Avoiding flashy, contrived strategies, her poems operate within what Donald Revell calls the poetry of

8 THE OBLIGATION TO BEAR TESTIMONY TO HUMAN RIGHTS ABUSES

attention. They trust "the opened eye to see."[23] For Revell the "poetry of attention proceeds not by acquisition but, rather, by plain accumulation. It doesn't add up; it goes. I see the light, but seeing doesn't make it mine."[24]

The title of Jabbeh Wesley's fourth collection of poetry, *Where the Road Turns*,[25] is a subtle allusion to Wole Soyinka's 1965 play, *The Road*, and Ben Okri's 1991 Booker Prize-winning novel, *The Famished Road*. These two books explore the riches of Yoruba mythology in order to shed light on the African condition. The characters in Soyinka's play live on the road and make their living from what it has to offer. There are some absurdist elements in Soyinka's conception of the road as a metaphor of Africa's instability, especially in the play's parallel with Samuel Beckett's *Waiting for Godot*. What is said of *The Road* also applies to Jabbeh Wesley's *Where the Road Turns*. Aided by the picture of the winding dirt road on the cover and at the beginning of each of the book's four sections, Jabbeh Wesley reminds us of the twisting road of Africa's existential journeys. The eponymous poem itself is representative of the poetry of attention:

> I'm right here on the road, in the open
> You will find me waiting where Gbarnga's
> hills curve into zigzags, and cars slow down
> because potholes have taken over the road,
> because potholes have taken over my life.[26]

The detailed description of the place where a lonely speaker waits enables us to see what the speaker sees: a crumbling world. We are even more troubled by the fact that the speaker sees a parallel between himself or herself and the road: "Potholes have taken over my life," just as they have taken over the road. This identification of one's self with the road is to be understood as a lamentation for the conditions of the speaker's life, and not as romanticizing the rural life of Africa.

The road in an unnamed country in Africa is representative of the condition of the entire continent; the speaker stands for its dispossessed, abused people. According to Mark Doty, the National Book Award-winning poet and critic, "every achieved poem inscribes a perceptual signature in the world."[27] "Where the Road Turns" achieves just that.

We are confronted with an environment that persists in our inner vision. For Doty:

> What descriptions—or good ones, anyway—actually describe then is consciousness, the mind playing over the world of matter, finding there a glass various and lustrous enough to reflect back the complexities of the self that's doing the looking.[28]

In the achieved poem, therefore, we are made to confront not only the world of the speaker, but also his consciousness, and ultimately that of the poet. By presenting this decayed part of the African world, the poet wants us to be troubled the way she has been. Indeed, the first poem in the collection, "Cheede, My Bride: A Grebo Man Laments— 1985" appears to have set the consciousness-raising tone for the rest of the poems.

> While we sleep, jumbo trucks haul timber
> to build needle houses and monkey bridges
> across the skies in some city far away.
> One day my wife, Cheede, will run away
> to Monrovia, that swallows its victims whole
> down boa-constrictor bellies.[29]

We meet a mind grappling with a world that is being ruthlessly exploited. The exploitation of the world plays itself out in the lives of the people, as the second stanza reveals. One is reminded of Africa's struggles with neo-imperialism. Its natural resources are being used for the development of other parts of the world. Such exploitation contributes to the implosion of different units of African life: the family, the village, the county, the city, and the country. What this and other poems aim to achieve, therefore, is to raise our consciousness of the precariousness of the African world as seen from Liberia. This is the most that poets or tragedians can do, and they do so in the knowledge or the hope that the audience or the reader will be moved to relate to that world, as Aristotle might have anticipated.

The Silence the Dead Refuse to Take

Though Jabbeh Wesley is not as demanding of her readers as Levi is of his, her testimonies are no less morally urgent. She too understands the importance of defeating the tyranny of silence. In the poem, "Requiem for Auntie," from the collection, *Becoming Ebony*,[30] she takes us through a maze of relationships between the dead and the living. The poem is spoken from the perspective of a little girl observing the body of her aunt. The first stanza begins with a general observation, but then quickly narrows to a particular person's experience, to the girl's perspective:

> When the dead first arrive in death, their eyes stand
> naked and wide and bare to the bone. This gaze
> numbed my girl eyes the day they brought my Auntie
> home...[31]

The reference to nakedness suggests the closure in the dead person's existence; at the same time, it recalls its parallel opposite: the fact that the living still have opportunities. The dead person's gaze constitutes a direct challenge to the girl, who is literally shocked into the realization of her own good fortune at being alive and of the possibilities open to her. In this short, powerful moment, there is an unspoken dialogue between the deceased and the bereaved, between an aunt and her niece; there is a simultaneous negotiation between nakedness and the urgent moral call to clothe that nakedness. The affinity between the dead aunt and her living niece is as much a moment of feminine solidarity as it is a universal experience of sympathy with the weak or with people in pain, as Susan Feagin suggested above. By the end of the poem, the speaker, the little girl, has grown into a woman with a profound sense of responsibility, and here meditations on the mysteries of the world are based on, or, inspired by, her original experience as a child:

> The mysteries of this world are not in the living.
> The mysteries of this world are in the dead cold of
> death, in the weathered things of this world, in
> the silence that the dead refuse to take along...[32]

In her musings, the niece reveals that her aunt has left something with her: the silence she refused to take along to the grave. That silence, like all silence about human suffering, is oppressive, and it urges the niece to do something. The niece therefore has the obligation to end the tyranny of silence and her aunt's helplessness by bearing testimony, by telling us about her aunt. In her requiem, her aunt, now standing for all the dead, speaks through her niece. The panorama that Jabbeh Wesley paints here calls to mind Giorgio Agamben's analysis of Levi's memoirs, cited above.

In *Survival in Auschwitz*, Levi recounts how the inmates of the camps used the word *Muselmann*[33] to designate those so debilitated by hunger and sickness that they resembled the living dead more than human beings. Giorgio Agamben describes them as comparable to the body "of the overcomatose person and the neomort attached to life-support systems today."[34] The existence of nearly every so-called *Muselmann* ended in the gas chamber. For Agamben, even though those who were eventually led to the gas chambers were the perfect witnesses of the evils of the Holocaust, they cannot bear witness because they took their experience to the grave. Agamben argues that a life that has become "bare, unassignable and unwitnessable" is not necessarily condemned to silence.[35] However, the only way it can speak is through the survivor, through the witness, whose authority "consists in his capacity to speak solely in the name of an incapacity to speak—that is, in his or her being a subject."[36] In light of Agamben's explanation, we understand that Levi, who barely survived extermination, speaks not just for himself, but also on behalf of all those who did not survive. Testimony consists of any action taken by the survivor of violence to ensure that the *Muselmann* is not forgotten. Agamben argues that:

> it is because there is testimony only where there is an impossibility of speaking, because there is a witness only where there has been desubjectification, that the *Muselmann* is the complete witness and that the survivor and the *Muselmann* cannot be split apart.[37]

Of particular relevance is this fact, that the survivor and the *Muselmann* cannot be separated. This fusion attests to the moral power of witnessing by binding the dead with the living, the privileged with the underprivileged. In speaking for those incapable of speaking, the survivor becomes one with the victim. What has this to do with women's writing and human rights? In Chapter 7, I argued that women are uniquely positioned to be the avatars of human rights because of their experience of pain from the system designed to exploit them. We can understand Agamben's idea that the survivor and *Muselmann* cannot be split apart in the above light. Those who have survived human rights abuses are welded together with the victims in the act of witnessing. The survivors have the obligation to speak out. The little girl in "Requiem for Auntie" can be understood as metonymic of the women writers who speak of abuses of women's rights. In being drawn into her aunt's world, in speaking about her, the niece's life can no longer be separated from that of her aunt. In the same way, the survivors of the Liberian war can no longer be separated from the dead. They are bound by a common fate, by the open wound of being, a wound which the poet, in line with Aristotelian thinking, seeks to heal.

Jabbeh Wesley is to Liberia what Levi is to the survivors of the Holocaust. She speaks through her characters, including the girl in "Requiem for Auntie," and lets us know that the survivor who turns his back on the dead will eventually be confronted with the moral vacuity of his existence. This awareness is enhanced by the experience of the speaker in "Coming Home to Iyeeh" from *Becoming Ebony*.[38] The speaker is the "child that wanders [and who] comes home only to graves." The poem reveals a tone of regret in the speaker who has been away from his homeland for a long time, and who never cared to find out what became of those who were lost. But it is now time for mourning, for paying respect to the dead:

> Every teardrop falling, every dirge sung, every wail or moan
> or sigh...all the drumming and praise songs must be hers.
> *Iyeeh*, Mother, *Khadi Wheh, Wahnjeh*, we praise you—
> it is your children who now praise you...your wandering
> stranger-children now coming home.
> Where there are trumpets, they will sound.
> We do not pour libation with ancestral hands or gourds.[39]

Jabbeh Wesley insinuates an atmosphere of moral urgency. The survivors who turn their back to their past are traitors. They refuse to bear witness to the suffering of their people. She seems to suggest that in regard to morality, the degree to which we relate to the innocent dead parallels the degree to which we relate to the living. *The River Is Rising* is,[40] of Jabbeh Wesley's four collections, the one most directly occupied with the memories of the dead by making an urgent moral plea. The poet provides specific details of the Liberian wars, and even names that ultimately confer humanity on places and incidents, and therefore bring them closer to the reader's axis of empathy. In the title poem, "The River is Rising," the image of a river stands for the ebb and flow of memory. The speaker announces that the river is "swelling with the incoming tide" and people, the speaker included, "stand at the banks" as witnesses to what the rising river will bring. Of course the rising river brings with it crabs and clams and shrimps, but the speaker's description of what they call the "river's creatures" describes much more than these natural inhabitants of the river.

The refrain, "The river is rising, but this is not a flood" is designed to calm those who stand by the river waiting for what will be washed up. The rising river will not sweep them away. Rather they should watch for what it has to show them, besides the life it contains:

> Do not let your eye wander away from this scene
> Yes, all bones below the Mesurado or the St. Paul
> or Sinoe or the Loffa River will be brought up
> to land so all the overwhelming questions
> can once more overwhelm us.[41]

We do not have answers to the overwhelming questions that the washed-up remains will raise, nor are the questions themselves revealed to the readers. They are left to the imagination, which at this stage has probably already been shocked into pity and fear. Being overwhelmed by questions about life implies experiencing an Aristotelian catharsis after which one's life can never return to what it had always been. But it will be a testimony to the humanity of the bystanders if they are overwhelmed by what they see, because the remains are not part of the "river's creatures"; human bones are not supposed to be washed up by rivers. This human wreckage could only have been the product of atrocities, and the tide of the river bears witness to them.

The history of Liberia is rife with instances of brutalities against innocent people. We recall the British and American-sponsored colonization of the nineteenth century as well as the brutal regimes and wars of Samuel Doe and Charles Taylor. The Mesurado, the Loffa, and other rivers must have born witness to those crimes. All of the victims we can imagine come together in the person of "a lost sister" washed up by the rivers, and who stands at the bank "waving at those /who in refusing to die, simply refuse to die." The redundancy in the phrase is designed to underscore the stubbornness of the dead. The dead refuse to die. They are the ones who literally set the rivers moving; however, with the help of their currents, they make their way to the feet of the living. The rivers are their vehicles. By being washed up into the memory of the living, they become one with the survivors—those who, in their own way, also refused to die.

The idea that the dead trouble the living sums up the moral goals of the women writers discussed thus far in regard to their concern with the human rights in society.

In a generous communal spirit, the speaker reminds us that the song is not for "Ellen alone." It is also a song "for Mapue and Tenneh and all the Ellens there are." It is also a song for Kimah and Musu and Massa and the many others. The poet, in having her speaker invoke names belonging to many ethnic groups, makes a gesture of inclusion; she casts the net of her community wide and reminds all Liberians that the healing duty of memory is for all. Healing cannot be partial. Healing that is not total or inclusive is, in effect, an oxymoron. It inflicts more wounds.

The last stanza, "Let no man stand between us /and the river again" hints at the necessity for all to confront the devastating evidence, which has raised overwhelming questions. No one should stand between people and what is remembered; if people lose sight of the latter, they will no longer grieve for the dead, and the failure to grieve, as is implied in Levi's testimonies, derides the living and makes the recurrence of war atrocities possible. Little surprise then that Jabbeh Wesley declared in the interview mentioned above that poetry was an outlet for her grief.

Remembering as Confronting Meaninglessness

Remembering is a function of the meaning-making process after the emptiness of loss. Spelder and Strickland state that "grief is the emotional response to bereavement, to the event of loss."[42] The theologian Todd J. DuBose explains that "grief gazes at an ever-receding present as it moves further and further into the past. The immediate reaction often involves bargaining for a reversal of the loss, denial, anger, shock, anguish, distress, sadness."[43] These reactions are the body's means of trying to make sense of the world in the wake of the emptiness created by bereavement. Interpreting Drew Leder and Maurice Merleau-Ponty's notion of the chiasmic structure of the body, DuBose explains that the body realizes its existence only in relation to, or in reaching out to the external world, to other bodies. It touches because it is being touched. Other bodies make ours perceptible. The disappearance of these other bodies in death is, in tune with the chiasmic structure of bodily existence, the disappearance of our own bodies. We experience that disappearance as pain, grief, sorrow.

These manifestations of pain are, indeed, the ways our bodies adjust to a vacuum and fill it with meaning. For DuBose,

> meaning-making processes, which *appear* to be immaterial processes, are embodied phenomena. Reflection, perception, feeling, language, even logic make sense only through the influx of the body's "reading" of space, time, action, and sensation.[44]

The body invents some immaterial entities or gestures to take the place of the material loss; they include consolation, hope, and love, sometimes even hallucinations and fantasies. The memory of the departed keeps alive the grief of their loss and so confers the present with meaning. For Jabbeh Wesley therefore, to write poetry is to make sense of the dysfunctional world of Liberia. The grief in her works comes with memories, sauntering into the survivor's consciousness like ghosts. Indeed, the persistence of ghosts is a metaphor for the persistence of the memory of the dead and for the attendant grief. This is particularly true in the poem, "Ghosts Don't Go Away Just Like That" from *Where the Road Turns*.

> Sometimes they lurk in hallways where they have lost
> the other side of them. They may hover over new wars
> like the wars that carried them away from their bodies,
> causing them to lose their world and us in the rush.
> Ghosts don't go away just like that, you know;
> they may come in that same huge crowd that was
> massacred together with them, and since that massacre
> may have happened at school, in a bar or at a church, they
> may be found, kneeling at the pulpit, singing and taking
> communion again and again, with everyone else.[45]

In her writing, Jabbeh Wesley performs rituals that acknowledge the existence of these ghosts in ways that bring peace not only to them, but also to the living. Might we interpret these ghosts as representing the absence of human rights? Ghosts, by implication, are the absence of bodies; they leave us to imagine what might have happened to those bodies. Bearing witness to oppression is comparable to grieving, a search for meaning. We fight abuse by creating meaning.

No other poem expresses the violence in Liberia during the civil war as does "An Elegy for the St. Peter's Church Massacred" from *The River is Rising*. It is a poem that details the massacre of 600 men, women, and children at St. Peter's Church, a horrible act that made international news.[46] Over 200 soldiers from the Armed Forces of Liberia (AFL) forced their way into the church and shot the people who had taken refuge there. For the speaker, the survival of such tragedies is more painful than death, and that is why he believes he is in a worse situation than the victims:

> I envy those who were massacred.
> Those who never saw their killers approach
> with heavy bootsteps that made no sound
> in the dark morning hours[47]

He also envies those people who died in the dark, who did not have to "see the faces of their murderers." Perhaps the advantage to the dead in not glimpsing the faces of their murderers is that they will never realize the depravity of their fellow humans. It is this truth of human existence that the speaker, the survivor of the whole horror, has had to live with: "It is a sad story when one survives." The speaker is perhaps feeling guilty of having survived the horrors that consumed others. One of the ways to assuage that guilt is to defy the silence that surrounds the horror. Through him the poet seems to put the survivors to shame and fill them with remorse.

Against the background of rampant violence, the most dramatic aspect of which was the massacre of those 600 unarmed civilians, we begin to understand the agony of a person searching for the members of his family in the poem, "Finding my Family" from *Before the Palm Could Bloom*.[48] The speaker is a man who sets out in search of his children, his "big boy, Nyema," and "the small one, Doeteh." He asks a stranger if he saw "a mother walking by their side." Having lost hope of finding them alive, his tone changes from desperation to one of mourning:

> Good friend, were they hungry
> when they met their end?
> Oh, good friend, I will follow
> to wrap up their bones.
> Thank you, good friend.
> But how will I know their bones?[49]

Are we in a position to provide him with answers to his bewildering questions? Do we know where his wife and children are? These questions are designed to put us on the spot, to embarrass us. We feel shame in the comfort of our living rooms. In our helplessness, we might be tempted to point fingers. We know that the major culprits in the war are the warlords who may have conscripted his boys and killed his wife. But knowing the names of the warlords is not enough. That is not even what the speaker or the poet demands of us. The search, the questions addressed to an unnamed passer-by, one whom the speaker calls friend, is an open invitation to the reader to take the place of this distraught questioner. It is an ethical call to empathize in the manner that Levi urged in the epigraphic poem above. By switching perspectives, which is exactly what empathy achieves, by putting ourselves in the position of the sufferer, or, in this case, the grieving person, we begin to understand the devastation so completely as to be compelled to prevent its recurrence. This, to me, is at the core of Jabbeh Wesley's poetics of testimony. She foresees that anyone capable of fully experiencing another's pain will not likely stand by and allow that pain to be inflicted on others. It is true that the human tendency toward aggression offers no assurance that such shifts of perspective will prevent anyone from inflicting more pain on others. Yet the writer hopes that much can be achieved by keeping the consciousness of the human condition alive.

In "Child Soldier" from *Before the Palm Could Bloom*, the speaker erects a spiritual monument for the "war children /who follow men who have lost all reason." Each of the poem's six stanzas begins with, or is constructed around, a different name. These names—Saye, Ghapu, Kahieh, Nimley, Kortu, Wlemunga—are drawn from the different tribes and ethnicities in Liberia. Ghapu is a Bassa name meaning "light skinned" or "white man." Nimley means "victor" or "I have survived." Kortu means "end the war."[50]

Of particular importance for Jabbeh Wesley's ethical attitude toward Liberia and the world is not only the universal, cosmopolitan spirit that guided the poet's choice of names, but also the fact that some of the names that might belong to one ethnic group were hybrids created from at least two languages and ethnicities. One such name is Nimley, which is both Grebo and Kru. Grebo and Kru, along with Bassa, are from the Kwa or Klao family of languages. These languages have common roots and are so intermeshed as to defy any search for linguistic purity. By choosing names from these language cultures, the poet raises the specter of wars of brothers against brothers. Given that these were child soldiers, the poet calls Africa's attention not only to senseless fratricidal murder, but also the smothering of the future of Africa itself. The poet thus insinuates a question: Why bring children into a world where they will turn against their parents like Frankenstein's creature? This idea of children turning against their parents is especially demonstrated by the existence of Dekuah, a spirit child, whose symbolic relevance we shall discuss more fully later.

In the poem "In the Ruined City: A Poem for Monrovia" from *The River is Rising*, the speaker laments the dearth of aesthetics and leisure.

> There are no more trumpets or drums.
> The Dorklor dancer who lost his legs
> in the war now sits by the roadside, waiting.
> It is something to lose your legs to a war,
> they say, to Charles Taylor's ugly war,
> where the fighter cannot recall why he still fights.[51]

The senselessness of Charles Taylor's war is demonstrated in a particularly painful way through the suggestion that the soldiers no longer know why they fight. But our attention remains with the dancer who has now lost the means for his art, for that which gave meaning to his life. And he sits by the roadside waiting. What exactly is he waiting for? Does he wait in the same way that the speaker in "Where the Road Turns" does? With the dancer's waiting, the poet leaves a hole in our hearts, a great longing symbolized by his missing limbs. We understand the missing limbs as the most visible scar of human rights abuse. But the man does not succumb to his condition; he searches for meaning, for love.

Jabbeh Wesley leaves us with more than just pictures of desolation in her poetics of testimony. Even as she explores the traumas of the war, she steers the reader's attention to the Liberian people's passion for life. In "I am Not Dekuah" from *Before the Palm Could Bloom*, the speaker addresses his/her clansmen:

> Dieh, I come knocking
> Clansmen, I come calling.
> I come crawling at your doors.
> There is a matter
> from my heart.
> Gather your sons from afar
> at *Tuwa Kai*
> *Kwee* must come to town today.[52]

The picture painted is that of a guest asking for accommodation. But we learn that the speaker is a child, and therefore his plea is existential; he wants to live and to thrive. The speaker's clan is representative of the larger world. He pleads with that world for a chance to grow. "I am not Dekuah; let me live". "I am not Dekuah" appears five times in the seven stanzas of the poem, underscoring the speaker's resolve to live. This anaphora draws attention to the precariousness of the situation that children, and, indeed everyone else was facing at during the war. People were making peace with the fact that children were not surviving childhood. As child soldiers, some of the children even turned against their parents. It is in this context that the speaker announces that he is not Dekuah.

Dekuah is a spirit child whose goal is to punish its birthing family as it is bound to slip into the birthing mother's womb again, only to die again after birth. It is to be assumed that Dekuah is a gratuitously malignant spirit that delights in the pain of those who gave it life. Some children, according to this mythology, succeed in being born up to three times. There is an obvious influence from Wole Soyinka's poem "Abiku" in Jabbeh Wesley's uses of Dekuah in her poetry. In "Abiku," the spirit child boasts in the first stanza that there is nothing his birthing family can do to keep him in the land of the living.

> In vain your bangles cast
> Charmed circles at my feet
> I am Abiku, calling for the first
> And repeated time[53]

Abiku children are given marks on their faces or other visible parts of the body so that when they are born again, those marks will reveal them for who they are: deceivers, spirit children. Some of the children, having been discovered and shamed, decide to stay in the land of the living. Some, nevertheless still return to the "spirit world" because of their stronger binding pacts with other children there.[54] The Grebo (Jabbeh Wesley's ethnicity), believe, as do most West African cultures, that such spirit children exist. In these cultures, children are given similar names. Dekuah in Grebo can be broken down as De "come," Kuah, "to die": a child who has come to die. Other names associated with the Dekuah (Abiku) phenomenon are Mudi, "Go Back," Sejlah "We don't want you," Kude "The devil's mother," et cetera.

If Dekuah signifies unwillingness to live, or reminds us of the Frankenstein syndrome, as we suggested above, it is no surprise that the child in the poem immediately announces that he is not Dekuah; he has not come to die. Emphasizing the singularity of his existence, his will to live, he says, "I've never been born before" and then goes on to announce what he is and what he desires. "My name is Nehklon / Let me live." Of particular relevance is the shift from the negative declaration "I am not" to a positive one, "I am". In this linguistic switch, the poet signals a deeper moral and existential consequence. In this shift from a reactionary attitude to life to one that is proactive, Jabbeh Wesley brings the challenges of life affirmation to the consciousness of her readers. Through Nehklon, she enables us to imagine people taking charge of their lives, as Levi does in his "If This Is a Man". It is therefore not only Nehklon who pleads; all Liberians plead for a chance to live, for a fair share in life's bounty. There is nothing to be happy about in the remembrance of the war's violence; there is no happy ending for the narrative other than the hope that people might be allowed to live and to thrive. People are not Dekuahs; they have not come to die.

I titled the concluding section of Chapter 5 "When Right Means Life." The title is in tune with one of the central ideas of this book, which is that the absence of rights disables women, and often leads to their death. In Petina Gappah's short story, "At the Sound of the Last Post" the denial of rights leads to the death of the hero's first wife. In Sefi Atta's novel, *Everything Good Will Come*, Arinola experiences the same fate. If rights mean life, the reverse is also the case. The love of life is precisely a call for rights. To put it differently, there can be no love of life without rights. The desire to live is universal. Might this be Jabbeh Wesley's appeal to universal human rights?

Carol Blessing rightly observes that Jabbeh Wesley's poetic tone "shifts between critical, bemused, revelatory, celebratory, and mournful, as she discusses both her American and Liberian lives."[55] Her style is generally narrative, predominantly free verse that lives primarily through her deft evocation of strong images. Adhering closely to formal stanzas often arranged in couplets, tercets, and quatrains, but dispensing with strict meters and rhymes, she delves into conversational rhythms that invoke a familial atmosphere. Her narrative is often reminiscent of folklore—as if the narrator were among friends, telling stories around the kitchen table. The moment of epiphany in such contexts comes when mournful tones sneak into the words of the speaker. For example, "Strange Lovers" from the collection *Before the Palm Could Bloom*, begins:

> So it is the moon that sends the Mesurado
> running to visit the Atlantic
> with its millions of troops?[56]

Here Jabbeh Wesley plays with elements that the listeners are very familiar with and which they can easily visualize. The personification of the Mesurado River achieves comic relief even in the midst of tragedy. Throughout the poem, a voice induces a dialogue between the river and its millions of troops— its fish–and, taking the position of the fish, goes on with questions, now directed at some other forces. One can imagine children chuckling at the narrative, and adults grinning, while they are all seated around the family hearth listening. The last three stanzas evince a change in tone, preparing the reader for a shocking realization. The fish, and the voice that has taken their perspective, are tired of being sent on rendezvous. One of these days the voice/fish will be gone

> Like a frog that cried and cried for the rain,
> and before the rains, withers beside the dried
> banks of the stream.
> I'll be gone, Mesurado, do you hear me?[57]

Even in her familial tone, and perhaps because of it, Jabbeh Wesley never forgets that the healing and meaning-making function of grief and mourning, as painful as the latter processes are, is not to be avoided. Rather, as DuBose, argues, based on the painful experience of his wife's miscarriage, as "'child' and 'parent' disappeared, our bodies and our society *dys*-appeared, and our connections and hopes re-appeared."[58] Jabbeh Wesley attaches the reappearance of hopes for the healing and reconstruction of her Liberian world to people's ability and willingness to truly experience the painful process of grief and, perhaps informed by that cathartic experience, to allow compassion and empathy to guide their relationship to others.

NOTES

1. Carol Blessing, "Exile and Maternal Loss in the Poems of Patricia Jabbeh Wesley," in *Exile and the Narrative/Poetic Imagination*, ed. Agnieszka Gutthy. Newcastle upon Tyne: Cambridge Scholars Publishing, 2010, 77–93 (Blessing 2010).
2. Charles Morrow Wilson, *Black Africa in Microcosm*. New York: Harper & Row, 1971, 25–30 (Wilson 1971).
3. Ibid., 52.
4. Yekutiel Gershoni, *Black Colonialism: The Americo-Liberian Scramble for the Hinterland*. Boulder and London: Westview Press, 1985, xi (Gershoni 1985).
5. Ibid., 95.

6. George Klay Kieh, *The First Liberian Civil War: The Crises of Underdevelopment*. New York: Peter Lang, 2008, 25–29 (Kieh 2008).
7. Melissa Beattie-Moss, "Word of Mouth. The Painful, Joyful Heart: A Conversation with Patricia Jabbeh Wesley." 2005. http://www.rps.psu.edu/jabbeh/index.html (Accessed October 26, 2012) (Beattie-Moss 2005).
8. Ibid.
9. Hal Herring, "Dreaming of Home: A Conversation with Liberian Poet Patricia Jabbeh Wesley," *Bloomsbury Review*, 23.5 (2003): no page. (Herring 2003)
10. James Dawes, "Human Rights in Literary Studies," *Human Rights Quarterly*, 31.2 (2009): 395 (Dawes 2009).
11. Richard Kearney, "Narrative and Ethics," *Proceedings of the Aristotelian Society*, 70 (1996): 31(Kearney 1996).
12. Susan L. Feagin, "The Pleasure of Tragedy," *American Philosophical Quarterly*, 20.1 (1983): 103 (Feagin 1983).
13. Geoffrey Hartman, "The Humanities of Testimonies: An Introduction," *Poetics Today*, 27.2 (2006): 249 (Hartman 2006).
14. Primo Levi, *The Drowned and the Saved*. New York: Simon and Schuster, 1988, 199 (Levi 1998).
15. Ibid., 199.
16. Primo Levi, *Survival in Auschwitz: The Nazi Assault on Humanity*. Trans. Stuart Woolf. New York: A Touchstone Book, 1996, 9 (Levi 1996).
17. Ibid., 9.
18. Nicholas Patruno, *Understanding Primo Levi*. Columbia, SC: The University of South Carolina Press, 1995, 9 (Patruno 1995).
19. Ibid., 10.
20. Jonathan Druker, "Ethics and Ontology in Primo Levi's 'Survival in Auschwitz': A Levinasian Reading," *Italica*, 83.3.4 (2006): 533 (Druker 2006).
21. Ibid., 534.
22. Levi, *The Drowned*, 15 (Levi 1998).
23. Donald Revell, *The Art of Attention: A Poet's Eye* (Minneapolis, MN: Graywolf Press, 2007), 13 (Revell 2007).
24. Ibid., 18.
25. Patricia Jabbeh Wesley, *Where The Road Turns*. Pittsburgh, PA: Autumn House Press, 2010 (Wesley 2010).
26. Ibid., 56
27. Mark Doty, *The Art of Description: World Into Word*. Minneapolis, MN: Graywolf Press, 2010, 21 (Doty 2010).
28. Ibid.
29. Patricia Jabbeh Wesley, *Where The Road Turns*, 7.
30. Patricia Jabbeh Wesley, *Becoming Ebony*. Carbondale, IL: Southern Illinois University Press, 2003 (Wesley 2003).
31. Ibid., 8.

32. Ibid., 9.
33. "Muslim" in German.
34. Giorgio Agamben, *Remnants of Auschwitz: The Witness and the Archive.* Trans. Daniel Heller-Roazen. New York: Zone Books, 1999, 156 (Agamben 1999).
35. Ibid., 156–157.
36. Ibid., 158.
37. Ibid., 158.
38. Wesley, *Becoming Ebony* (Wesley 2003).
39. Ibid. 27.
40. Patricia Jabbeh Wesley, *The River is Rising*. Pittsburgh, PA: Autumn House Press, 2007 (Wesley 2007).
41. Ibid., 11.
42. Cited in J. Todd DuBose, "The Phenomenology of Bereavement, Grief, and Mourning," *Journal of Religion and Health*, 36.4 (1997): 368 (DuBose 1997).
43. Ibid., 368.
44. Ibid., 370.
45. Ibid., 39.
46. Reuters, "Liberia Troops Accused Of Massacre in Church." 1990 (Reuters 1990). http://www.nytimes.com/1990/07/31/world/liberia-troops-accused-of-massacre-in-church.html.
47. Ibid., 44.
48. Patricia Jabbeh Wesley, Before The Palm Could Bloom: Poems of Africa. New Issues Press Kalamazoo, Western Michigan University, 1998.
49. Ibid., 20.
50. I am grateful to Patricia Jabbeh Wesley for translating these names and guiding me through Liberian cultures and languages.
51. Jabbeh Wesley, The River is Rising, 34.
52. Jabbeh Wesley, Before the Palm Could Bloom, 9.
53. Wole Soyinka, "Abiku." www.cafeafrikana.com/poetry.html.
54. Chidi T. Maduka, "African Religious Beliefs in Literary Imagination: Ogbanje and Abiku in Chiuna Achebe, J.P. Clark and Wole Soyinka," *Journal of Commonwealth Literature*, 22.1 (1987): 18 (Maduka 1987).
55. Blessing, "Exile and Maternal Loss in the Poems of Patricia Jabbeh Wesley," 78–79 (Blessing 2010).
56. Jabbeh Wesley, Before the Palm Could Bloom, 33.
57. Ibid., 33–34.
58. DuBose, "The Phenomenology of Bereavement," 374 (DuBose 1997).

BIBLIOGRAPHY

Achebe, Chinua. 1975. *Morning Yet on Creation Day*. New York: Anchor Press/Doubleday.
Achebe, Chinua. 1988. *Hopes and Impediments*. New York: Doubleday.
Achebe, Chinua. 1994. *Things Fall Apart* (original 1958). New York: Anchor Books.
Achebe, Chinua. 2000. *Home and Exile*. New York: Oxford University Press.
Acholonu, Catherine Obianuju. 2002. *Motherism: The Afrocentric Alternative*. Owerri, Nigeria: Afa Publications.
Adams, Tony E. 2008. A Review of Narrative Ethics. *Qualitative Inquiry* 14.2: 175–194.
Adeleke, Tunde. 1998. "Black Americans and Africa: A Critique of the Pan-African and Identity Paradigms." *The International Journal of African Historical Studies* 31.3: 505–536.
Adichie, Chimamanda Ngozi. 2003. *Purple Hibiscus*. New York: Anchor Books.
Adichie, Chimamanda Ngozi. 2009. *The Thing Around Your Neck*. Lagos: Farafina Books.
Adichie, Chimamanda Ngozi. 2011. The Dangers of a Single Story. www.ted.com/talks/chimamanda_adichie_the_danger_of_a_single_story.html. Accessed January 2, 2012.
Adichie, Chimamanda Ngozi. 2013. "We Should All Be Feminists." http://tedxtalks.ted.com/video/We-should-all-be-feminists-Chim.
African Commission on Human and Peoples' Rights. 2015. African Charter on Human and Peoples' Rights. http://www.achpr.org/instruments/achpr/#a29. Accessed March 2, 2015.

© The Author(s) 2016
C. Eze, *Ethics and Human Rights in Anglophone African Women's Literature*, Comparative Feminist Studies,
DOI 10.1007/978-3-319-40922-1

Afrol.com. 2012. http://www.afrol.com/Categories/Women/wom005_fgm_norway.htm. Accessed April 22, 2012.

Agamben, Giorgio. 1999. *Remnants of Auschwitz: The Witness and the Archive.* Trans. Daniel Heller-Roazen. New York: Zone Books.

Ahmed, Nabaz, Shara Amin, Patrick Farrelly, Sinead Kinnane, Jordan Montminy, Maggie O'Kane and Alex Rees. 2014. "FGM: The Film That Changed the Law in Kurdistan" – video. www.theguardian.com/society/video/2013/oct/24/fgm-film-changed-the-law-kurdistan-video. Accessed August 24, 2014.

Aidoo, Ama Ata. 1993. *Changes.* New York: The Feminist Press at CUNY.

Ake Festival. 2013. www.akefestival.org. Accessed November 8, 2013.

Akung, Jonas E. 2012. "Feminist Dimensions in Sefi Atta's *Everything Good Will Come.*" *Studies in Literature and Language* 4.1: 114–122. http://cscanada.net/index.php/sll.article/view/j.sll.1923156320120401.1930. Accessed October 10, 2012.

Ali, Ayaan Hirsi. 2007. *Infidel.* New York: Simon and Schuster.

Allen, Amy. 2008. *The Politics of Our Selves: Power, Autonomy, and Gender in Contemporary Critical Theory.* New York: University of Columbia Press.

Althusser, Louis. 1971. *Lenin and Philosophy.* Trans. Ben Brewster. New York: Monthly Review Press.

Amadiume, Ifi. 1987. *Male Daughters, Female Husbands: Gender and Sex in an African Society.* London: Zed Books Ltd.

Amede Obiora, L. 2003. "The Little Foxes that Spoil the Vine: Revisiting the Feminist Critique of Female Circumcision." *African Women and Feminism: Reflecting on the Politics of Sisterhood*, ed. Oyeronke Oyewumi, 197–230. Trenton, NJ: Africa World Press Inc

Amina, Mire. 1998. "In/Through the Bodies of Women: Rethinking Gender in African Politics." *POLIS* 6 2. www.polis.sciencespobordeaux.fr/vol8ns/mire.pdf. Accessed June 3, 2012.

Amore, K.P., Bamgbose, G.S. and A.O. Lawani. 2011. "Gender Politics: Reflection of Inter-Genpolitism in Buchi Emecheta's Second-Class Citizen." *i-Hurage: International Journal for Human Right and Gender Education* 2.2: 204–215.

Anderson, Amanda. 2006. *The Way We Argue Now: A Study in the Culture of Theory.* Princeton University Press.

Andrade, Susan Z. 2011. *The Nation Writ Small: African Fictions and Feminisms, 1958–1988.* Durham: Duke University Press Books.

Andrade, Susan Z. 2011. "Adichie's Genealogies: National and Feminine Novels." *Research in African Literatures.* Achebe's World: African Literature at Fifty 42.2: 91–101.

Anker, Elizabeth S. 2012. *Fictions of Dignity: Embodying Human Rights in World Literature.* Ithaca: Cornell University Press.

An-Na'im, Abdullahi Ahmed, and Francis M. Deng, eds. 1990. *Human Rights in Africa: Cross-Cultural Perspectives.* Washington, DC: The Brookings Institute.

Anya, Ike. 2005. "Sefi Atta: Something Good Comes to Nigerian Literature." http://www.africanwriter.com/sefi-atta-something-good-comes-to-nigerian-literature/. Accessed June 30, 2005.

Anyadike, Chima. 2008. "The Global North in Achebe's *Arrow of God* and Adichie's *Half of a Yellow Sun.*" *Global South* 2.2: 139–149.

Anzaldua, Gloria. 1999. *Borderlands/La Frontera: The New Mestiza.* San Francisco: Spinsters/aunt lute.

Appiah, Kwame Anthony. 1992. *In My Father's House: Africa in the Philosophy of Culture.* New York: Oxford University Press.

Appiah, Kwame Anthony. 2006. *Cosmopolitanism: Ethics in a World of Strangers.* New York: W.W. Norton.

Arendt, Hannah. 1998. *The Human Condition.* Chicago: University of Chicago Press.

Aristotle. 1996. *Poetics.* Trans. Malcolm Heath. London: Penguin Books.

Aristotle. 1999. *Nicomachean Ethics.* Trans. Terence Irwin. Indianapolis: Hackett Publishing Co.

Arndt, Susan. 2001. *The Dynamics of African Feminism: Defining and Classifying African-Feminist Literatures.* Trans. Isabel Cole. Trenton, NJ: Africa World Press.

Ashcroft, Bill, Gareth Griffiths, and Helen Tiffin. 1989. *The Empire Writes Back: Theory and Practice in Post-Colonial Literatures.* London: Routledge.

Assah, Augustine H. 2007. "Images of Rape in African Fiction: Between the Assumed Fatality of Violence and the Cry for Justice." *Annales Aequatoria* 28: 333–355.

Assah, Augustine H. 2008. "Challenges of Our Times: Responses of African/Diasporan Intellectuals to FGM." *Afroeuropa: Journal of Afro-European Studies* 2.1: no page. http://journal.afroeuropa.eu/index.php/afroeuropa/article/viewFile/62/73.

Assah, Augustine H., and Tobe Levin, eds. 2009. *Empathy and Rage: Female Genital Mutilation in African Literature.* Banbury, UK: Ayebia Clarke Pub.

Associated News. 2007. "Europe, Africa Seek New Relationship at Summit." www.iht.com/articles/ap/2007/12/08/europe/EU-GEN-EU-Africa-Summit.php. Accessed January 30, 2008.

Atta, Sefi. 2004. *Everything Good Will Come.* Boston: Interlink Books.

Atta, Sefi. 2011. *Swallow.* Boston: Interlink Books.

Attfield, Robert, and Susanne Gibson. 1996. "Ethics." In *A Dictionary of Cultural and Critical Theory,* ed. Michael Payne. Oxford, UK: Blackwell Publishers.

Attree, Lizzy. 2013. "The Caine Prize and Contemporary African Writing." *Research in African Literatures* 44.2: 35–47.
Atwood, Margaret. 2010. "Why We Tell Stories." *Big Think.* www.bigthink.com/ideas/24259. Accessed June 3, 2012.
Azuah, Unoma. 2008. "Of Phases and Faces: Unoma Azuah Engages Sefi Atta and Chika Unigwe. *Research in African Literature. Nigeria's Third-Generation Novel: Preliminary Theoretical Engagement* 39.2: 108–116.
Bâ, Mariama. 1989. *So Long a Letter.* London: Heinemann.
Bady, Aaron. 2001. "Blogging the Caine Prize." *Zungu Zungu.* May 30. Accessed March 7, 2014.
Bae, Sangmin. 2007. *When the State No Longer Kills: International Human Rights Norms and Abolition of Capital Punishment.* New York: State University of New York Press.
Baingana, Doreen. 2003. *Tropical Fish: Stories Out of Entebbe.* Amherst: University of Massachusetts.
Baron-Cohen, Simon. 2011. *Zero Degrees of Empathy.* London: Allen Lane.
Barton, Edwin J., and Glenda A. Hudson. 2004. *Contemporary Guide to Literary Terms: With Strategies for Writing Essays About Literature.* 2nd edition. Boston: Houghton Mifflin Company.
Bazin, Nancy Topping. 1985. "Venturing Into Feminist Consciousness: Two Protagonists from the Fiction of Buchi Emecheta and Bessie Head." *Sage II.* 2.1: 32–36.
BBC News. 2008. "UK Caused Cholera, Says Zimbabwe." http://news.bbc.co.uk/2/hi/7780728.stm.
BBC News. 2014, April 29. "President Uhuru Kenyatta Signs Kenya Polygamy Law." www.bbc.com/news/world-africa-27206590.
Beattie-Moss, Melissa. 2005. Word of Mouth. The Painful, Joyful Heart: A Conversation with Patricia Jabbeh Wesley. http://www.rps.psu.edu/jabbeh/index.html. Accessed Friday, October 26, 2012.
Beech, Dave. 2009. "Beauty, Ideology and Utopia." http://www.uwe.ac.uk/sca/research/vcrg/proj_beech.htm.
Beech, Dave, ed. 2009. *Beauty* (Whitechapel: Documents of Contemporary Art). Cambridge, MA:, The MIT Press.
Bekers, Elisabeth. 2010. *Rising Anthills: African and African American Writing on Female Genital Excision,* 1960–2000. Madison, WI: University of Wisconsin Press.
Benjamin, Walter. 2013. *On the Concept of History.* www.marxist.org. Accessed September 7, 2013.
Blessing, Carol. 2010. "Exile and Maternal Loss in the Poems of Patricia Jabbeh Wesley." In *Exile and the Narrative/Poetic Imagination,* ed. Agnieszka Gutthy, 77–93. Newcastle upon Tyne: Cambridge Scholars Publishing.
Boehmer, Elleke. 2005. *Gender and Narrative in Postcolonial Nation.* Manchester University Press.

Buber, Martin. 1970. *I and Thou*. New York: Simon Schuster.
Buell, Lawrence. 2000. "What We Talk About When We Talk About Ethics." In *The Turn To Ethics*, ed. Marjorie Garber, et al. New York: Routledge.
Buergenthal, Thomas. 2000. "International Human Rights in an Historical Perspective." In *Human Rights: Concept and Standards*, ed. Janusz Symonides, 3–30. Aldershot, UK: Dartmouth Publishing Company Ltd.
Bulawayo, NoViolet. 2013. *We Need New Names*. New York: Little Brown.
Burke, Kenneth. 1945. *Grammar of Motives*. Berkeley: University of California Press.
Butler, Judith. 1997. *The Psychic Life of Power: Theories in Subjection*. Stanford, CA: Stanford University Press.
Butler, Judith. 2001. "Giving an Account of Oneself." *Diacritics* 31.4: 22–40.
Butler, Judith. 2005. *Giving an Account of Oneself*. New York: Fordham University Press.
Cary, Joyce. 1951. *Mister Johnson*. New York: Harper and Brothers.
Castle, Stephen. 2007. Mugabe's Presence Hijacks European-African Meeting. *New York Times*. http://www.nytimes.com/2007/12/09/world/africa/09summit.html?fta=y&_r=0.
Catholic Commission for Justice and Peace. 2006. *Gukurahundi in Zimbabwe: A Report Into the Disturbances in Matabeleland and the Midlands 1980–1988*. South Africa: Jacana Media (Pty) Ltd.
Cazenave, Odile, and Patricia Célérier. 2011. *Contemporary Francophone African Writers and the Burden of Commitment*. Charlottesville, VA: University of Virginia Press.
Chennells, Anthony. 2009. "Inculturated Catholicisms in Chimamanda Ngozi Adichie's *Purple Hibiscus*." *English Academy Review* 26.1: 15–26.
Chinweizu. 1975. *The West and the Rest of Us*. New York: Vintage Publishers.
Chinweizu. 1990. *Anatomy of Female Power: A Masculinist Dissection of Matriarchy*. Lagos: Nigeria Pero Press.
Chukukere, Glo. 1995. *Gender Voices and Choices: Redefining Women in Contemporary African Fiction*. Enugu: Fourth Dimension.
Chukukere, Glo. 1998. "An Appraisal of Feminism in the Socio-Political Development of Nigeria." In *Sisterhood, Feminism and Power: From Africa to the Diaspora*, ed. Obioma Nnaemeka. Trenton, NJ: Africa World Press.
Cixous, Hélène. 1976. "The Laugh of the Medusa." Trans. Keith Cohen and Paula Cohen. *Signs* 1.4: 875–893.
Clinton, Hillary Rodham. 2013. "Helping Women Isn't Just a "Nice" Thing to Do." http://www.thedailybeast.com/witw/articles/2013/04/05/hillary-clinton-helping-women-isn-t-just-a-nice-thing-to-do.html. Accessed May 15, 2013.
Clinton, Hillary Rodham. 2013. "Women's Rights are Human Rights." http://gos.sbc.edu/c/clinton.html. Accessed May 15, 2013.
Coly, Ayo A. 2010. *The Pull of Postcolonial Nationhood: Gender and Migration in Francophone African Literatures*. Lanham: Lexington Books.

Conrad, Joseph. 1990. *Heart of Darkness* (original 1899). New York: Dover Thrift Editions.

Cooper, Brenda. 2008. *A New Generation of African Writers: Migration, Material Culture and Language*. Suffolk, UK: James Currey.

Culbertson, Carolyn. 2013. "The Ethics of Relationality: Judith Butler and Social Critique." *Continental Philosophy Review* 46: 449–463.

D'Almeida, Irène. 1994. *Francophone African Women: Destroying the Emptiness of Silence*. Gainesville, FL: University of Florida Press.

Dangarembga, Tsitsi. 1988. *Nervous Conditions*. New York: Seal Press.

Dathorne, O.R. 1976. *African Literature in the Twentieth Century*. Minnesota: University of Minnesota Press.

Davies, Carol Boyce. 1986. "Introduction: Feminist Consciousness and African Literary Criticism." In *Ngambika: Studies of Women in African Literature*, ed. Carol Boyce Davies and Anne Adams Graves, 1–23; 8–12. Trenton, NJ: Africa World Press.

Dawes, James. 2007. *That the World May Know: Bearing Witness to Atrocity*. Cambridge, MA: Harvard UniversityPress.

Dawes, James. 2009. "Human Rights in Literary Studies." *Human Rights Quarterly* 31.2: 394–409.

De Waal, Frans. 2009. *The Age of Empathy: Nature's Lessons for a Kinder Society*. New York: Harmony Books.

Dembour, Marie-Bénédicte. 2010. "What Are Human Rights? Four Schools of Thought." *Human Rights Quarterly* 32.1: 1–20.

Diamond, Larry. 1989. "Fiction as Political Thought." *African Affairs* 88: 435–445.

Didion, Joan. 2006. *We Tell Ourselves Stories in Order to Live: Collected Nonfiction*. New York: Alfred Knopf.

Dirie, Waris. 1998. *Desert Flower: The Extraordinary Life of a Desert Nomad*. London: Virago.

Donnelly, Jack. 2003. *Universal Human Rights in Theory and Practice*. Ithaca, NY: Cornell University Press.

Doty, Mark. 2010. *The Art of Description: World into Word*. Minneapolis, MN: Graywolf Press.

Druker, Jonathan. 2006. Ethics and Ontology in Primo Levi's "Survival in Auschwitz": A Levinasian Reading. *Italica* 83.3 4: 529–542.

DuBose, J. Todd. 1997. "The Phenomenology of Bereavement, Grief, and Mourning." *Journal of Religion and Health* 36.4: 367–374.

Eagleton, Terry. 2003. *After Theory*. New York: Basic Books.

Egejuru, Phanuel A., and Ketu H. Katrak, eds. 1997. *Nwanyibu: Womanbeing and African Literature*. Trenton: Africa World Press.

Ekpo, Denis. 2010. "Introduction: From Negritude to Post-Africanism." *Third Text* 24.2: 177–187.

Emecheta, Buchi. 1980. *The Joys of Motherhood*. London: George Braziller, Inc.
Emecheta, Buchi. 1980. *The Slave Girl*. New York: George Braziller, Inc.
Emecheta, Buchi. 1988. "Feminism with a Small "f"!" In *Criticism and Ideology. Second African Writers' Conference*, ed. Kirsten Holst Petersen, 173–185. Uppsala: Scandinavian Institute of African Studies.
El Saadawi, Nawal. 2007. *The Hidden Face of Eve*. New York: Zed Books.
Eze, Emmanuel, ed. 1997. *Race and the Enlightenment: A Reader*. Malden, MA: Wiley-Blackwell.
Eze, Chielozona. 2011. *Postcolonial Imagination and Moral Representations in African Literature Culture*. Lanham: Lexington Books.
Eze, Chielozona. 2013. "Death, Here I Am: Violence and Redemption in Zakes Mda's *Ways of Dying*." *Journal of Narrative Theory* 43.1 (Spring): 87–107.
Eze, Chielozona. 2014. "Rethinking African Culture and Identity: The Afropolitan Model." *Journal of African Cultural Studies* 26.2: 234–247.
Eze, Chielozona. 2015. "Transcultural Affinity: Thoughts on the Emergent Cosmopolitan Imagination in South Africa." *Journal of African Cultural Studies* 17.2: 216–228.
Fanon, Frantz. 1967. *Black Skin, White Masks*. New York: Grove Press.
Fanon, Frantz. 1967. *The Wretched of the Earth*. Trans. Constance Farrington. London: Penguin Books.
Feagin, Susan L. 1983. "The Pleasures of Tragedy." *American Philosophical Quarterly* 20.1: 95–104.
Foucault, Michel. 1978. *The History of Sexuality*. Vol. 1. Trans. R. Hurley. New York: Random House.
Foucault, Michel. 1997. *Ethics: Subjectivity and Truth: The Essential Works of Michel Foucault. 1954–1984*. Edited by Paul Rabinow. New York: The New Press.
Frank, Arthur W. 1995. *The Wounded Storyteller: Body, Illness, and Ethics*. Chicago: University of Chicago Press.
Frank, Arthur W. 2010. *Letting Stories Breathe*. Chicago: The University of Chicago Press.
Gappah, Petina. 2009. *An Elegy for Easterly*. London: Faber and Faber.
Garland Thomson, Rosemarie. 1997. *Extraordinary Bodies: Figuring Physical Disability in American Culture and Literature*. New York: Columbia University Press.
Garland-Thomson, Rosemarie. 2002. "Integrating Disability, Transforming Feminist Theory." *NWSA Journal* 14.3: 1–32.
Garuba, Harry. 2005. "The Unbearable Lightness of Being": Re-Figuring Trends in Recent Nigerian Poetry. *English in Africa:New Nigerian Writing*. 32.1: 51–72.
Gershoni, Yekutiel. 1985. *Black Colonialism: The Americo-Liberian Scramble for the Hinterland*. Boulder and London: Westview Press.

Gert, Bernard. 2012. "The Definition of Morality." *The Stanford Encyclopedia of Philosophy*. Edited by Edward N. Zalta. http://plato.stanford.edu/archives/fall2012/entries/morality-definition/. Accessed May 20, 2013.

Gikandi, Simon. 2001. "Chinua Achebe and the Invention of African Culture." *Research in African Literature*. 32.3: 4–8.

Gilchrist, J. J., M. Fernandes, L. Poulton, G. Grandjean, and M. Tait. 2009. "Zimbabwe: Cholera Country." www.guardian.co.uk/world/video/2009/feb/26/zimbabwe-cholera. Accessed Wednesday, February 25, 2009.

Gqola, Pumla Dineo. 2005. "Editorial: Yindaba kaban' u'ba ndilahl' umlenze? Sexuality and Body Image." *Agenda: Empowering Women for Gender Equity*. 63, African Feminisms. 2.2: Sexuality and Body Image: 3–9.

Gqola, Pumla Dineo. 2015. *Rape: A South African Nightmare*. Johannesburg: Jacana Media.

Greenspan, P.S. 1994. "Guilt and Virtue." *The Journal of Philosophy* 92.2: 57–70.

Habila, Helon. 2013. We Need New Names by NoViolet Bulawayo—Review. http://www.theguardian.com/books/2013/jun/20/need-new-names-bulawayo-review.

Habila, Helon, ed. 2011. *The Granta Book of African Short Story*. London: Granta Books.

Halliwell, Stephen. 1998. *Aristotle's Poetics*. Chicago: University of Chicago Press.

Harris, Hugh. 1927. "The Greek Origins of the Idea of Cosmopolitanism." *The International Journal of Ethics* 38: 1–10.

Harrow, Ken. 2002. *Less Than One and Double: A Feminist Reading of African Women's Writing*. Portsmouth, NH: Heinemann.

Hartman, Geoffrey. 2006. "The Humanities of Testimonies: An Introduction." *Poetics Today* 27.2: 249–260.

Hawthorne, Susan. 2005. "Ancient Hatred and Its Contemporary Manifestation: The Torture of Lesbians." *Journal of Hate Studies* 4.1: 33–58.

Hegel, Wilhelm Gottfried. 1971. *Philosophy of Mind: Being Part Three of the Encyclopedia of the Philosophical Sciences* (1830). Edited by William Wallace. Oxford: Clarendon Press.

Herring, Hal. 2003. "Dreaming of Home: A Conversation with Liberian Poet Patricia Jabbeh Wesley." *Bloomsbury Review* 5: 23.

Hetherington, Penelope. 1998. "The Politics of Female Circumcision in the Central Province of Colonial Kenya, 1920–30." *The Journal of Imperial and Commonwealth History* 26.1: 93–126.

hooks, bell. 2000. *Feminism is for Everybody*. Cambridge, MA: Pluto Press.

hooks, bell. 2004. "Feminism: A Movement to End Sexist Oppression." In *Readings in Feminist Rhetorical Theory*, ed. Cindy L. Griffin, Karen A. Foss, and Sonja K. Foss, 47–56. Thousand Oaks, CA: Sage Publications.

Hope, Lewis. 1995. "Between Irua and Female Genital Mutilation: Feminist Human Rights Discourse and the Cultural Divide." *Harvard Human Rights Journal* 8.1: 1–55.

Huffington Post. 2014, March 20. "Nearly 4,000 Treated For Female Genital Mutilation in London." http://www.huffingtonpost.com/2014/03/20/female-genital-mutilation_n_5000214.html.

Hunt, Lynn. 2008. *Inventing Human Rights: A History*. New York: W.W. Norton & Company.

Ikheloa, Ikhide. 2011. "The 2011 Caine Prize: How Not to Write About Africa." www.xokigbo.wordpress.com. Accessed February 5, 2014.

IRIN: Humanitarian News and Analysis. 2005, March 17. "In-depth: Razor's Edge—The Controversy of Female Genital Mutilation: KENYA: Justifying Tradition: Why Some Kenyan Men Favour FGM." http://www.irinnews.org/indepthmain.aspx?InDepthId=15&ReportId=62471&Country=Yes.

IRIN: Humanitarian News and Analysis. 2005, March 17. "Razor's Edge—The Controversy of Female Genital Mutilation SIERRA LEONE: Female Circumcision Is a Vote Winner. http://www.irinnews.org/indepthmain.aspx?InDepthId=15&ReportId=62473&Country=Yes.

Iser, Wolfgang. 1978. *The Act of Reading: A Theory of Aesthetic Response*. Baltimore: The Johns Hopkins Press.

Jabbeh Wesley, Patricia. 1998. *Before The Palm Could Bloom: Poems of Africa*. New Issues Press Kalamazoo, MI: Western Michigan University.

Jabbeh Wesley, Patricia. 2003. *Becoming Ebony*. Carbondale, IL: Southern Illinois University Press.

Jabbeh Wesley, Patricia. 2007. *The River Is Rising*. Pittsburgh, PA: Autumn House Press. 2007.

Jabbeh Wesley, Patricia. 2010. *Where the Road Turns*. Pittsburgh, PA: Autumn House Press.

JanMohamed, Abdul. 1986. "The Economy of Manichean Allegory: The Function of Racial Difference in Colonialist Literature." In *Race, Writing and Difference*, ed. Henry Louis Gates, Jr., 59–87. Chicago: University of Chicago Press.

Jobson, Liesl. 2013. "Author Interview: A Love Letter to All Zimbabweans." http://www.bdlive.co.za/life/books/2013/10/22/author-interview-a-love-letter-to-all-zimbabweans.

Johnson, James D., Carolyn H. Simmons, Amanda Jordav, Leslie Maclean, Jeffrey Taddei, Duane Thomas, John F. Dovidio, and William Reed. 2002. "Rodney King and O.J. Revisited: The Impact of Race and Defendant Empathy Induction on Judicial Decisions." *Journal of Applied Social Psychology* 32.6: 1208–1223.

Jolly, Rosemary Jane. 2010. *Cultured Violence: Narrative, Social Suffering, and Engendering Human Rights in Contemporary South Africa.* Liverpool: Liverpool University Press.

Judkis, Maura. 2015. "Always Super Bowl 2015 Commercial: Redefining 'Throw Like a Girl.'" *Washington Post.* http://www.washingtonpost.com/blogs/style-blog/wp/2015/02/01/always-super-bowl-2015-commercial-redefining-throw-like-a-girl/.

Kant, Immanuel. 1997. *Foundations of the Metaphysics of Morals.* Translated with an Introduction by Lewis White Beck. Upper Saddle River, NJ: Pearson.

Karimi, Faith, and Lillian Leposo. 2014. "New Kenya Law Legalizes Polygamy; Women's Group Applauds It." http://www.cnn.com/2014/05/01/world/africa/kenya-polygamy-law/.

Kassindja, Fauziya. 1998. *Do They Hear You When You Cry.* New York: Delta.

Kearney, Richard. 1996. "Narrative and Ethics." *Proceedings of the Aristotelian Society* 70: 29–45.

Keen, Suzanne. 2006. "A Theory of Narrative Empathy." *Narrative* 14.3: 207–236.

Keen, Suzanne. 2007. *Empathy and the Novel.* New York: Oxford University Press.

Keen, Suzanne. 2014. "Narrative Empathy." In *The Living Handbook of Narratology,* ed. Peter Hühn et al. Hamburg: Hamburg University Press. hup.sub.uni-hamburg.de/lhn/index.phpndex.phpni-hamburg.de/lhn/oldid=2044. Accessed April 20, 2014.

Kehinde, Ayo, and Joy Ebong Mbipom. 2011. "Discovery, Assertion and Self-Realisation in Recent Nigerian Migrant Feminist Fiction: The Example of Sefi Atta's *Everything Good Will Come.*" *African Nebula* 3: 62–77.

Kenyatta, Jomo. 1938. *Facing Mount Kenya.* London: Secker and Warburg.

Kieh, George Klay. 2008. *The First Liberian Civil War: The Crises of Underdevelopment.* New York: Peter Lang.

Kolawole, Mary E. 1997. *Womanism and African Consciousness.* Trenton, NJ; Asmara: Africa World Press.

Kouba, Leonard, and Judith Muasher. 1985. "Female Circumcision in Africa: An Overview." *African Studies Review* 28: 95–110.

Krithika, R. 2013. "I am a Happy Feminist." www.hindu.com/mag/2009/08/09/stories/2009080950020200.htm. Accessed January 25, 2013.

Kruger, Marie. 2011. *Women's Literature in Kenya and Uganda: The Trouble with Modernity.* New York: Palgrave.

Kumar, Palash. 2006, December 15. "India Has Killed 10 Million Girls in 20 Years." http://abcnews.go.com/Health/story?id=2728976

Larson, Charles. 1976. *The Novel in the Third World.* Washington DC: Inscape.

Leaning, Jennifer, Susan Bartels, and Hani Mowafi. 2009. "Sexual Violence During War and Forced Migration." In *Women, Migration, and Conflict:*

Breaking a Deadly Cycle, ed. Susan Forbes Martin and John Tirman, 173–199. New York: Springer.

Levi, Primo. 1996. *Survival in Auschwitz: The Nazi Assault on Humanity*. Trans. Stuart Woolf. New York: A Touchstone Book.

Levi, Primo. 1998. *The Drowned and the Saved*. New York: Simon and Schuster.

Levinas, Emmanuel. 1969. *Totality and Infinity*. Trans. Alphonso Lingis. Pittsburgh, PA: Duquesne University Press.

Levinas, Emmanuel. 1985. *Ethics and Infinity: Conversations with Phillip Nemo*. Trans. Richard Cohen. Pittsburgh, PA: Duquesne University Press.

Lionnet, Françoise. 1995. *Postcolonial Representations: Women, Literature, Identity*. Ithaca: Cornell University Press.

Lipps, Theodor. 1913. *Zur Einfühlung*. Leipzig: Engleman.

Lockhat, Haseena. 2004. *Female Genital Mutilation: Treating the Tears*. London: Middlesex University Press.

Lorde, Audre. 1984. *Sister Outsider: Essays and Speeches*. Freedom, CA: The Crossing Press.

Lyotard, Jean-Francois. 1984. *The Postmodern Condition: A Report on Knowledge*. Trans. Geoff Bennington and Brian Massumi. Minnesota: University of Minnesota Press.

MacIntyre, Alasdair. 1984. *After Virtue*. South Bend, Indiana: University of Notre Dame Press.

MacIntyre, Alasdair. 1999. *Dependent Rational Animals: Why Human Beings Need the Virtues*. Peru, IL: Open Court.

Maduka, Chidi T. 1987. "African Religious Beliefs in Literary Imagination: Ogbanje and Abiku in Chiuna Achebe, J.P. Clark and Wole Soyinka." *Journal of Common Wealth Literature* 22.1: 17–31.

Mann, Susan Archer, and Ashly Suzanne Patterson, eds. 2015. *Reading Feminist Theory: From Modernity to Postmodernity*. New York: Oxford University Press.

Marcel, Gabriel. 1963. *The Existential Background of Human Dignity*. Cambridge, MA: Harvard University Press.

Mbembe, Achille. 2002. "African Modes of Self-Writing." *Public Culture* 14.1: 239–273.

Mekgwe, Pinkie. 2008. "Theorizing African Feminism(s): The 'Colonial' Question." *QUEST: An African Journal of Philosophy/Revue Africaine de Philosophie* XX: 11–22.

Memmi, Albert. 1990. *The Colonizer and the Colonized* (original 1965). Trans. Howard Greenfield. London: Earthscan Publications.

Mencius. 1970. Trans. D.C. Lau. London: Penguin Classics.

Mkhwanazi, Nolwazi. 2013. "Miniskirts and Kangas: The Use of Culture in Constituting Postcolonial Sexuality." http://www.darkmatter101.org/site/2008/05/02/miniskirts-and-kangas-the-use-of-culture-in-constituting-postcolonial-sexuality/. Accessed May 15, 2013.

Mohamed, Fahma. "Tell Schools to Teach Risks of Female Genital Mutilation Before the Summer." http://www.change.org/en-GB/petitions/educationgovuk-tell-schools-to-teach-risks-of-female-genital-mutilation-before-the-summer-endfgm.

Mohanty Talpade, Chandra, Ann Russo, and Lourde Torres. 1991. *Third World Women and the Politics of Feminism*. Bloomington, IN: Indiana University Press.

Moller Okin, Susan. 1989. *Justice, Gender and the Family*. New York: Basic Books.

Moller Okin, Susan. 1999. *Is Multiculturalism Bad for Women?* New Jersey: Princeton University Press.

More, Nicholas. 2011. "Nietzsche's Last Laugh: Ecce Homo as Satire." *Philosophy and Literature* 35.1: 1–15.

Morrell, Robert, and Edgewood Campus. 2007. "Men, Masculinities and Gender Politics in South Africa: A Reply to Macleod." *Psychology in Society* 35.1: 15–25.

Mugo, Micere Githae. 2004. *African Orature and Human Rights in Gikuyu, Shona and Ndebele Zimani Cultures*. Harare, Zimbabwe: Sapes Books.

Mushava, S. 2013. "Is NoViolet a Victim of West's Propaganda?" *The Herald*. http://www.herald.co.zw/is-noviolet-a-victim-of-wests-propaganda/. Accessed November 10, 2013.

Mushava, S. 2013. "Zimbabwe: African Literature Reduced to a Commodity." http://allafrica.com/stories/201312300593.html?viewall=1. Accessed November 10, 2013.

Mwangi, Evan. 2009. *Africa Writes Back to Self: Metafiction, Gender, Sexuality*. New York: State University of New York Press.

Nako, Nontassa. 2003. "Possessing the Voice of the Other: African Women and the 'Crises of Representation' in Alice Walker's Possessing the Secret of Joy." In *African Women and Feminism: Reflecting on the Politics of Sisterhood*, ed. Oyeronke Oyewumi, 187–196. Trenton, NJ: Africa World Press.

Ndlovu-Gatsheni, Sabelo J. 2009. "Africa for Africans or Africa for 'Natives' Only? 'New Nationalism' and Nativism in Zimbabwe and South Africa." *Africa Spectrum* 44.1: 61–78.

Neblett, William. 1974. "The Ethics of Guilt." *The Journal of Philosophy* 71.18: 652–663.

Newell, Stephanie. ed., 1997. *Writing African Women: Gender, Popular Culture and Literature in West Africa*. London: Zed.

Newton, Adam Zachary. 1995. *Narrative Ethics*. Cambridge, MA: Harvard University Press.

Nfah-Abbenyi, Juliana Makuchi. 1997. *Gender in African Women's Writing*. Bloomington, IN: Indiana University Press.

Nietzsche, Friedrich. 1977. *The Portable Nietzsche*. Edited by Walter Kaufman. New York: Penguin Books.

Nnaemeka, Obioma, ed. 1998. *Sisterhood, Feminism and Power. From Africa to the Diaspora*. Trenton, NJ: Africa World Press.

Nnaemeka, Obioma, ed. 2005. *Female Circumcision and the Politics of Knowledge. African Women in Imperialist Discourse*. Westport, CT: Praeger.
Nnaemeka, Obioma. 2005. "African Women, Colonial Discourses, and Imperialist Interventions: Female Circumcision as Impetus." In *Female Circumcision and the Politics of Knowledge: African Women in Imperialist Discourse*, ed. Obioma Nnaemeka, 274–276. Westport, CT: Praeger.
Nnoromele, Salome C. 2002. "Representing the African Woman: Subjectivity and Self in *The Joys of Motherhood*." *Critique: Studies in Contemporary Fiction* 2: 43.
Norridge, Zoe. 2012. *Perceiving Pain in African Literature*. New York: Palgrave Macmillan.
NPR. 2014. http://www.pbs.org/speaktruthtopower/issue_female.html. Accessed November 10, 2014.
Nussbaum, Martha. 1990. *Love's Knowledge: Essays on Philosophy and Literature*. New York: Oxford University Press.
Nussbaum, Martha. 1996. "Patriotism and Cosmopolitanism." In *For Love of Country: Debating the Limits of Patriotism*, ed. Joshua Cohen, 3–17. Boston: Beacon Press.
Nussbaum, Martha. 2001a. *Upheavals of Thought: The Intelligence of Emotions*. Cambridge, UK: Cambridge University Press.
Nussbaum, Martha. 2001b. *Women and Human Development: The Capabilities Approach*. Cambridge University Press.
Nuttall, Sarah. 2009. *Entanglement: Literary and Cultural Reflections on Post-Apartheid*. Johannesburg: Wits University Press.
Nwapa, Flora. 1966. *Efuru*. London: Heinemann Publishers.
Nzegwu, Nkiru Uwechia. 2006. *Family Matters: Feminist Concepts in African Philosophy of Culture*. New York: State University of New York.
O'Kane, Maggie Patrick Farrelly, Alex Rees, and Irene Baqué. 2014. FGM: "It's like neutering animals" –The Film That Is Changing Kurdistan. http://www.theguardian.com/society/2013/oct/24/female-genital-mutilation-film-changing-kurdistan-law. Accessed December 10, 2014.
Ogundipe-Leslie, Morala. 1994. *Re-Creating Ourselves: African Women and Critical Transformations*. Trenton, NJ: African World Press.
Ojo-Ade, Femi. 1983. "Female Writers, Male Critics." *African Literature Today* 13: 158–179.
Okeke-Ihejirika, P. E., and S. Franceschet. 2002. "Democratization and State Feminism: Gender Politics in Africa and Latin America." *Development and Change* 33: 439–466.
Okonjo Ogunyemi, Chikwenye. 1996. *Africa Wo/Man Palava: The Nigerian Novel by Women*. Chicago: University of Chicago Press.
Okonjo Ogunyemi, Chikwenye. 2006. "Womanism: The Dynamics of the Contemporary Black Female Novel in English." In *The Womanist Reader*, ed. Layli Phillips, 21–36. New York: Routledge.

Okorafor, Nnedi. 2010. *Who Fears Death?* New York: Daw Books.
Okparanta, Chinelo. 2013. *Happiness, Like Water.* London: Granta.
Okri, Ben. 1991. *The Famished Road.* London: Jonathan Cape.
Olaniyan, Tejumola, T, and A. Quayson, eds. 2007. *African Literature: An Anthology of Criticism and Theory.* Malden, MA: Wiley-Blackwell.
Oloka-Onyango, J. and Sylvia Tamale. 1995. "'The Personal Is Political', or Why Women's Rights Are Indeed Human Rights: An African Perspective on International Feminism." *Human Rights Quarterly*, 17(4): 691–731.
Ouma, Christopher E.W. 2011. "Daughters of Sentiment, Genealogies, and Conversations Between *Things Fall Apart* and *Purple Hibiscus.*" In Chinua Achebe's *Things Fall Apart: 1958–2008*, ed. David Whittaker, 89–105. Amsterdam and New York: Rodopi.
Ovid. 1955. *Metamorphoses.* Trans. Mary M. Innes. London: Penguin Books.
Oxford English Dictionary. 1933. London: Oxford University Press.
Oyewumi, Oyeronke. 1997. *The Invention of Women: Making an African Sense of Western Gender Discourses.* Minneapolis, MN: University of Minnesota Press.
Oyewumi, Oyeronke. 2003a. "Alice in Motherland: Reading Alice Walker on Africa and Screening the Color 'Black'." *African Women and Feminism: Reflecting on the Politics of Sisterhood*, ed. Oyeronke Oyewumi, 159–186. Trenton, NJ: Africa World Press.
Oyewumi, Oyeronke. 2003b. "The White Woman's Burden: African Woman in Western Feminist Discourse." *African Women and Feminism: Reflecting on the Politics of Sisterhood*, ed. Oyeronke Oyewumi, 25–44. Trenton, NJ: Africa World Press.
Palumbo-Liu, David. 2012. *The Deliverance of Others: Reading Literature in a Global Age.* Durham: Duke University Press.
Patruno, Nicholas. 1995. *Understanding Primo Levi.* Columbia, SC: The University of South Carolina Press.
Pham, John-Peter. 2004. *Liberia: Portraits of a Failed State.* New York: Reed.
Phelan, James, and Peter J. Rabinowitz, eds. 1994. *Understanding Narrative.* Columbus, OH: Ohio State University Press.
Phelan, James. 2014. Narrative Ethics. In *The Living Handbook of Narratology*, eds. Peter Hühn, Wolf Schmid, Jörg Schönert, and John Pier. Hamburg: Hamburg University. http://www.lhn.unihamburg.de/article/narrative-ethics. Accessed March 23, 2014.
Phillips, Layli, ed. 2006. *The Womanist Reader.* New York: Routledge.
Priebe, Richard. 2005. "Literature, Community, and Violence: Reading African Literature in the West, Post-9/11." *Research in African Literatures* 362: 46–58.
Primorac, Ranka. 2006. *The Place of Tears. The Novel and Politics in Modern Zimbabwe.* London: Taurus Academic Studies.

Pucherová, Dobrota. 2012. "A Continent Learns to Tell Its Story at Last": Notes on the Caine Prize. *Journal of Postcolonial Writing* 48.1: 1–13.

Rancière, Jacques. 2006. "The Ethical Turn of Aesthetics and Politics." *Critical Horizons* 7.1: 1–20.

Rawls, John. 2001. *Justice as Fairness: A Restatement*. Edited by Erin Kelly. Cambridge, MA: Harvard University Press.

Rege, Josna E. 2000. "Gender Voices and Choices: Redefining Women in Contemporary African Fiction." *Research in African Literatures* 31.3: 209–210.

Reuters. 1990. "Liberia Troops Accused Of Massacre in Church." http://www.nytimes.com/1990/07/31/world/liberia-troops-accused-of-massacre-in-church.html. Accessed Friday, October 26, 2012.

Revell, Donald. 2007. *The Art of Attention: A Poet's Eye*. Minneapolis, MN: Graywolf Press.

Ricoeur, Paul. 1984. *Time and Narrative* 1. Trans. Kathleen McLaughlin and David Pellauer. Chicago: The University of Chicago Press.

Ricoeur, Paul. 1991. "Life in Quest of Narrative." In *On Paul Ricoeur: Narrative and Interpretation*, ed. David Wood, 20–33. London: Routledge.

Riding, Alan. 2006. "Rap and Film at the Louvre? What's Up With That?" *The New York Times*. www.nytimes.com/2006/11/21/books/21morr.html. Accessed October 5, 2011.

Rorty, Richard. 1989. *Contingency, Irony and Solidarity*. Cambridge, UK: Cambridge University Press.

Russell-Robinson, Joyce.1997. "African Female Circumcision and the Missionary Mentality." *A Journal of Opinion: Commentaries in African Studies: Essays about African Social Change and the Meaning of Our Professional Work* 25.1: 54–57.

Samuelson, Meg. 2007. *Remembering the Nation Dismembering Women? Stories of the South African Transition*. Scottsville, South Africa: University of Kwazulu Natal Press.

Scarry, Elaine. 1985. *The Body in Pain: The Making and Unmaking of the World*. New York: Oxford University Press.

Scheffer, David. 2013. "Sudan and the ICC: Rape as Genocide." http://www.nytimes.com/2008/12/03/opinion/03iht-edscheffer.1.18365231.html?_r=0. Accessed November 10, 2013.

Shestack, Jerome. 2000. "The Philosophical Foundations of Human Rights." In *Human Rights: Concept and Standards*, ed. Janusz Symonides, 31–68. Aldershot, UK: Dartmouth Publishing Company Ltd.

Shire, Warsan. 2011. *Teaching My Mother How to Give Birth*. United Kingdom: Mouthmark.

Shire, Warsan. 2014. "Tribe of Woods." http://badilishapoetry.com/radio/WarsanShire/. Accessed November 10, 2014.

Shoneyin, Lola. 2010. *The Secret Lives of Baba Segi's Wives*. New York: William Morrow.
Slaughter, Joseph R. 2007. *Human Rights, Inc: The World Novel: Narrative Form, and International Law*. New York: Fordham University Press.
Smith, Adam. 2002. *The Theory of Moral Sentiments*. Edited by Knud Haakonssen. Cambridge: Cambridge University Press.
Soyinka, Wole. 1965. *The Road*. Oxford: Oxford University Press.
Soyinka, Wole. 2012. "Abiku." www.cafeafrikana.com/poetry.html. Accessed November 2, 2012.
Stobie, Cheryl. 2010. "Dethroning the Infallible: Religion, Patriarchy and Politics in Chimamanda Ngozi Adichie's Purple Hibiscus." *Literature and Theology* 24.4: 421–435.
Stobie, Cheryl. 2012. "Gendered Bodies in Chimamanda Ngozi Adichie's Purple Hibiscus." In *Literature of Our Times: Postcolonial Studies in the Twenty-First Century*, ed. Bill Ashcroft, Ranjini Mendis, Julie McGonegal, and Arun Mukherjee, 307–326. Amsterdam and New York: Rodopi.
Stratton, Florence. 1994. *Contemporary African Literature and the Politics of Gender*. New York: Routledge.
Strong-Leek, Linda. 2009. *Excising the Spirit: A Literary Analysis of Female Circumcision*. Trenton, NJ: Africa World Press.
Sullivan, Shannon. 2006. *Revealing Whiteness: The Unconscious Habits of Racial Privilege*. Bloomington, IN: Indiana University Press.
Tamale, Sylvia. 2005. "Eroticism, Sensuality and 'Women's Secrets' Among the Baganda: A Critical Analysis." *Feminist Africa Issue: Sexual Cultures* 5: 9–36. http://agi.ac.za/sites/agi.ac.za/files/fa_5_feature_article_1.pdf. Accessed March 8, 2016.
Tamale, Sylvia. 2006. "African Feminism: How Should We Change?" *Development: Supplement: Women's Rights and Development* 49.1: 38–41.
Tamale, Sylvia. 2008. "The Right to Culture and the Culture of Rights: A Critical Perspective on Women's Sexual Rights in Africa." *Feminist Legal Studies* 16.1: 47–69.
The Chambers Dictionary. 1998. Edinburgh, UK: Chambers Harrap Publishers Ltd.
The Guardian. 2014. "Female Genital Mutilation Denies Sexual Pleasure to Millions of Women." http://www.theguardian.com/science/blog/2008/nov/13/female-genital-mutilation-sexual-dysfunction. Accessed March 24, 2014.
The Guardian. 2014. "Shire, Warsan: Young Poet Laureate Wields Her Pen Against FGM." http://www.theguardian.com/society/2014/feb/17/warsan-shire-young-poet-laureate-michael-gove. Accessed March 24, 2014.
Thiam, Awa. 1978. *Speak Out, Black Sisters: Feminism and Oppression in Black Africa*. London: Pluto Press.

Tong, Rosemarie, and Nancy Williams. 2014. "Feminist Ethics." *The Stanford Encyclopedia of Philosophy*. (Fall 2014. Edition). Edited by Edward N. Zalta. http://plato.stanford.edu/archives/fall2014/entries/feminism-ethics/.

Toye, Deji. 2005. "Unmasking the Okonkwo Complex in Purple Hibiscus." *Nigerian Guardian*. January 24, 2005.

Trawalter, Sophie. Kelly M. Hoffman, and Adam Waytz. 2014. "Racial Bias in Perceptions of Others' Pain." http://www.plosone.org/article/info:doi/10.1371/journal.pone.0048546. Accessed March 24, 2014.

Tunca, Daria. 2012. "Appropriating Achebe: Chimamanda Ngozi Adichie's Purple Hibiscus and 'The Headstrong Historian'." In *Adaptations and Cultural Appropriation*, ed. Pascal Nicklas and Oliver Lindner, 230–250. Berlin: De Gruyter.

Tutu, Desmond. 1999. *No Future Without Forgiveness*. New York: Image Doubleday.

Ullman, B.L. 1942. "History and Tragedy." *Transactions and Proceedings of the American Philological Association* 73: 25–53.

Umeh, Marie. 1998. *Emerging Perspectives on Flora Nwapa: Critical and Theoretical Essays*. Trenton, NJ: Africa World Press.

UNHCR. 2001. "The Gambia: Report on Female Genital Mutilation (FGM or Female Genital Cutting (GC)." www.refworld.org/docid/46d5787732.html.

Unigwe, Chika. 2004. *In the Shadow of Ala. Igbo Women Writing as an Act of Righting*. Thesis (Ph.D.) Leiden University.

Unigwe, Chika. 2009. *On Black Sisters' Street*. London: Vintage.

United Nations. 2015. The Universal Declaration of Human Rights. www.un.org/en/documents/udhr/. Accessed March 2, 2015.

United Nations. 2015. "What Are Human Rights?" http://www.ohchr.org/EN/Issues/Pages/WhatareHumanRights.aspx. Accessed March 2, 2015.

Vera, Yvonne. 2004. *The Stone Virgins*. New York: Farrar, Straus and Giroux.

Vice, Samantha. 2010. "How Do I Live in This Strange Place?" *Journal of Social Philosophy* 42.3: 323–342.

Wa Thiong'o, Ngugi. 1965. *The River Between*. London: Heinemann.

Wainaina, Binyanvanga. 2012. "How to Write About Africa." *Grant 92: The View from Africa*. www.granta.com/Archive/92. Accessed January 2, 2012.

Walker, Alice. 1992. *Possessing the Secret of Joy*. New York: New Press.

Walker, Margaret Urban. 2007. *Moral Understandings: A Feminist Study Ethics*. New York: Oxford University Press.

Wallace, Cynthia R. 2012. "Chimamanda Ngozi Adichie's Purple Hibiscus and the Paradoxes of Postcolonial Redemption." *Christianity and Literature* 61.3: 465–483.

Watson, Christie. 2013. "Ake Festival, Nigeria—Where Kids Want to Fly in Colour." www.bookbrunch.co.uk/article_free.asp?pid=ake_festival_nigeria_where_kids_want_to_fly_in_colour.

Weisgerber, Jean. 1973. "Satire and Irony as Means of Communication." *Comparative Literature Studies* 10.2: 157–172.

Wilson, Charles Morrow. 1971. *Black Africa in Microcosm*. New York: Harper & Row.

Wollstonecraft, Mary. 2008. "To M. Talleyrand-Perigord, Late Bishop of Autun." In *Masters of British Literature*, ed. David Damrosch and Kevin J.H. Dettmar. New York: Pearson, Longman.

Woolf, Virginia. 1989. *A Room of One's Own* (original 1929). New York: A Harvest Book.

Young, Iris Marion. 1980. "Throwing Like a Girl: A Phenomenology of Feminine Body Comportment Motility and Spatiality." *Human Studies* 3.2: 137–156.

Young, Iris Marion. 1990. *Throwing Like a Girl and Other Essays in Feminist Philosophy and Social Theory*. Bloomington, IN: Indiana University Press.

Zabus, Chantal. 2007. *Between Rites and Rights: Excision in Women's. Experiential Texts and Human Contexts*. Palo Alto, CA: Stanford University Press.

Zylinska, Joanna. 2005. *The Ethics of Cultural Studies*. New York: Continuum.

Index

A

Abstractions as enablers of pain, 59
Achebe, 8, 12, 69, 70, 72, 88, 146, 165
Acholonu, Catherine Obianuju, 10, 35
Adichie, Chimamanda Ngozi, 2, 3, 43, 44, 45, 46, 47, 48, 50, 51, 52, 53, 55, 56, 57, 58, 59, 60, 63, 64, 65, 72, 84, 90, 104, 107
African feminism, 3, 7, 8, 9, 10, 11, 12, 13, 20, 43, 70, 98
Africanism, 88
Agamben, Giorgio, 187, 196, 208
Althusser, Louis, 54, 55, 67, 93, 100, 118, 148, 161, 172
Amadiume, Ifi, 8, 9, 35
Andrade, Susan Z., 3, 13, 32, 56, 67
Anker, Elizabeth S., 19, 20, 23, 29, 39, 105, 119, 135
Aristotle, 6, 27, 28, 51, 115, 124, 190, 192, 194
Atta, Sefi, 2, 165, 166, 167, 168, 169, 171, 172, 174, 175, 176, 177, 178, 179, 180, 182, 183, 205

B

Bâ, Mariama, 3, 13, 122
Baingana, Doreen, 2
Banjul Charter, 20
Baron-Cohen, Simon, 16, 37, 46, 156
Bekers, Elisabeth, 96, 117
Bildungsroman, 23, 64
Body, 6, 13, 15, 19, 20, 22, 30, 51, 53, 57, 58, 59, 95, 97, 102, 123, 135, 145, 196, 199
Boehmer, Elleke, 11, 36
Boyce Davies, Carol, 8, 14, 35, 155
Buell, Lawrence, 5, 33, 155
Buergenthal, Thomas, 18, 38
Bulawayo, NoViolet, 2, 69, 70, 71, 72, 73, 74, 76, 77, 78, 79, 81, 83, 88, 89, 171
Butler, Judith, 3, 4, 5, 24, 25, 27, 33, 54, 58, 67, 81, 100, 118, 127, 154, 172

C

Caine Prize, 69, 71
Categorical imperative, 19
Cavarero, Adriana, 4, 24, 27, 127, 154
Cixous, Hélène, 30, 42, 55, 67, 96, 106, 116
Colonial trap, 12, 69, 88
Cooper, Brenda, 1, 31

D

Dawes, James, 25, 29, 40, 189, 207
Dembour, Marie-Bénédicte, 18, 38, 147, 166
De Waal, Frans, 15, 17, 37, 47
Didion, Joan, 24, 40
Dogon Myth, 97, 104
Donnelly, Jack, 19, 24, 38, 146, 161

E

Eagleton, Terry, 14, 37, 124, 141, 154, 155, 162
Ekpo, Denis, 88, 93
Emecheta, Buchi, 3, 13, 36, 146
Empathy, 7, 15–18, 24, 28, 30, 46, 47, 48, 51, 52, 61, 78, 79, 83, 87, 114, 115, 139, 140, 155, 157, 168, 182, 189, 206
Empathy blockage, 48
Enlightenment, 19, 20, 135, 167
Ethical turn, 1–29
Ethics, 3, 5, 27, 30, 74, 80, 187, 189

F

Fairness, 2, 29, 43, 44, 45, 48, 50, 52, 56, 57, 60, 61, 62, 63, 69, 81, 82, 86, 156
Female genital mutilation, 6, 71, 110, 135
Female subjectivity, 11, 13–15
Feminism, 3, 7, 9, 10, 29, 43–45, 56, 63, 70, 124, 152
Feminist Empathy, 7, 14, 15, 18, 29, 30, 86
Forced marriage, 6
Frank, Arthur W., 25, 40

G

Gappah, Petina, 2, 131, 132, 133, 134, 135, 136, 137, 139, 140, 142, 205
Grammar of motive, 73, 155

H

Harrow, Ken, 1, 31
Hooks, bell, 44, 45, 66
Human flourishing, 7, 23, 27, 46, 53, 56, 62, 70, 115, 139, 154, 189
Human Rights, 2, 5, 7, 18–24, 26, 29, 30, 63, 85, 102, 110, 125, 129, 131, 132, 145, 146, 149, 150, 151, 155, 158, 165, 166, 167, 174, 179, 187, 196
Hunt, Lynn, 19, 26, 29, 38, 125, 126, 166, 167

I

Ideology as abstraction, 23, 115, 135, 174
Iser, Wolfgang, 5, 33, 162

J

JanMohamed, Abdul, 16, 37
Justice as fairness, 45

K

Kant, Immanuel, 19, 25, 39, 49, 93, 123
Keen, Suzanne, 16, 28, 30, 37, 42, 91
Kolawole, Mary, 10, 35

L

Levi, Primo, 189, 190, 191, 192, 194, 196, 197, 202, 205, 207
Levinas, Emmanuel, 5, 24, 33, 123, 125, 141, 169, 174, 183, 192

Liberia, 188, 194, 197, 200, 202, 205
Lipps, Theodor, 15, 37

M

MacIntyre, Alasdair, 4, 33, 49, 66, 115, 120
Medusa, 160
Mekgwe, Pinkie, 11, 12, 36, 69, 93
Memmi, Albert, 16, 37
Mencius, 15
Merleau-Ponty, Maurice, 199
Morrison, Toni, 160
Motherism, 10
Mugabe, Robert, 71, 87, 88, 89, 131, 132
Mugabe Syndrome, 88, 89, 131
Mugo, Micere Githae, 21, 22, 39, 167
Mwangi, Evan, 1, 31

N

Narrative as Ethics, 27, 28
Narrative understanding, 28, 80, 81, 189
Nego-feminism, 10
Newton, Adam, 27, 41, 70, 73, 74, 90
Nfah-Abbenyi, Juliana Makuchi, 14, 37, 78, 91, 175
Nnaemeka, Obioma, 10, 36, 101, 118
Norridge, Zoe, 1, 2, 31
Nussbaum, Martha, 15, 28, 37, 46, 49, 51, 66, 83, 87, 92, 93, 126, 142, 154, 162, 189
Nwapa, Flora, 3, 13, 83, 92, 146, 158, 159
Nzegwu, Nkiru Uwechia, 10, 50, 67

O

Ogundipe-Leslie, Molara, 10, 36
Ojo-Ade, Femi, 7, 34
Okin, Susan Moller, 3, 32, 49, 66
Okonjo Ogunyemi, Chikwenye, 9, 10, 35, 122
Okorafor, Nnedi, 2, 102, 103, 104, 107, 108, 115, 119, 135, 142
Okparanta, Chinelo, 2, 69, 70, 72, 73, 74, 75, 76, 77, 79, 81, 82, 83, 85, 88, 89, 91, 156
Original position, 49–51, 59
Oyewumi, Oyeronke, 9, 35, 98, 99, 100, 101, 118

P

Pain, 6, 12, 14, 23–29, 56, 59, 60, 62, 63, 74–88, 100, 103, 105, 107, 110, 124, 125, 134, 145, 146, 152, 175, 180, 189, 199
Practical Imperative, 19
Primorac, Ranka, 1, 31

R

Rawls, John, 46, 49–51, 59, 66
Ricoeur, Paul, 28, 41, 73, 80, 81, 82, 91, 92, 189
Rorty, Richard, 80, 92, 160

S

Samuelson, Meg, 11, 36
Scarry, Elaine, 86, 93, 105, 153, 162
Shire, Warsan, 2, 95, 102, 107, 108, 110, 112
Shoneyin, Lola, 2, 123, 124, 125, 126, 127, 128, 129, 130, 136, 137, 138, 139, 141
Slaughter, Joseph R., 23, 40, 64, 68
Smith, Adam, 15, 28, 37, 50, 67, 78
Stiwanism, 10

Stratton, Florence, 11, 12, 36
Sullivan, Shannon, 26, 40

T
Tamale, Sylvia, 12, 20, 21, 36, 39, 79, 91, 101, 118
Thomson, Rosemary Garland, 6, 33
Trawalter, Sophie, 17, 38
Tutu, Demons, 22, 39

U
Ubuntu, 15, 21, 22, 26, 87, 115, 168
Unigwe, Chika, 2, 37, 145, 146, 147, 148, 150, 151, 152, 153, 154, 155, 158, 159, 160, 161
United Nations, 18, 145
Universal Declaration of Human Rights, 18, 19, 20, 126, 146

V
Veil of ignorance, 46, 49, 50, 55, 65
Vice, Samantha, 26, 62

W
Walker, Alice, 9, 98, 99, 100, 117
Wesley, Patricia Jabbeh, 2, 187, 188, 190, 192, 193, 194, 196, 197, 199, 200, 202, 203, 204, 205, 206, 208
Wollstonecraft, Mary, 44, 65, 66, 76
Write back, 1, 2, 69

Z
Zabus, Chantal, 29, 30, 42, 96, 97, 117
Zylinska, Joanna, 80, 91